I0793216

IMAGES
of America

THE HARRISON AREA

ON THE COVER: The lady is walking northeast down the main street of Harrison in the summer of 1917. Wooden buildings were destroyed in the fire on July 21, 1917. The large brick building in the center of the picture, Schuster's Department Store, was damaged and rebuilt. The steeple of the Methodist Episcopal Church is in the distance on the left. Chester Russell took this photograph and many others in this book.

IMAGES
of America

THE HARRISON AREA

Crane Historical Society
Harrison, Idaho

ARCADIA
PUBLISHING

ISBN 978-0-7385-7448-6

Published by Arcadia Publishing
Charleston, South Carolina

Printed in the United States of America

Library of Congress Control Number: 2010937736

For all general information, please contact Arcadia Publishing:
Telephone 843-853-2070
Fax 843-853-0044
E-mail sales@arcadiapublishing.com
For customer service and orders:
Toll-Free 1-888-313-2665

Visit us on the Internet at www.arcadiapublishing.com

To those hardy pioneers who settled the beautiful Harrison area

Contents

ACKNOWLEDGMENTS

All images are courtesy of the Crane Historical Society archives, which include photographs donated by the following families: Addington, Bishop, Carns, Cope, Corskie, Custer, Damiano, DeLuca, Drissen, Fabricius, Freeman, Fries, Foster, Heikkila, Hodge, Jensen, Jones, Justus, Kiger, Klein, Kroetch, Lamb, Lavigne-Gunter, Lund, Lundhal, Miller, Newton, Pugh, Rose, Russell, Sala, Selby, Smith, Thompson, Wark, and Wood. We cherish all of them.

This book is indebted to the editorial staff of the *Harrison Searchlight Celebration Issues*, published annually since 1953. With editors Bert Russell, Joyce Russell, Lorine M. Wilkinson, and, since 1968, Donald Heikkila, the staff has collected pictures, recorded personal interviews, and written historical articles. Thanks to all those writers and photographers whose contributions to the *Searchlight* provided much of the background for this book.

Thanks to the following authors who have written books about local history from which we were able to glean valuable information: Iva (Hollingsworth) Carns, Charles Custer, Ruby El Hult, John D. Pugh, Bert and Marie Russell, Orland A. Scott, Louise Shadduck, Clarence C. Strong, and Clyde S. Webb. Their books listed in the bibliography were treasures and provided stories and details that made history come alive.

A special thanks goes to Mary Mills. Without her expertise and dedication in collecting and cataloging the photographs, this book would not have been possible.

Introduction

This book tells the story of many of the events and people that shaped Harrison—the logging, the mills, the homesteaders, the pioneer families, the businesses, and the fire of 1917.

The Harrison story really begins before the town was settled. When fur traders and explorers came to the area in the early 1800s, they found a tribe of Indians living in the forests and along the shores of Coeur d'Alene Lake. They called themselves "camas people," but the French Canadian trappers and traders named them the Coeur d'Alenes. Two definitions have been brought forward as to the meaning. One is "heart-like-an-awl," comparing their sharp bargaining capabilities with the sharp tool. The other is "strong-breathed," recognizing their strong-hearted endurance. Regardless of the meaning, the name was used not only for the tribe but also for the river, the mountains, and the lake. The Indians made fishing camps along the shores of the lake at Shingle Bay, Lacon, East Point, and Powderhorn Bay. Undocumented sources claim the point where Harrison eventually was built was originally called Willow Springs or Spring Point.

The first permanent settlers in the Harrison area were two Jesuit missionaries who, in 1842, founded a mission at an Indian fishing camp about 11 miles south of Harrison. Father Nicholas Point and Brother Charles Huet built a cabin where they taught Christianity and farming, which the Indians readily embraced. In 1846, the mission was abandoned due to continued flooding, and a new mission was established at Cataldo, about 35 miles up the Coeur d'Alene River. The Mission of the Sacred Heart is the oldest standing building in Idaho.

Also in 1846, a treaty between Great Britain and the United States ceded title of the land west of the Rocky Mountains to the United States. Capt. John Mullan established quarters at Mission Point in 1859 and began constructing a road from the site to Black Lake. That route later became State Highway 3, connecting Harrison Flats with the interstate at Rose Lake.

Idaho became a territory on March 3, 1863, but northern Idaho remained remote. Soon, however, the following outside forces came together, which affected Harrison's future: the establishment of Fort Coeur d'Alene (later Fort Sherman) in 1878 and the discovery of gold in 1893 and silver in 1895. The Silver Valley mining district encompasses the cities of Wallace and Kellogg east of Cataldo. Eastern lumbermen began sending agents to buy timberland.

The first steamboat, the *Amelia Wheaton*, was built in 1880 to carry supplies to the fort. The Oregon Railroad and Navigation Company's rail line reached Harrison in 1890 and continued on to the Silver Valley. Harrison would become a transportation hub for both steamboats and trains.

The Crane family, consisting of brothers Addison, Edwin, and William, their father Silas, and grandfather George Jones, found a point that was the perfect location to establish lumber mills along the lake. The following is from an account by Helene (Crane) Kroetch, Edwin Crane's daughter:

"Our family came here in 1889. At first we lived in a log cabin with dirt floors below the Cope store, by the lake . . . There were no trains at that time, but they had begun to build the railroad. The first trains were work trains and then freight trains. When the first passenger train was put on, it brought the mail. Before the railroad was completed, the boats traveled from Coeur d'Alene to the Mission at Cataldo . . . Where my home is, was all a deep forest."

The Coeur d'Alene reservation had been established by treaty in 1887, and the town site selected was in the reservation. Silas Crane contacted Pres. Benjamin Harrison, a close family friend, and persuaded him to have the US government purchase a section of the reservation. Negotiations were begun. On March 4, 1891, President Harrison signed an executive order, which was ratified by congress on July 6, 1892. In 1894, a one-mile strip of land including a portion of the lake was ceded for a payment of $15,000.

Needing to pick a date for the town's founding, historians have settled on 1891, the year Silas Crane built the first home. The site incorporated as a village in August 1899 and was named after the president, Harrison. By 1903, Harrison had a population of 1,200, making it the largest city in the county.

The Homestead Law of 1862 (along with its amendments), the extensive railroad land grants, the Timber and Stone Act of 1878, the statehood grants, and the Forest Homestead Act of 1906, served to expand the population of the outlying area.

Tragically, the fire of 1917 changed the face of the city forever. Soon after, economic decline and the scarcity of readily available timber took its toll. The steamboats were expensive to maintain. Passenger traffic by steamboat ended in the 1920s and freight traffic in 1932. The last passenger train went through Harrison in 1957. The last remaining mill in the area closed in 1962. The rail line closed on April 29, 1993.

Harrison remains the urban center for a large portion of Kootenai County. The train's route is now the internationally known bicycle trail, the Trail of the Coeur d'Alenes.

Descendents of the original settlers are scattered throughout the world; some have remained in the area, others have returned after living in larger cities. As they read this book, we hope it brings back memories of stories their families told. This beautiful part of north Idaho has been rediscovered as a place for vacationing, to raise a family, and to retire. The hope also is that visitors and new residents will revel in the glorious past and appreciate the dedication of the early settlers. Enjoy!

One

Logging

Many factors came together to fuel the growth of logging in the Northwest. The supply of old-growth white pine in the Northeast and upper Midwest was shrinking. The growing agricultural industry required wooden crates. Railroads needed ties. Mines required timber for shoring underground tunnels. New towns needed lumber for building. Public lands were opening up for homesteading, and this land needed to be cleared for farming.

Lumber company agents, known as cruisers, were impressed with the quality and the vastness of the area's white pine forests. In addition, the rivers, streams, and lakes were available to provide electric power and transportation. The Northern Pacific Railroad had reached Spokane, and local railroads were in the process of being built. This assured goods could be shipped out of the area.

Lumber companies bought tracts of land aided by the Timber and Stone Act of 1878, where land could be purchased for $2.50 per acre. According to the act, a person could buy a maximum of 160 acres, though not for speculation. Despite this requirement, most of the land was sold immediately to big buyers. On Harrison Flats, East Point, and other farmable land around Harrison, families cleared their land and sold the logs to pay for it.

With the never-ending demand for logs from the mills in Harrison and the rest of the Coeur d'Alenes, thousands of loggers were kept busy. They soon filled the camps that were set up by the lumber companies.

Lumberjacks had their own language and names for the specialized jobs and tools used. Walking into an early day logging camp would be like stumbling into a foreign city. A "river pig" described a man who drove logs down the river. A "skinner" drove a team of horses, oxen, or mules. A "road monkey" sanded the sled road in the winter. A "swede-fiddle" was a crosscut saw. A "sisserbill" was someone who did not belong to the union. Someone "blew it in" when he went to Harrison to spend his "stake."

Today's logging procedures, equipment, and life are a world apart from the early days.

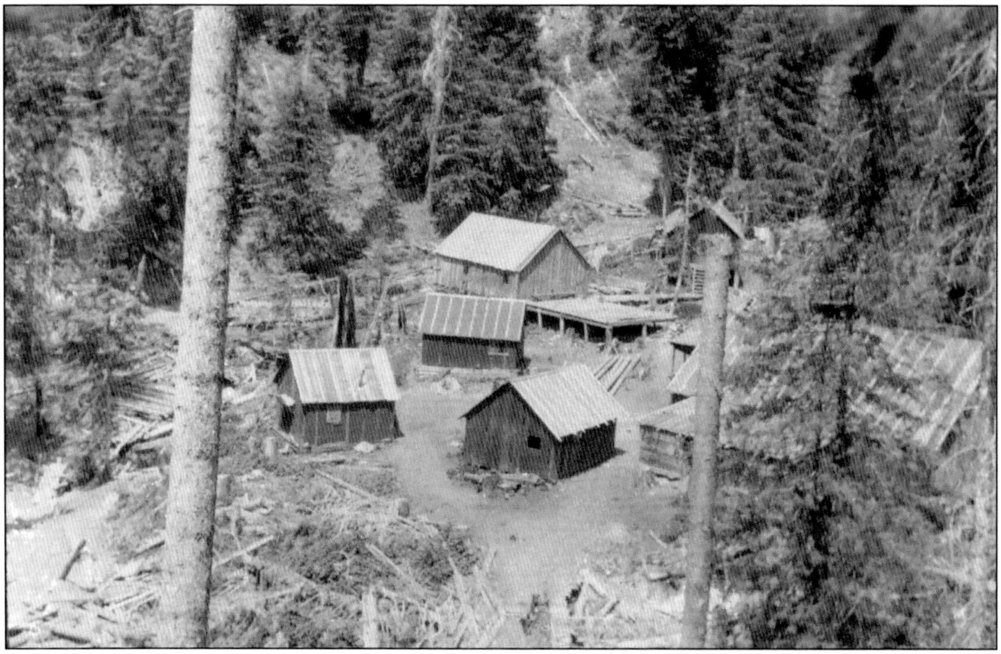

A typical logging camp had an office, bunkhouse, cook shack, and horse corral. Early bunk beds had no springs, only straw mattresses. The "bull cook" kept the large barrel stove in the bunkhouse supplied with wood. Each lumberjack supplied his own bedroll and washed his own clothes on Sunday, which was called "boil up day."

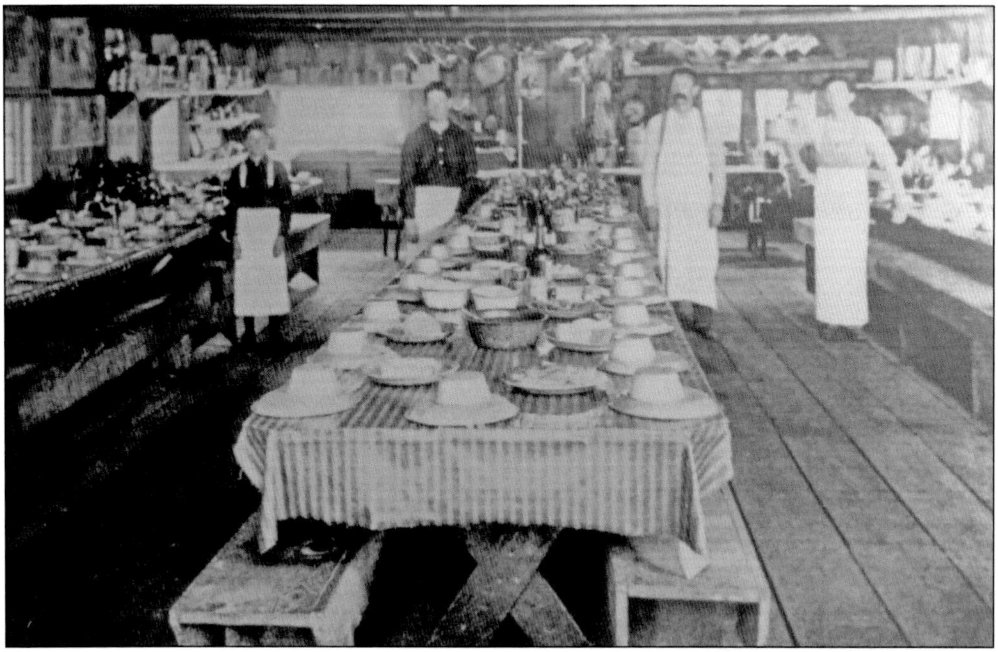

Camps took pride in supplying plentiful, excellent meals, which were prepared in a cook shack, like this one. Larger camps had a pastry chef who baked all night with the help of a flunky. Regardless of the weather, supplies were delivered daily, even to remote camps. Depending on the size of the camp, it could take up to 20 mules to carry the wooden crates, which held a day's supply.

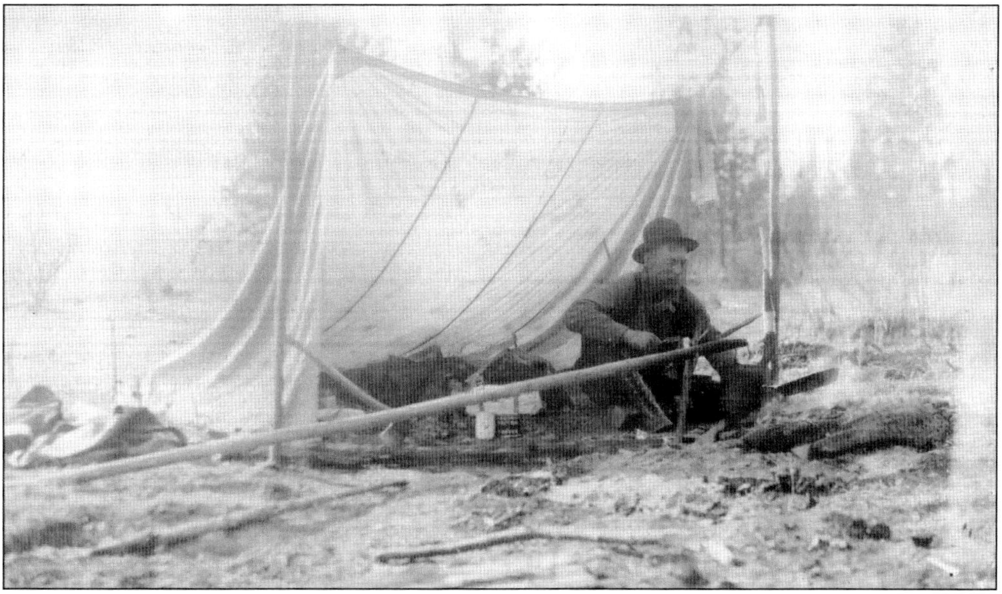

Logger Jack Murphy is shown here in an undated photograph. Long hours of hard labor for poor pay made for almost intolerable working conditions. Room and board were deducted from the already low pay. Straw bosses were pressured by their bosses, or "brains," to meet quotas. Unionization in 1917 brought the eight-hour work day and other improvements for camp workers.

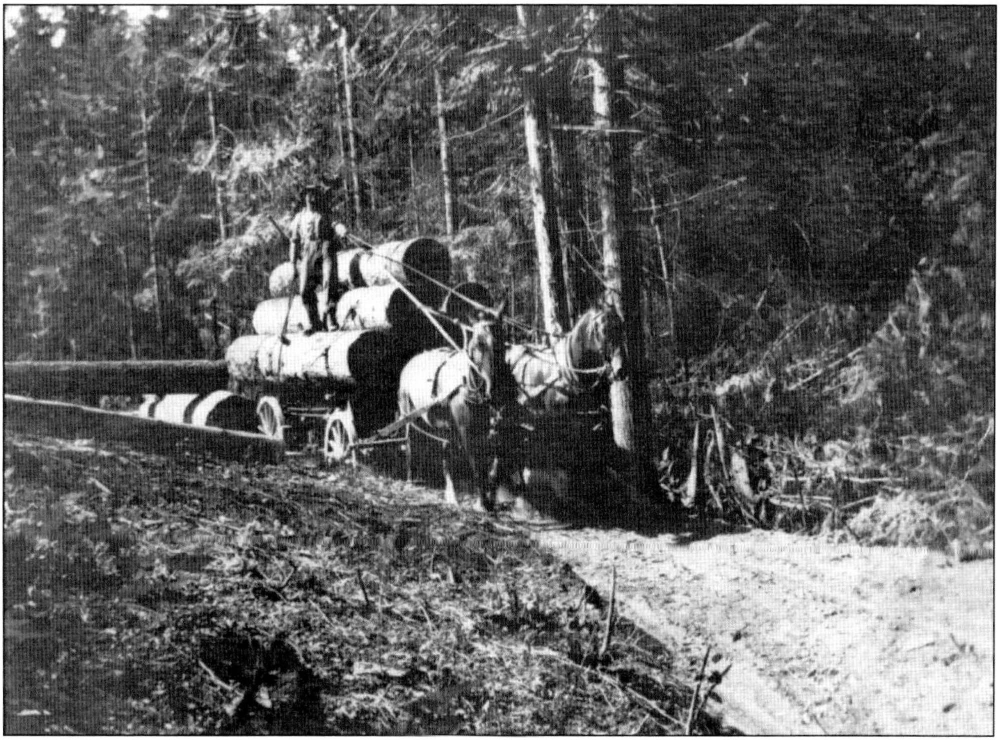

Logs were hauled by team and wagon, as in this photograph featuring John Justus. Horses also pulled pole-cars. The cars had concave rimmed wheels, which ran on round pole tracks much like a railroad. Two pole railroads operated in the Harrison area, one at Powderhorn Bay and the other at Carlin Bay.

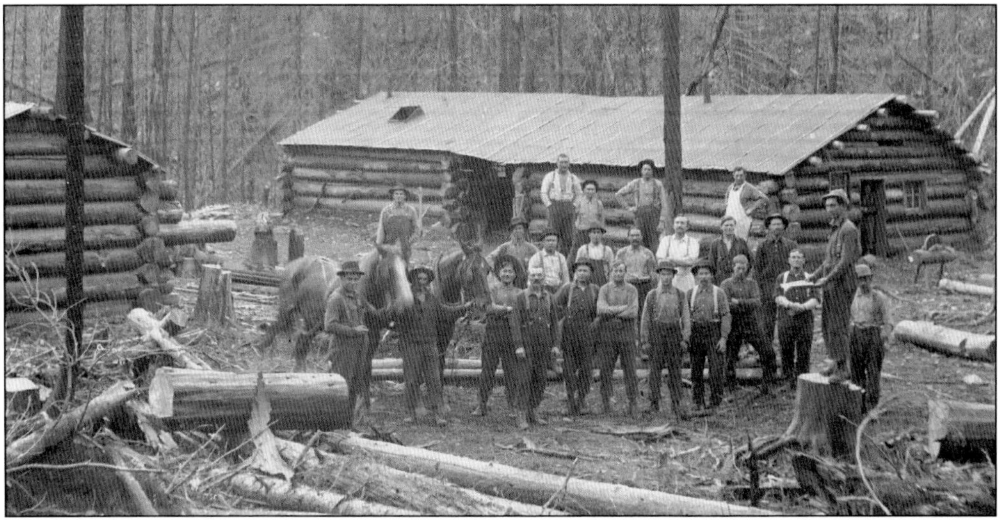

The logging camp crew is standing in front of Henry Morin (at the right, standing on a stump). He is either giving work instructions or preaching a Sunday sermon. Morin came to Harrison from Michigan in 1901 at age 12 with his family. He was considered an expert lumberjack and was hired to run several logging camps throughout his career. He shared his stories with local historians Bert and Marie Russell, who published them in the book *Rock Burst*.

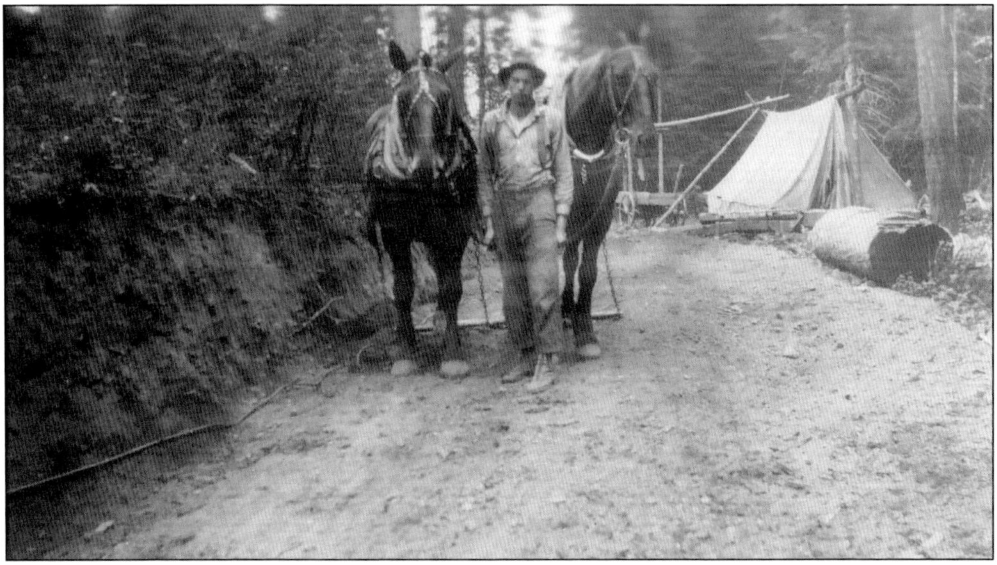

Before 1910, oxen were often used in logging, but horses were faster and soon replaced the slow-moving oxen. James Carns is holding his team used to pull wagons and, in the winter, sleighs or go-devils. A go-devil lifted one end of the log, and the other end was skidded on the snow. Because of the heavy workload, logging horses were usually retired after 10 years for lighter farm work.

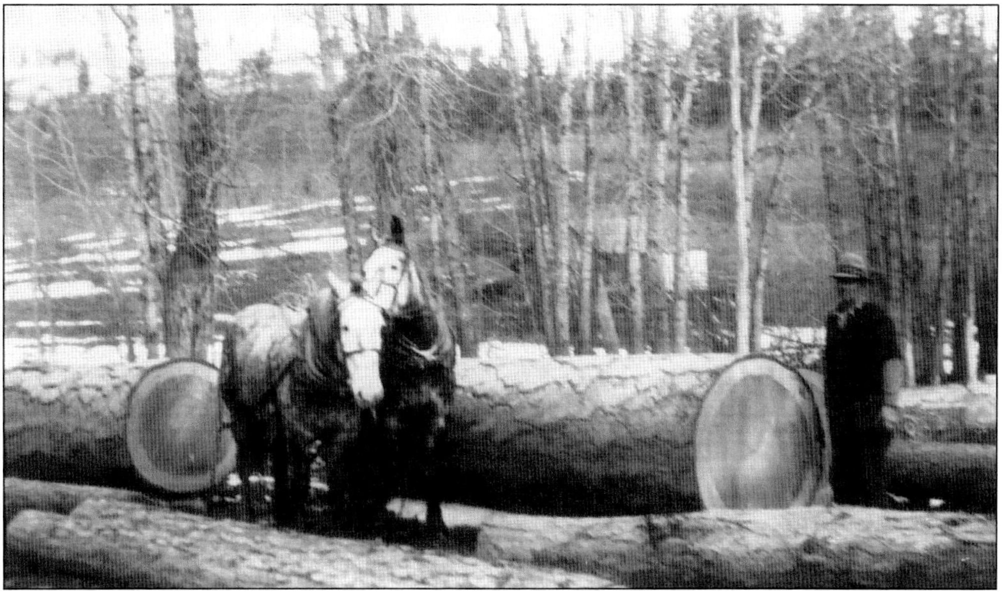

John Justus lived above Thompson Lake and worked at William Tucker's Peterson Gulch logging camp, which is where this April 24, 1919, picture was probably taken. The horses are Maggie and Molly.

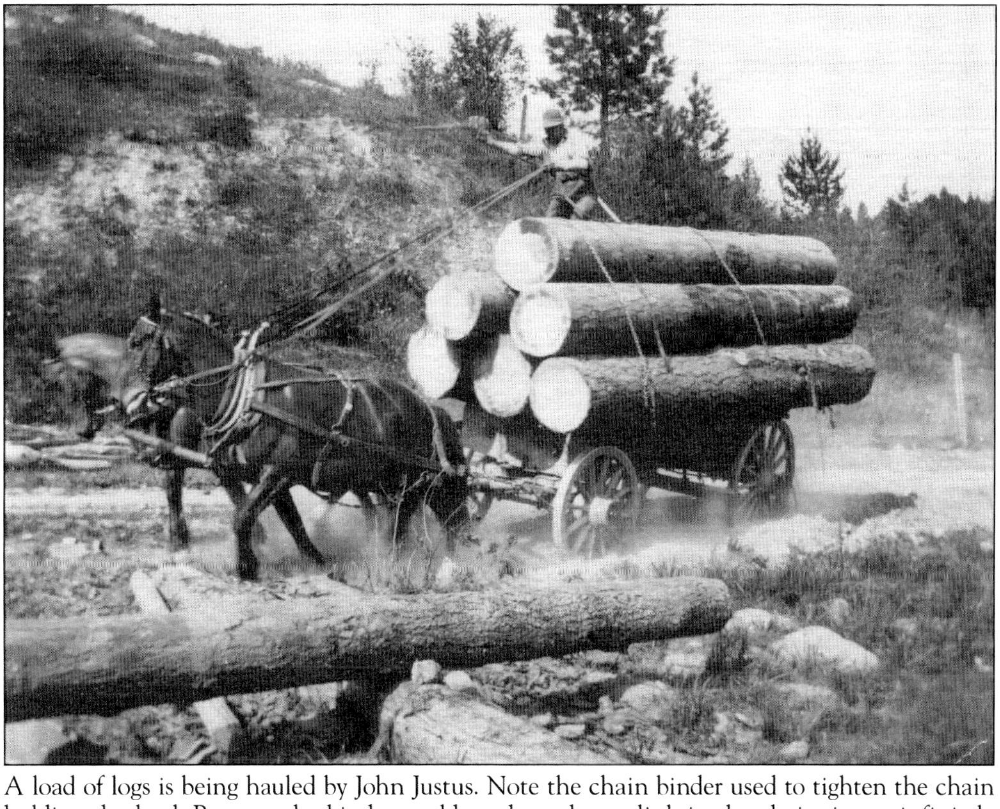

A load of logs is being hauled by John Justus. Note the chain binder used to tighten the chain holding the load. Because the binder could go through any link in the chain, it was infinitely adjustable. When the lever was pulled down, it tightened the chain against the logs.

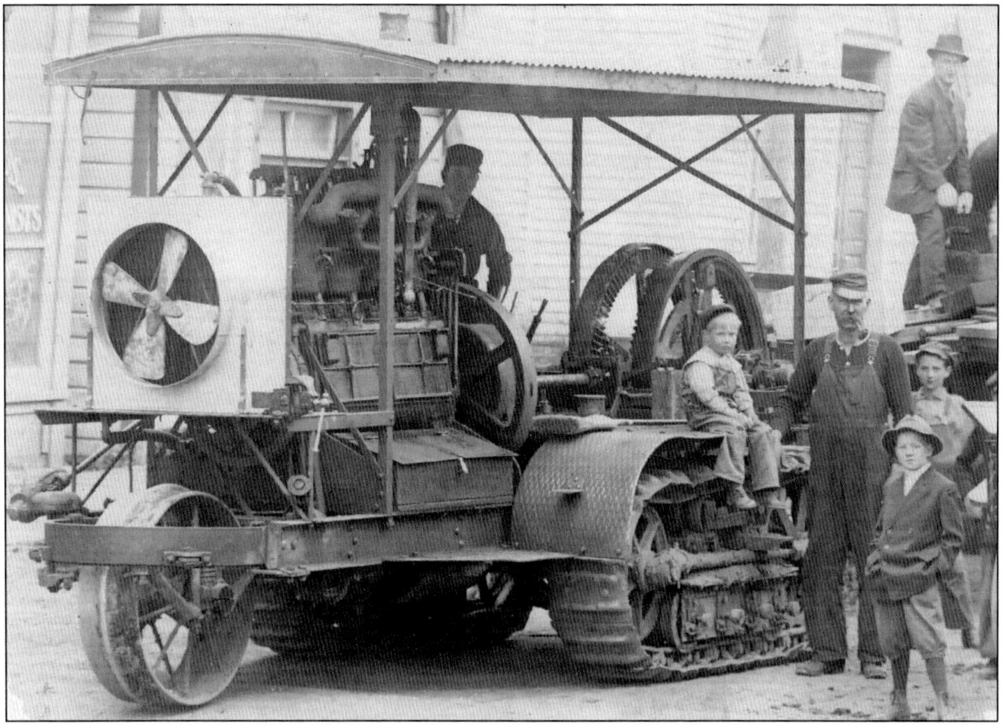

This early gas-powered Holt tiller-wheel cat was used to haul loads from the woods. Where a horse could only pull a single wagonload, this equipment could pull six. In this photograph, taken about 1913, three-year-old William "Bill" Lamb is sitting on the machine. His father, Thomas, is standing next to him.

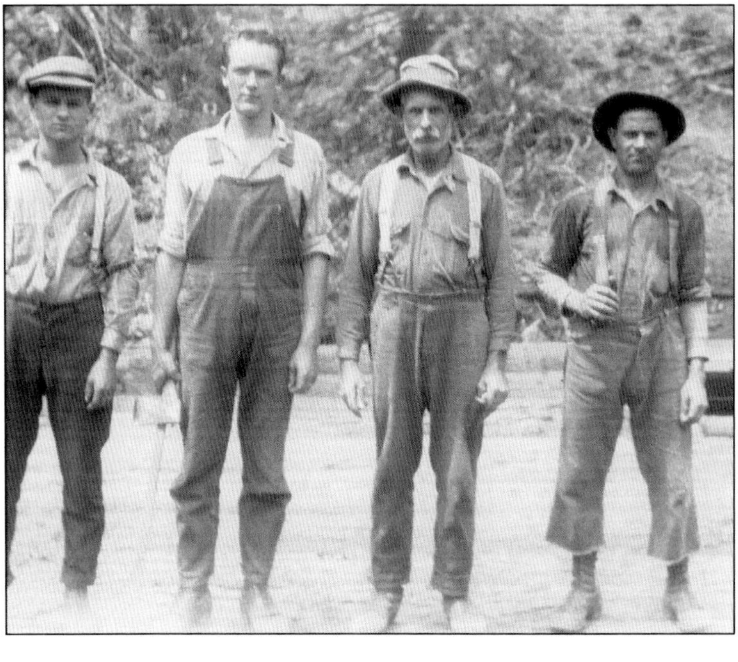

Chester Justus is second from the left in this undated photograph of four typically dressed logging camp workers. The others are unidentified. The logger on the right is wearing "stagged off" overalls. He has used his jackknife to cut the hem from his waist overalls, as they were called then, so if his pant leg was caught by a limb it would tear, allowing him to run from the falling tree.

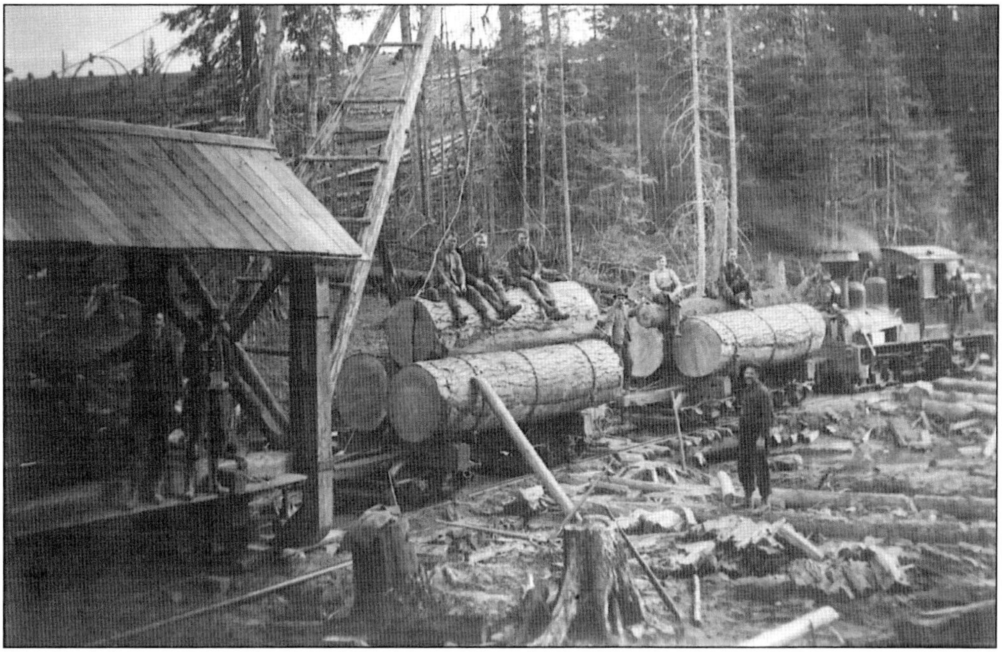

Lumber companies owned timberland, mills, tugboats, logging trains, and logging camps. Russell and Pugh owned more virgin white pine than any other company in the state. This photograph of logs being loaded on the logging train was taken at the Russell and Pugh logging camp at Powderhorn Bay around 1905.

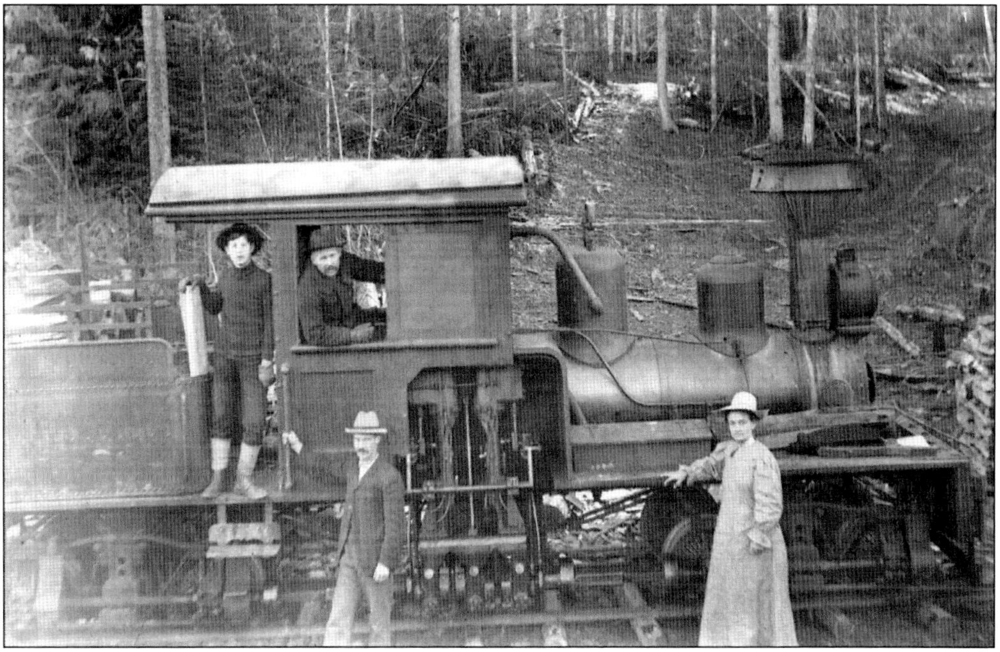

The Russell and Pugh Lumber Company had a logging railroad, which followed the Powderhorn drainage from the upper end of Stott Road to Powderhorn Bay. This c. 1905 photograph is of the engine of the Russell and Pugh train. The Grant Lumber Company also had a railroad, which ran from their camp on Harrison Flats west to Shingle Bay.

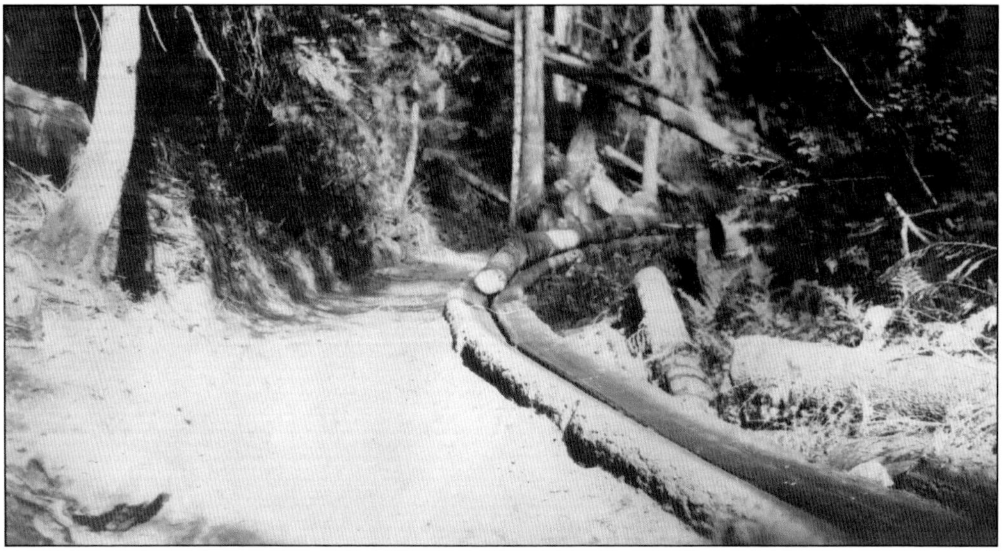

Chutes were constructed of hewn logs, laid end to end. On relatively flat terrain, horses did the dangerous job of pulling logs out of the woods, traveling the tote road beside the chute. If the terrain was steep, logs were hauled to the top of the chute and gravity took over. It took skill to keep logs moving at the right speed. If logs moved too swiftly, they either jumped the chute, causing pile-ups, or friction created sparks, causing fires. A gooseneck hook was put in the chute, or it was sprinkled with sand to slow the logs. Speed could be increased by greasing the chute. In winter, ice was used to speed the logs, or hot sand melted the ice and slowed the logs. These are two views of a chute with the tote road alongside.

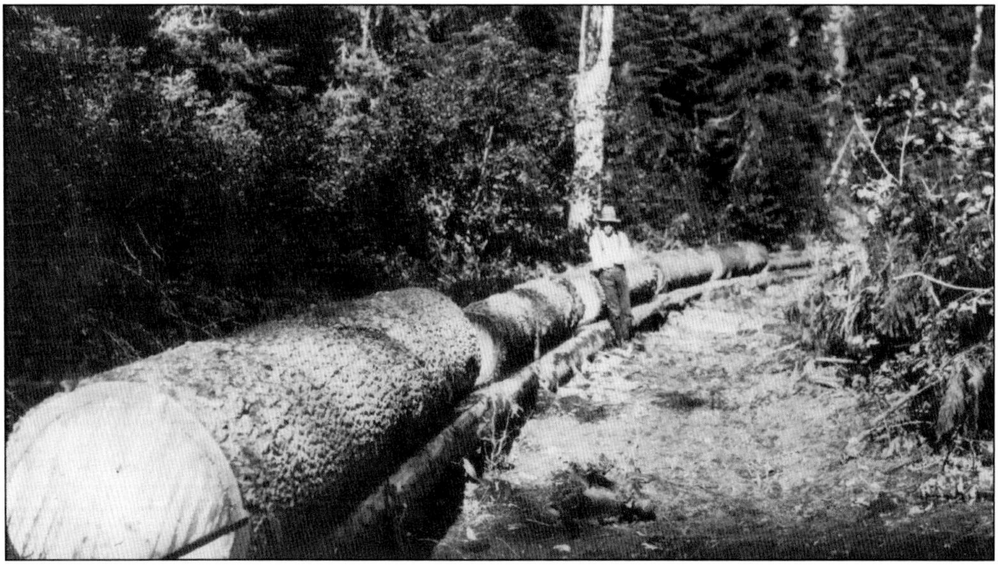

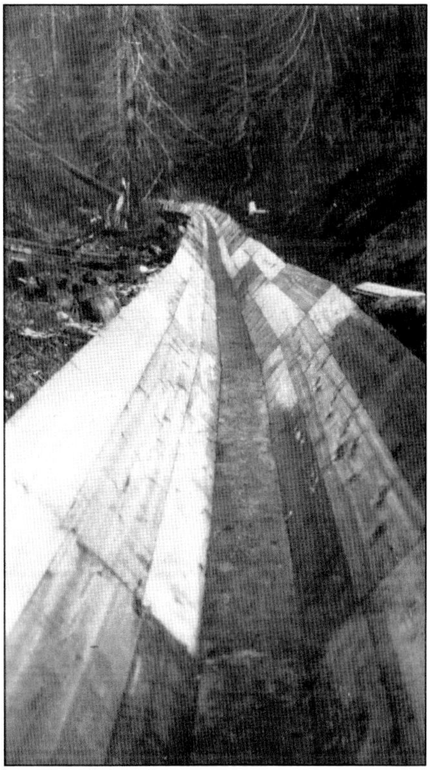

Chutes took logs directly to the lake, or they were stacked or "decked" on a rollway and then rolled into a flume. Flumes were filled with water from streams or ponds that "washed" the logs down to the lake. It took about 250,000 feet of lumber to build one mile of flume, a foot wide at the bottom and four feet wide at the top. Before a log left the woods, it was stamped on the end with the owner's distinguishing brand. This assured that the owner would be given credit at the mill for his logs. All logs were floated down the rivers together and were separated at the sorting gap.

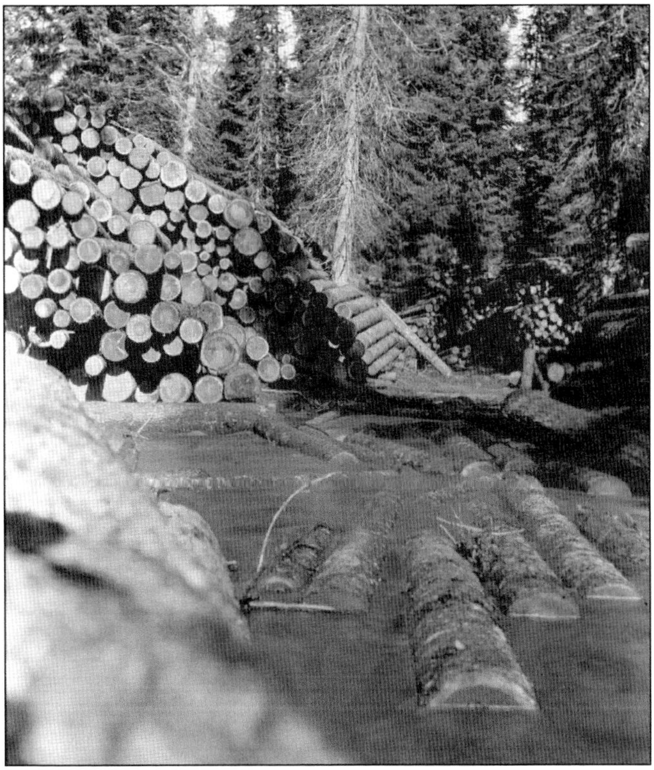

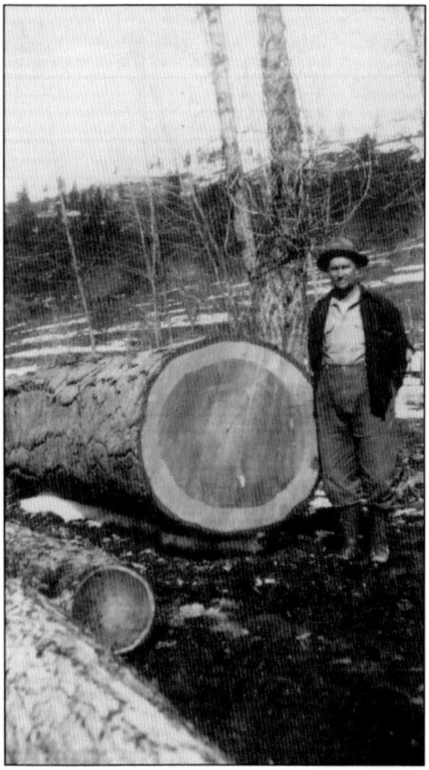

Logging camps were expensive to construct and operate. Besides the camp, there were chutes, roads, skid roads, and, occasionally, railroads and flumes to build. Wages and equipment for work at all stages of the operation needed to cover sawing, chute trailing, decking, loading, hauling, landing, scaling, cooking, and, before trucks, teamsters and blacksmiths. William K. Tucker, shown here on April 24, 1929, had several logging camps in the area at various times.

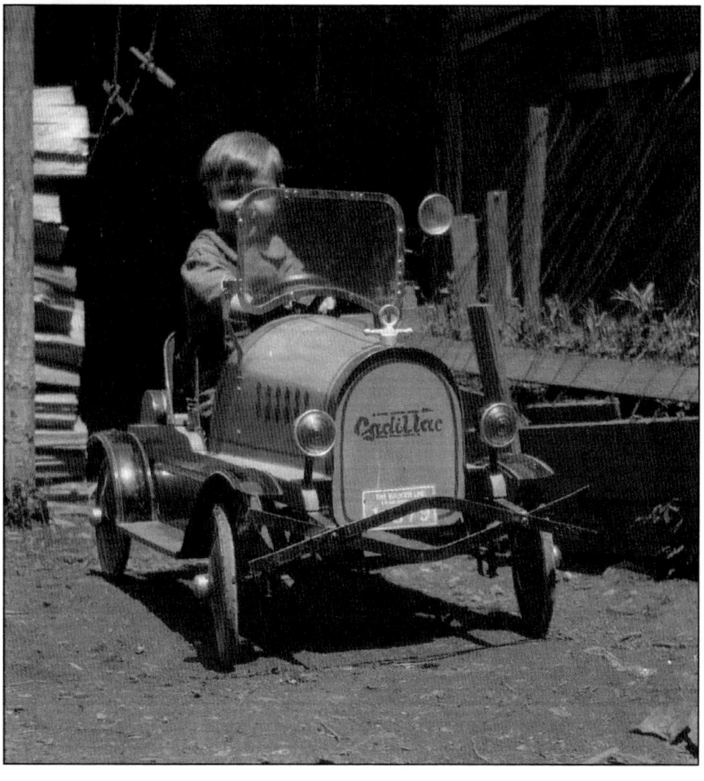

James Leslie Carns, age two in 1924, is driving his own Cadillac at his uncle William Tucker's Peterson Gulch logging camp. It was purchased for "Leslie" as a Christmas present by a camp worker who had no one else to buy for. This shows that not all loggers were rough or blew their money at the local establishments.

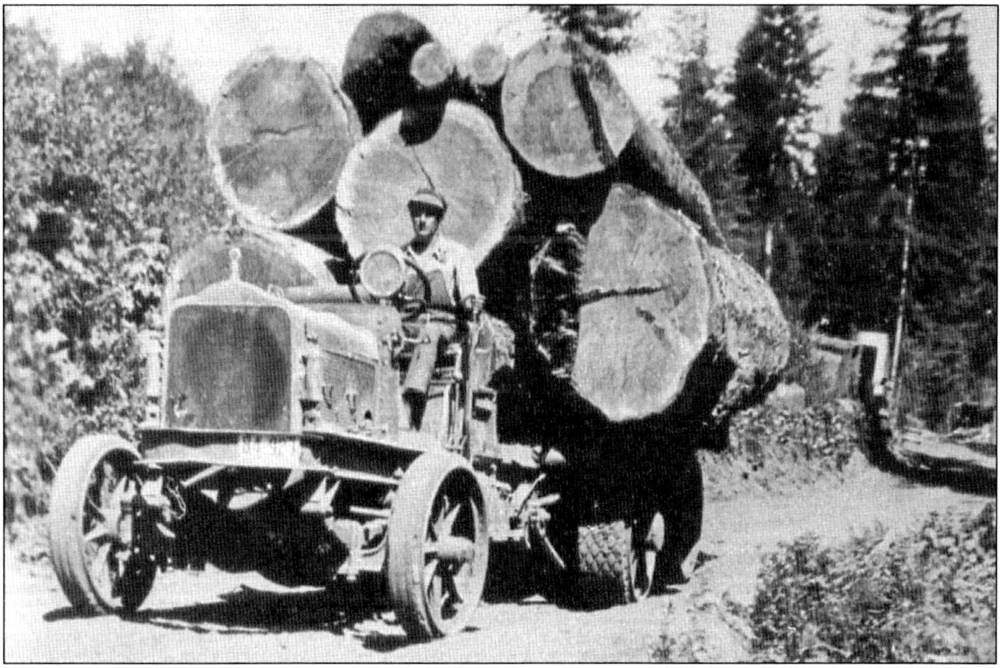

By the 1920s, horses were being replaced by trucks. This 1925 photograph shows Chester Justus driving a loaded truck from William Tucker's camp. With this heavy load, brakes were vital. However, early brakes were a woven lining riveted onto a band. The driver's feet were "boosters." When they got hot and expanded, there were no brakes. There was an emergency brake, but it was also a band.

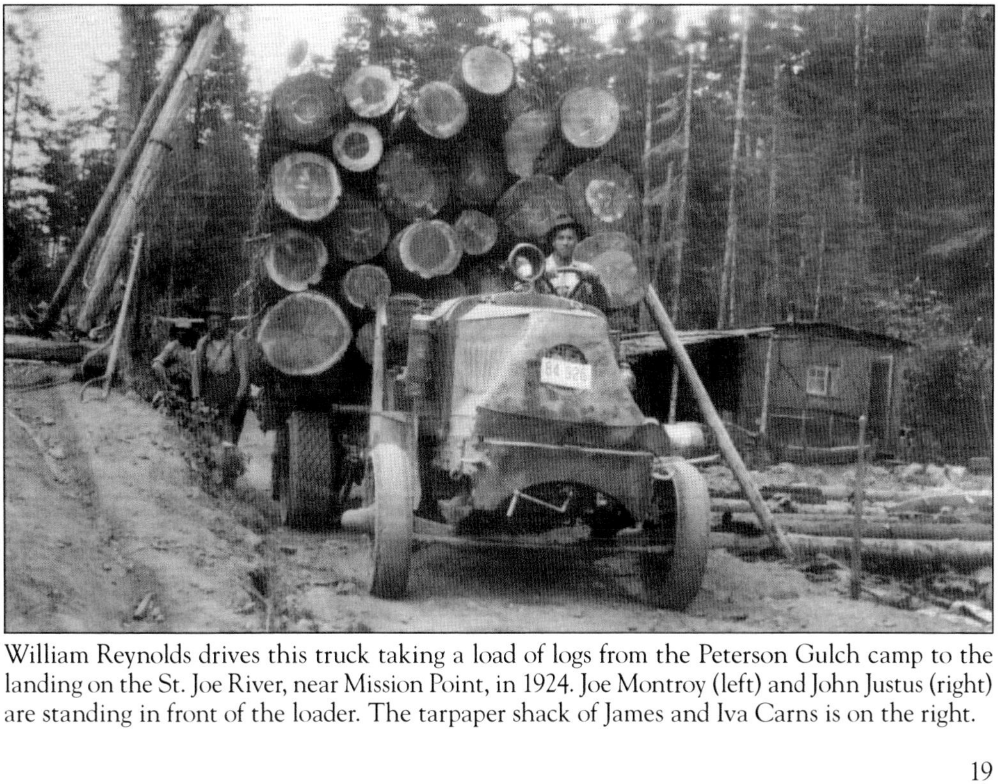

William Reynolds drives this truck taking a load of logs from the Peterson Gulch camp to the landing on the St. Joe River, near Mission Point, in 1924. Joe Montroy (left) and John Justus (right) are standing in front of the loader. The tarpaper shack of James and Iva Carns is on the right.

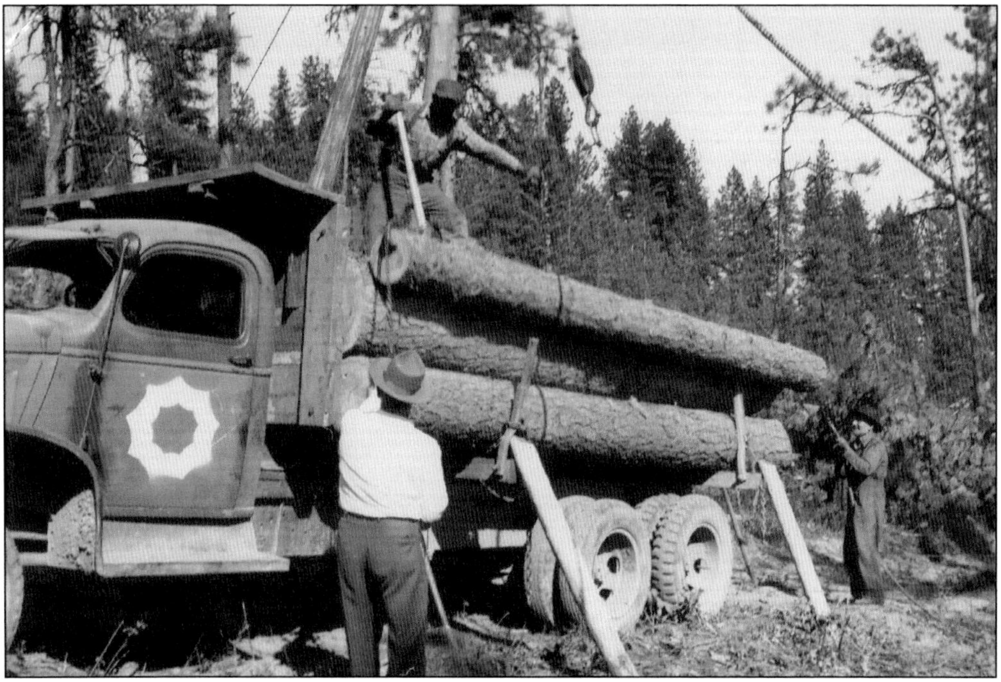

The job of the top loader was well respected, better paying, and important. It was his responsibility to be sure the load was properly balanced so it did not tip the truck over. Sandie Baillie is standing at the rear of the truck.

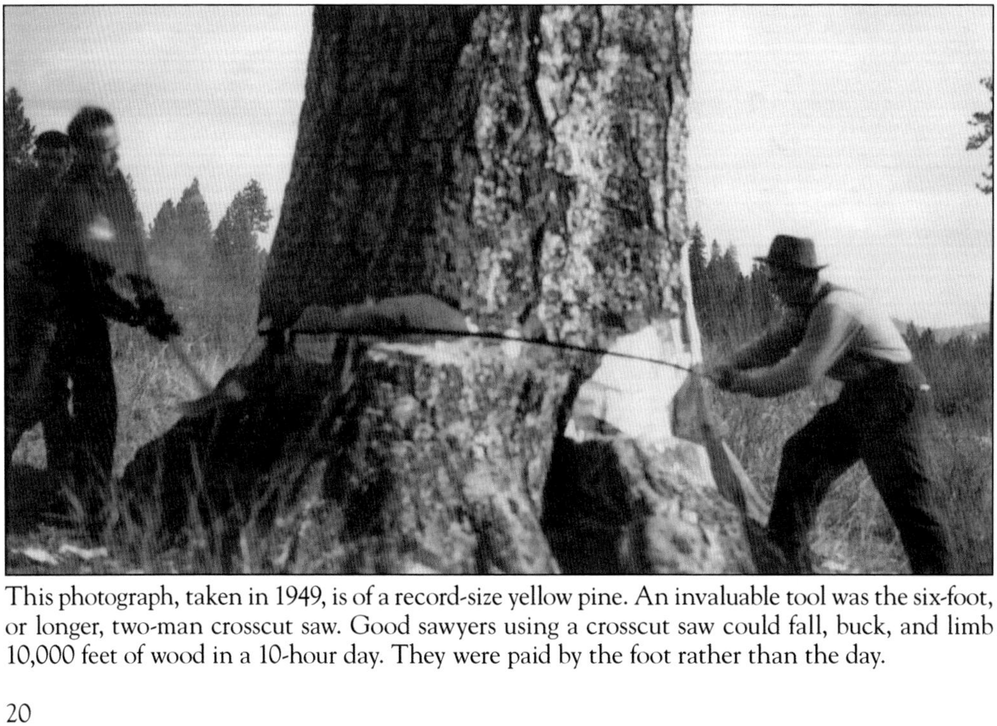

This photograph, taken in 1949, is of a record-size yellow pine. An invaluable tool was the six-foot, or longer, two-man crosscut saw. Good sawyers using a crosscut saw could fall, buck, and limb 10,000 feet of wood in a 10-hour day. They were paid by the foot rather than the day.

Sandie Baillie and Joseph Jenecik (front) are working in the woods in June 1951. Joseph is using a peavey, a pole with a hook near the end, which was used to move and load logs.

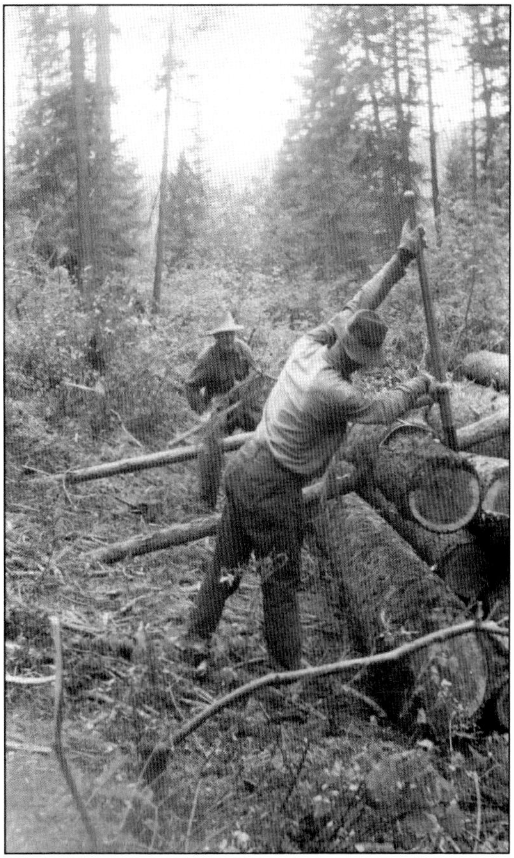

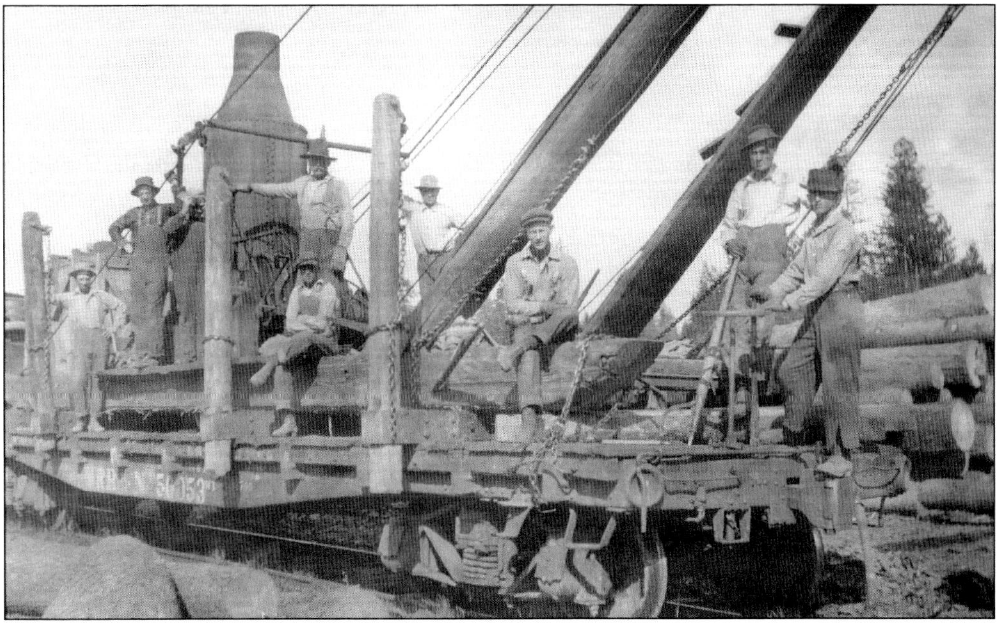

Trains were used to ship finished lumber and rough logs out of the area. This unidentified photograph shows a crew loading logs on a train.

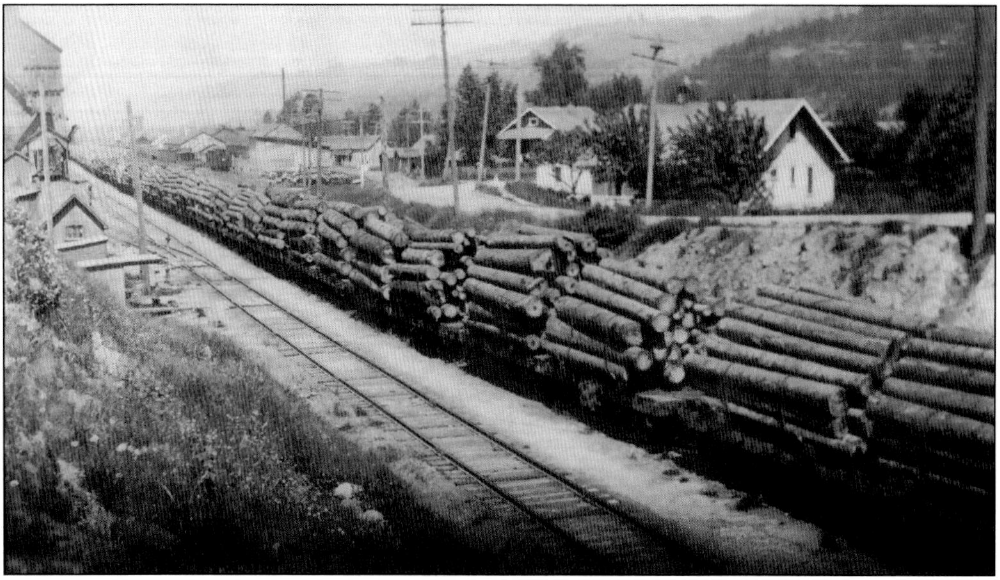

A train loaded with logs is waiting at a siding. The location of the train is not identified, but logs extend as far as the eye can see.

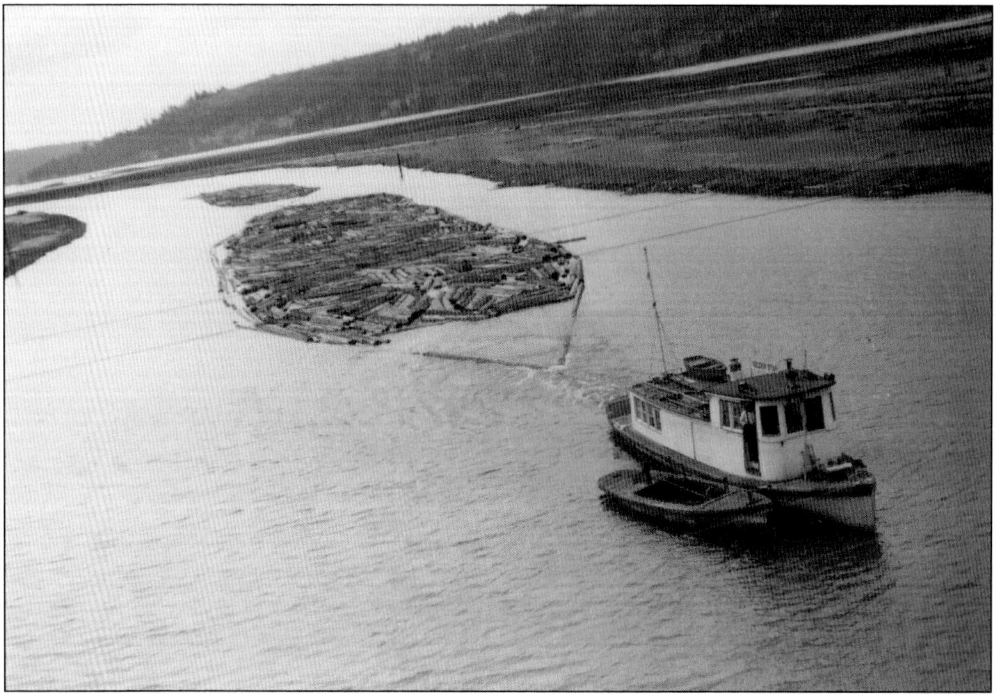

Railroad and lumber companies used tugboats for many tasks, like towing log booms. In this undated photograph, the *Golden Star* is towing a log boom on the Coeur d'Alene River heading to the Russell and Pugh mill in Springston. The outer logs are "boom sticks," which are peeled logs with a three-inch hole at each end. A "boom chain" goes through the holes and lashes them together.

Two

Mills

The City of Harrison came into being to support lumber mills. In 1889, three Crane brothers, William, Edwin, and Addison, along with their father, Silas W. Crane, and grandfather, George Jones, found the perfect site for a mill town. Timber in the surrounding countryside was plentiful and easily accessible. The lakefront was an ideal location for sawmills. The lake and nearby Coeur d'Alene and St. Joe Rivers made transport of logs and finished lumber products convenient and fairly inexpensive.

The first Harrison mill (1892) was located on railroad land, which bordered the lake. The finished mill products were piled for drying and shipping on the same platform over the water on which the mill stood. Soon the one mile of available waterfront was lined with sawmills and lumberyards.

If the city supported the lumber mills, the mills in turn supported the city of Harrison. The city's population would balloon to 2,000 when the mills were operating at full capacity. A full range of businesses to serve the workers soon flourished—hotels, saloons, food purveyors, general merchandise, hardware, a bank, and an opera house. The workers built homes and churches. The city could afford schools, electricity, phones, and public utilities.

The fire of 1917 altered the city's history. Many businesses burned and were not rebuilt. Three or four mills that had not burned operated for a few years, but then eventually closed due to the weak economy. The Russell and Pugh Lumber Company moved three miles up the Coeur d'Alene River to Springston. Employing about 100 men, it provided the economic base for Harrison until it closed in 1962. With no mills for employment, workers left town. The fire had started in a mill. It is an ironic twist of fate that the mills that built the town were the beginning of its decline.

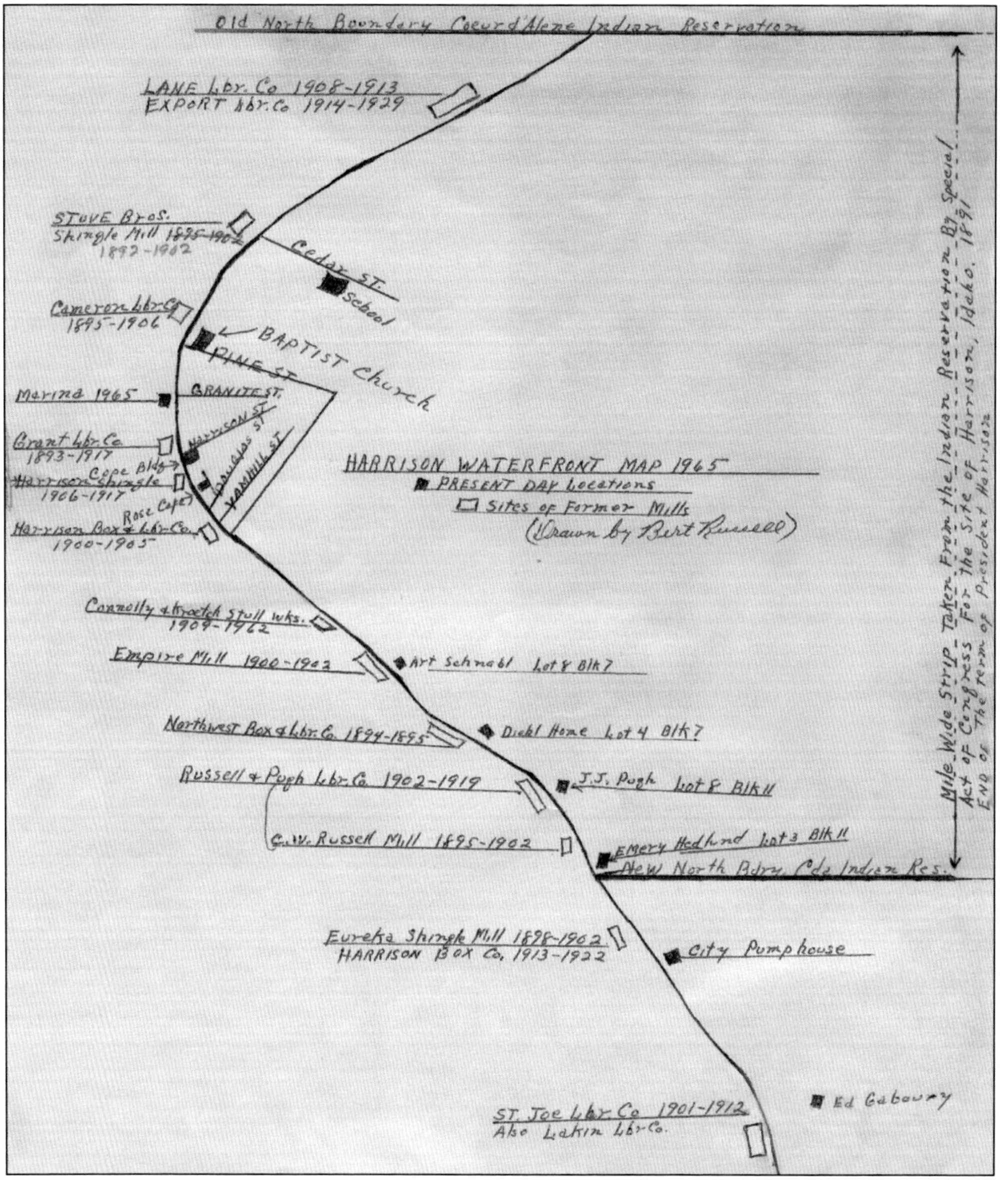

Here is a map of the Harrison mills, including their dates of operation, drawn by Bert Russell in 1965. In this chapter the mills are discussed in order from north to south.

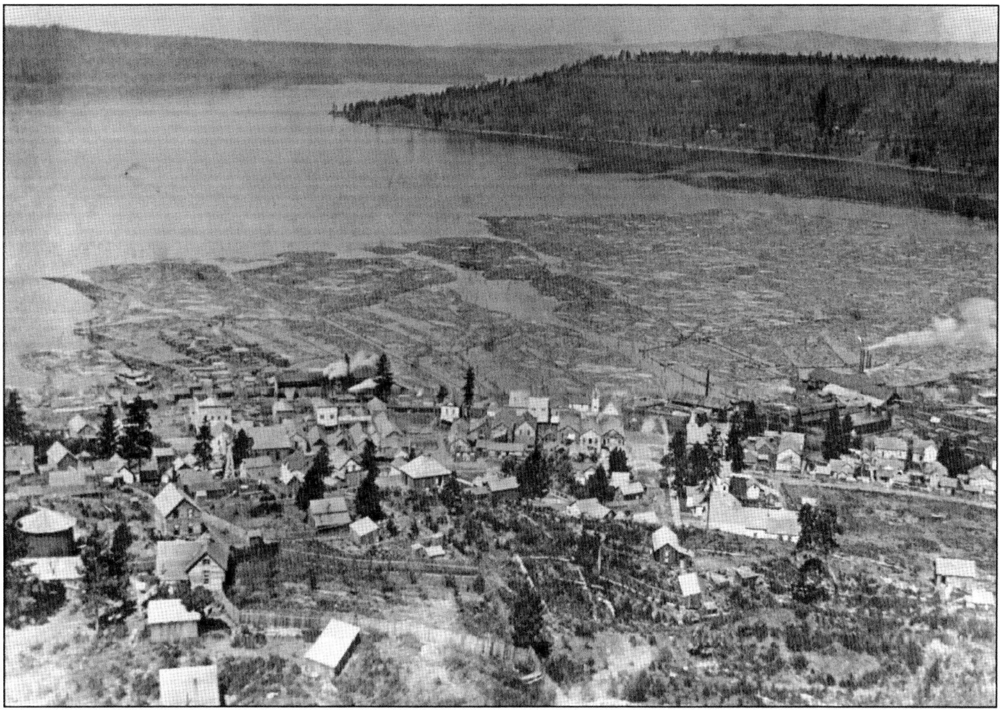

Looking west toward Harlow Point, this is a view of Harrison from the hill above town. The mouth of the Coeur d'Alene River, where Edwin Crane operated a sorting works, is toward the right. Stored logs can be seen floating in the lake. The Export Lumber Company sawmill is at the far right.

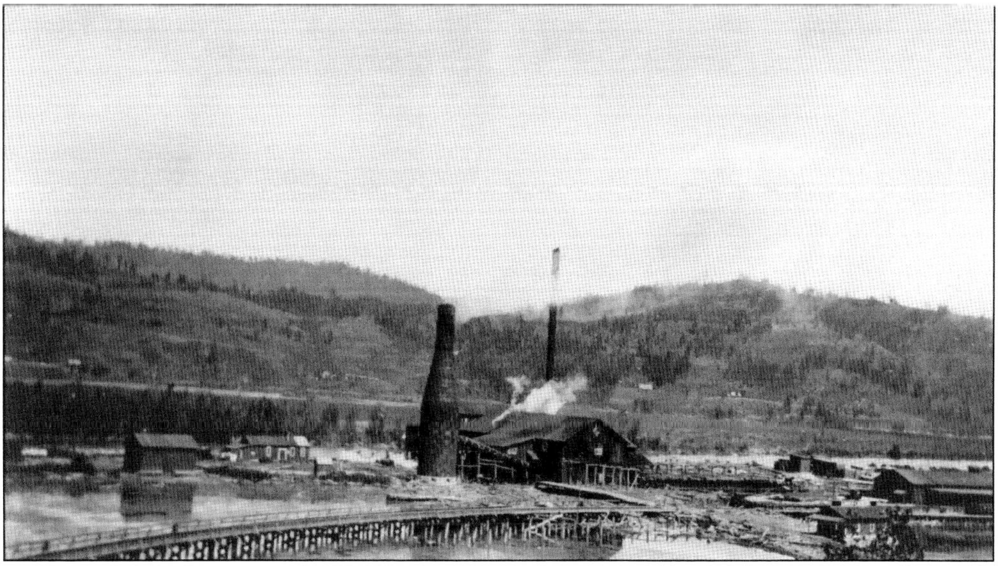

The Lane Lumber Company was moved to Harrison in 1908. In 1914, it was purchased by Fred Herrick and renamed the Export Lumber Company, pictured here in 1918. He owned the Milwaukee Lumber Company in St. Maries and other lumber investments in Idaho, Montana, and Oregon. Floods, forest fires, high costs, and the Depression were the leading factors of the bankruptcy of the Herrick empire and closure of his Harrison enterprise in 1929.

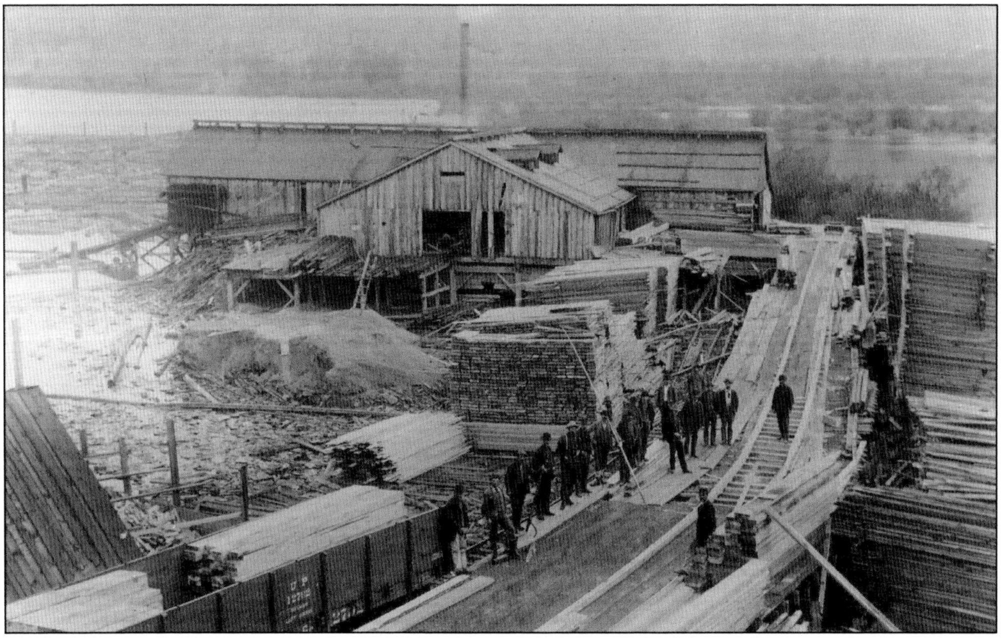

One of the first mill owners in Harrison was Martin Sexton, who moved his sawmill from Tensed to Harrison in 1892. That same year, he sold the mill to Donald Cameron and his brother. The merger with their existing mill created one of the largest mills in the country. This photograph is of the Cameron Lumber Company in 1901.

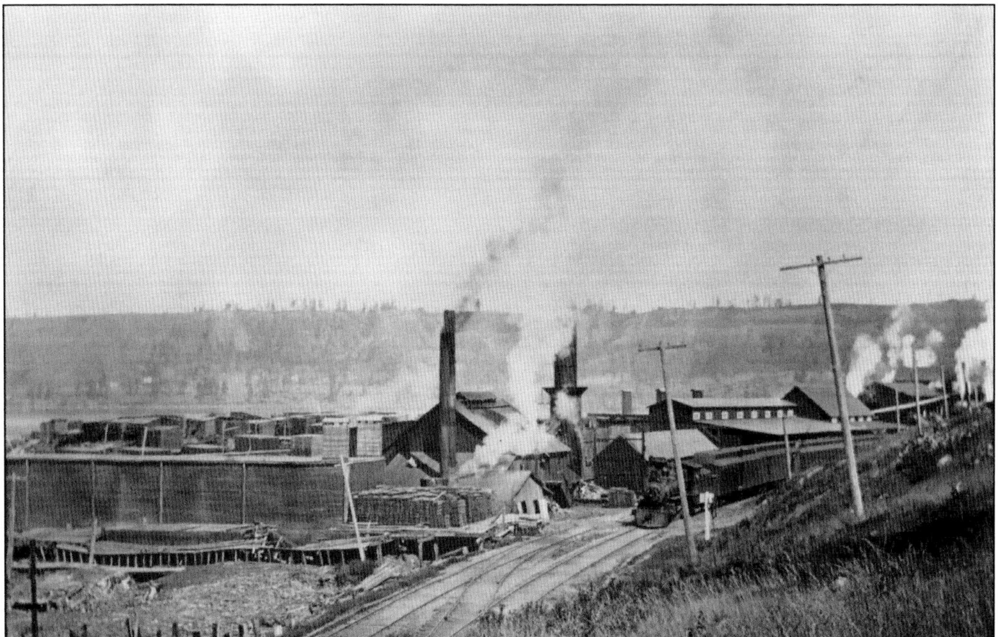

The Grant brothers, Fred and Ernest, bought the Fisher Brothers mill (formerly Hogue-Fisher) in St. Maries, moved it by barge to Harrison, and set up business in 1893 as the Grant Lumber Company. This very successful mill was enlarged and modernized over the years. It was at this mill that the July 21, 1917, fire started, which devastated Harrison. Today, a marina sits on the site.

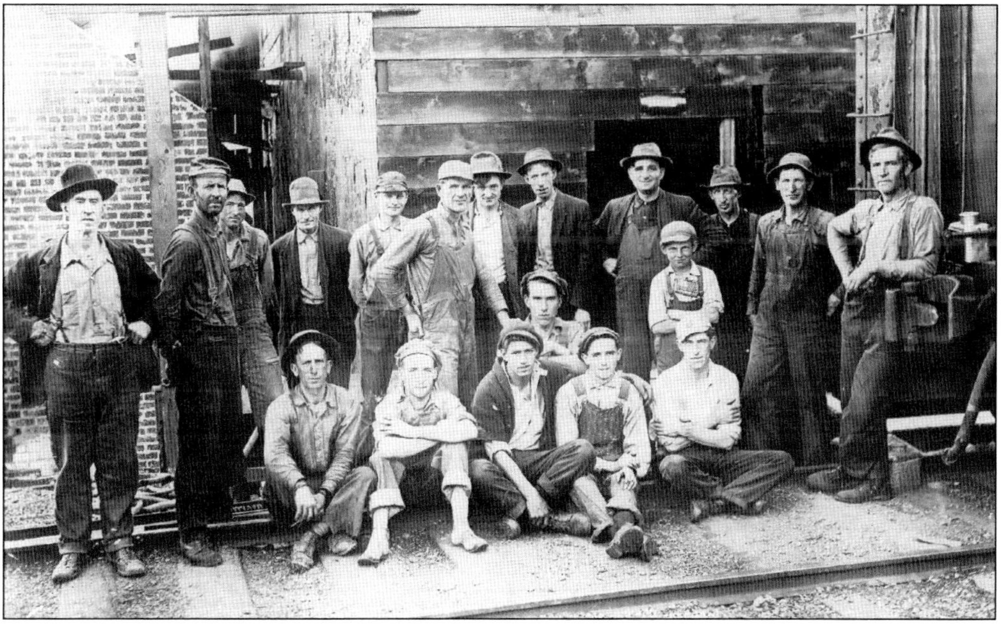

By 1892, Harrison had two shingle mills, Bacon-Herrin and Stuve Brothers. Victor Carlson and Samuel and Joseph Avery started the Eureka Shingle Company in 1899. Over the years, ownership and its name were changed, and eventually the building burned and was later rebuilt. In 1915, Joseph Avery and partners started a new business, the Harrison Shingle Company, in a new location. This photograph of the crew was taken in 1915.

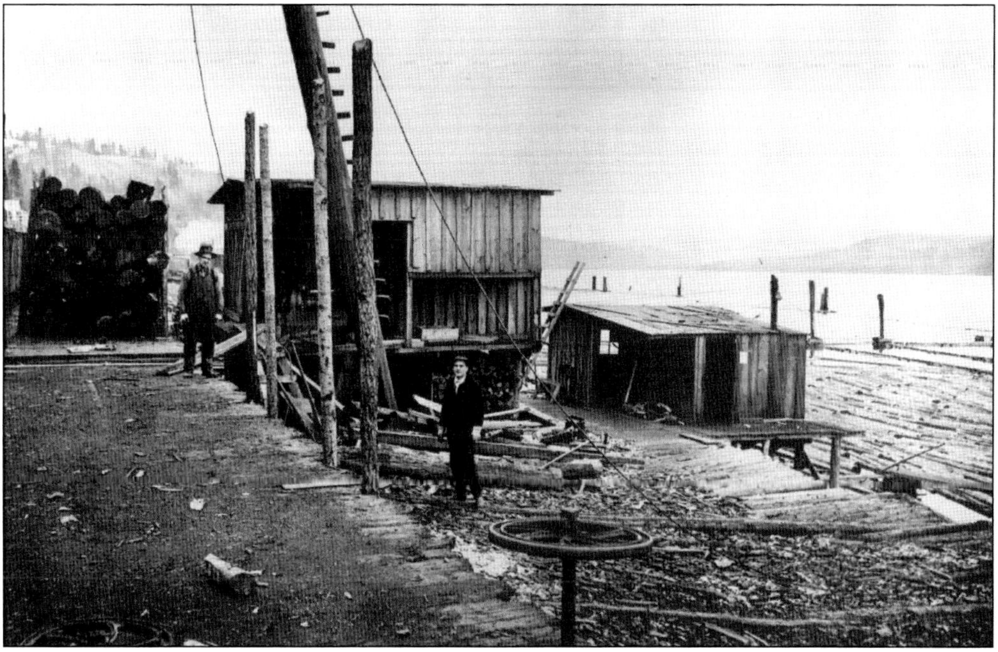

Logs lay in the lake in front of the Connolly and Kroetch Stull Works around 1915. Except in a few big mines, shoring material is composed of peeled logs, which are called stulls. Due to pressure and moisture, timbers did not last long in the days before wood was pressure treated. Many stulls would be shipped to Silver Valley mines between 1909 and 1962 while the stull works was in operation.

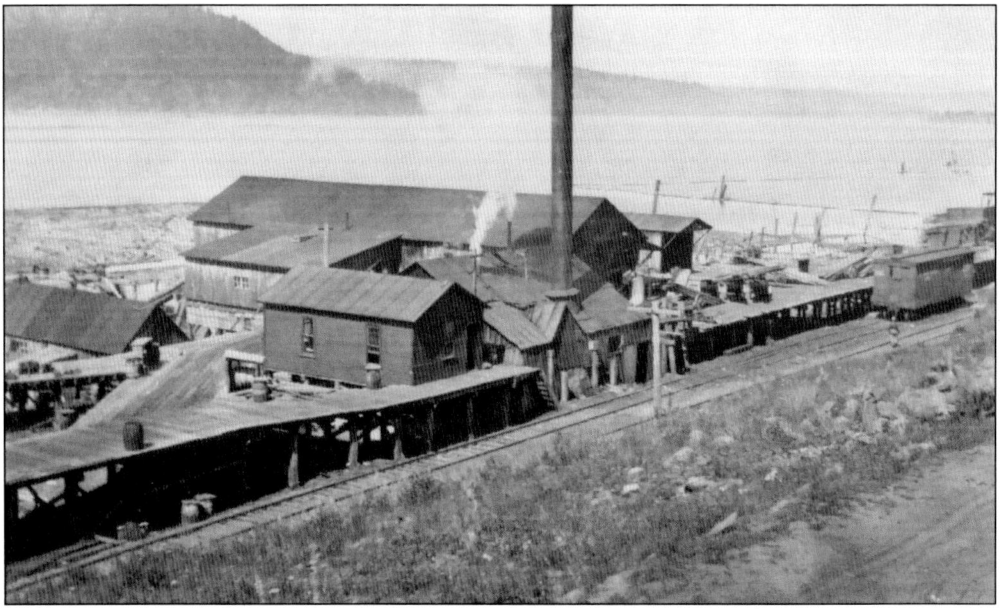

Charles W. Russell was an example of those who followed the woods from Vermont to Minnesota to Idaho. In 1894, he moved a sawmill to Harrison. This photograph of the Charles W. Russell mill, taken about 1900, shows the tramway between the mill and the railroad. Lumber was pushed on two-wheeled carts to where it could be handed down from the tram instead of being lifted up from the ground.

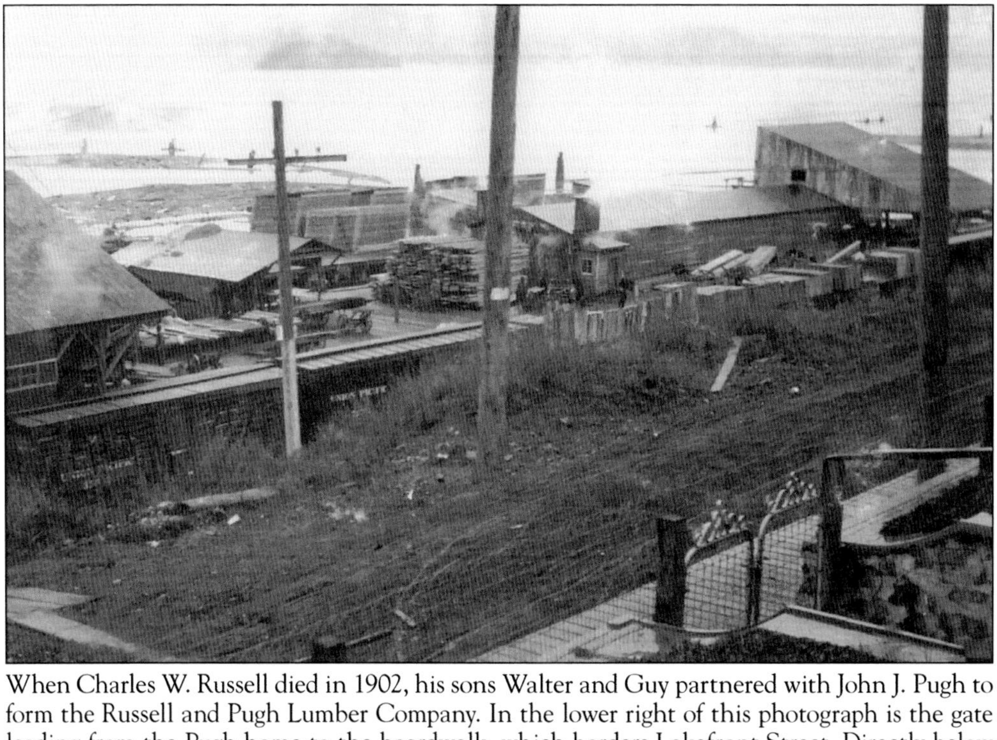

When Charles W. Russell died in 1902, his sons Walter and Guy partnered with John J. Pugh to form the Russell and Pugh Lumber Company. In the lower right of this photograph is the gate leading from the Pugh home to the boardwalk, which borders Lakefront Street. Directly below the street are the railroad, mill, and lumberyard. The mill was destroyed by fire in 1919.

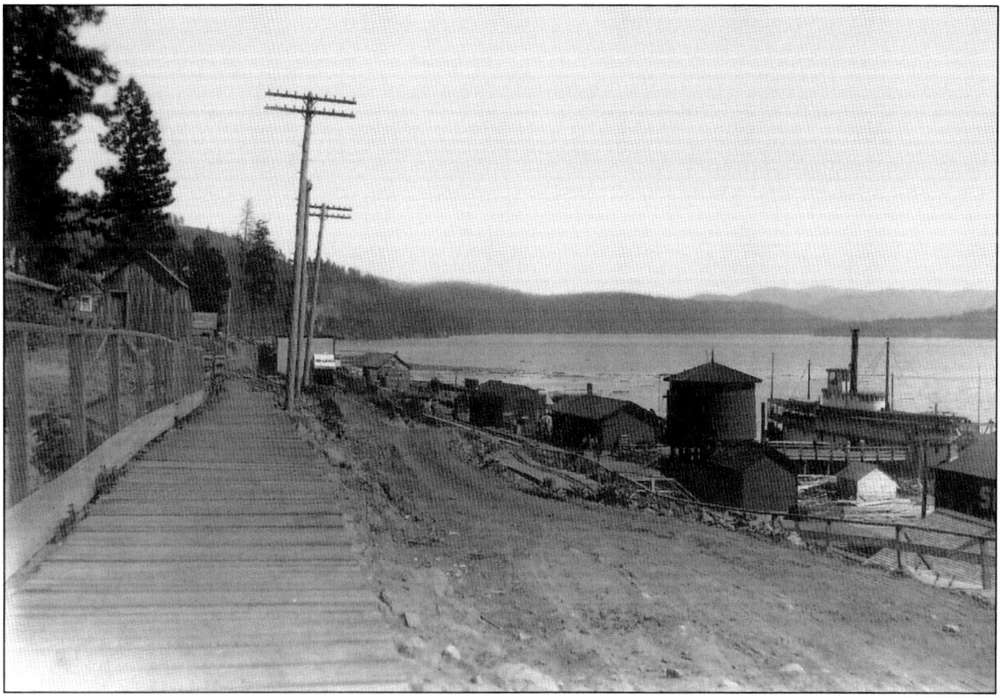

Since wood was plentiful, sidewalks in town were made of boards. This boardwalk ran along Front Street from the main business district south to the Box Factory. Parts of the boardwalks, which stretched gracefully over much of the town, lasted until the 1970s. The *Georgie Oakes* is docked at the waterfront about 1900.

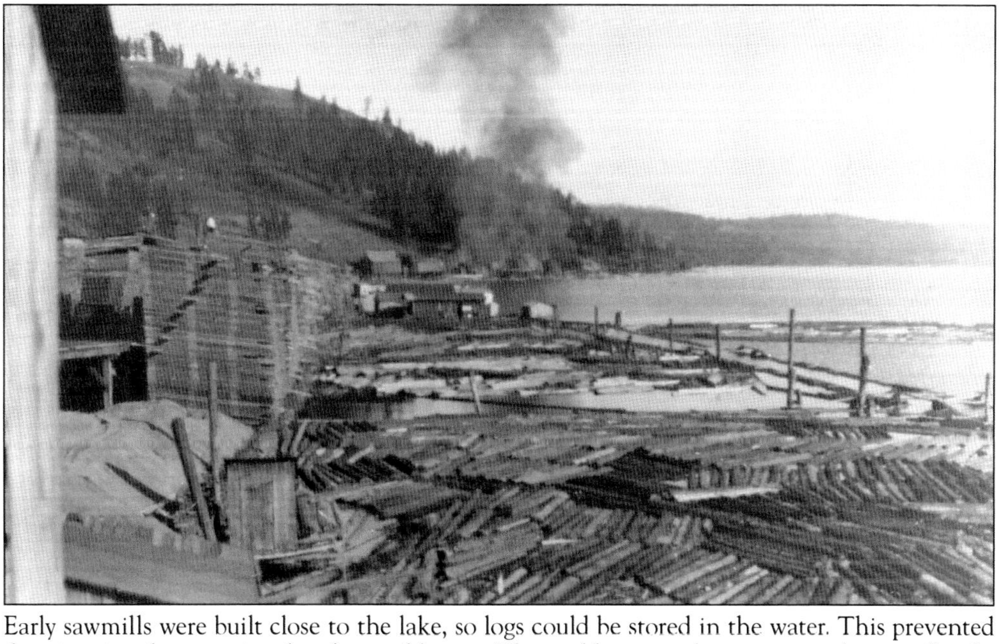

Early sawmills were built close to the lake, so logs could be stored in the water. This prevented deterioration from rotting, beetles, and borers. The problem was that winter and spring floods, which occurred almost every year, caused a lot of damage to mills and stacked lumber. The lakebed is still littered with sunken logs, which are in excellent condition.

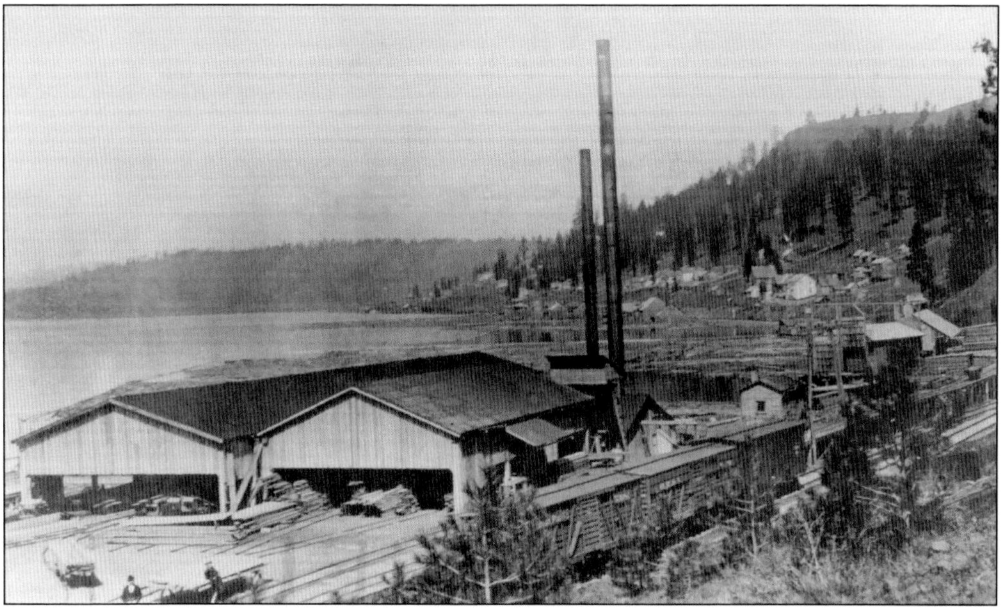

The St. Joe Lumber Company was built in 1900 and destroyed by fire in 1908. This picture was taken in 1903. From 1913 to 1916, the Duluth Lumber Company operated a mill on the site. For some reason, it was still called the St. Joe Mill. To add to the confusion, it was also called the Lakin Mill, probably for the mill manager. It was also destroyed by fire.

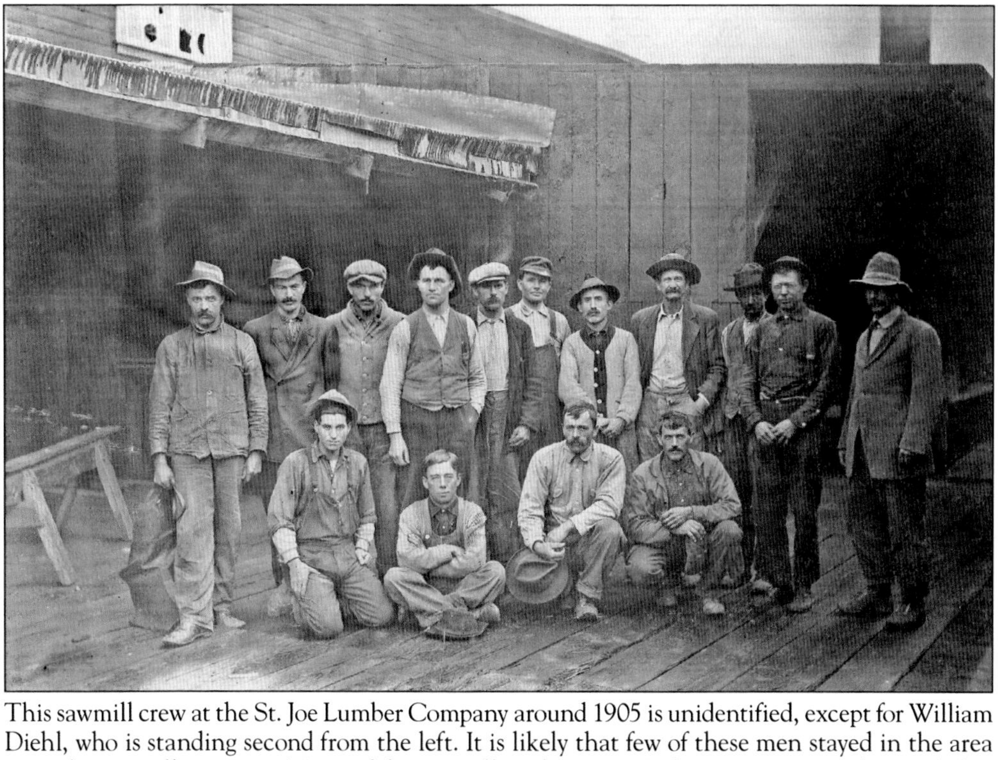

This sawmill crew at the St. Joe Lumber Company around 1905 is unidentified, except for William Diehl, who is standing second from the left. It is likely that few of these men stayed in the area once the sawmill was gone. Many of the sawmill workers were Italian immigrants who resided in a boarding and rooming house or a tent city operated by Jim Pedro.

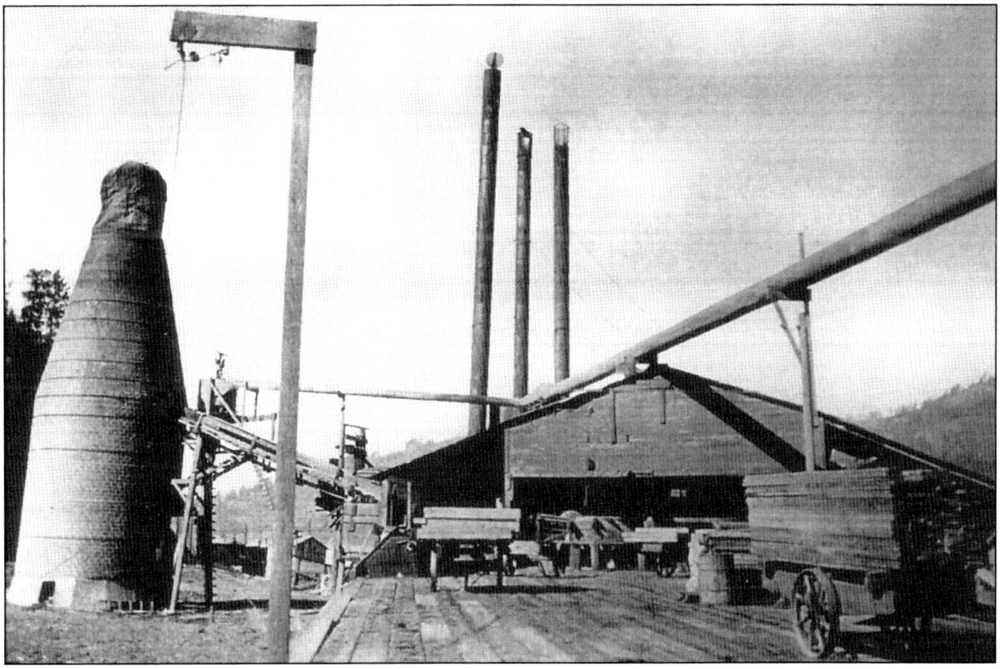

This photograph of the Russell and Pugh mill in Springston was taken in the 1930s. At the left is the burner, which burned log trimmings and sawdust. This heated a system of water pipes, which fed the boiler room. Steam was piped to the generator that ran the carriage and the saw. Early mills were located on a lake or river to have a continual source of water.

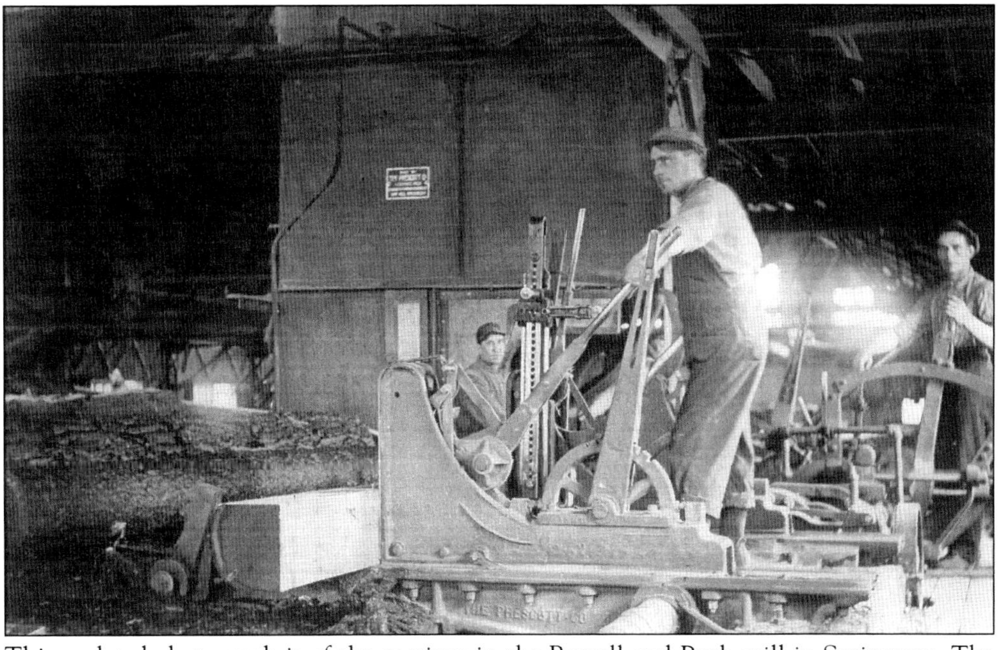

This undated photograph is of the carriage in the Russell and Pugh mill in Springston. The carriage was operated by the sawyer. The "dogger" rode the carriage and turned the logs as they moved through the saw. The job of sawyer was most integral to mill operations; the job of "dogger" was the most dangerous.

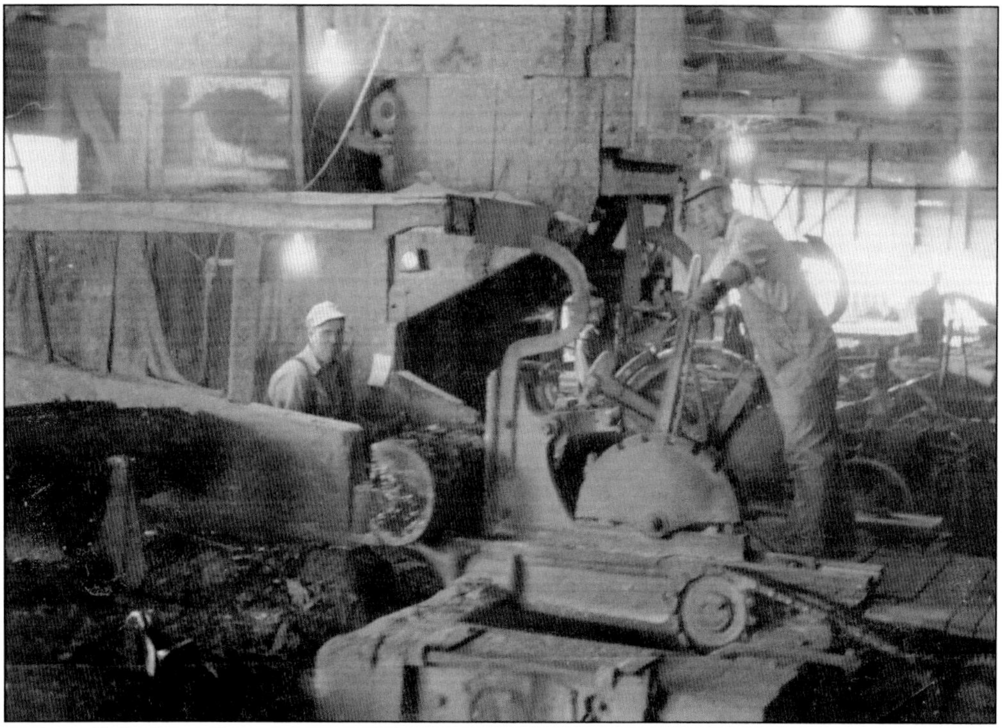

Early mills had circular saws. Few of these were large enough to cut entirely through the largest logs. The top saw was supposed to be in line with the bottom saw, which was not always the case. As sawmills were improved and modernized, they were equipped with band saws, which could saw boards from any size log. This is the interior of the Russell and Pugh mill in Springston.

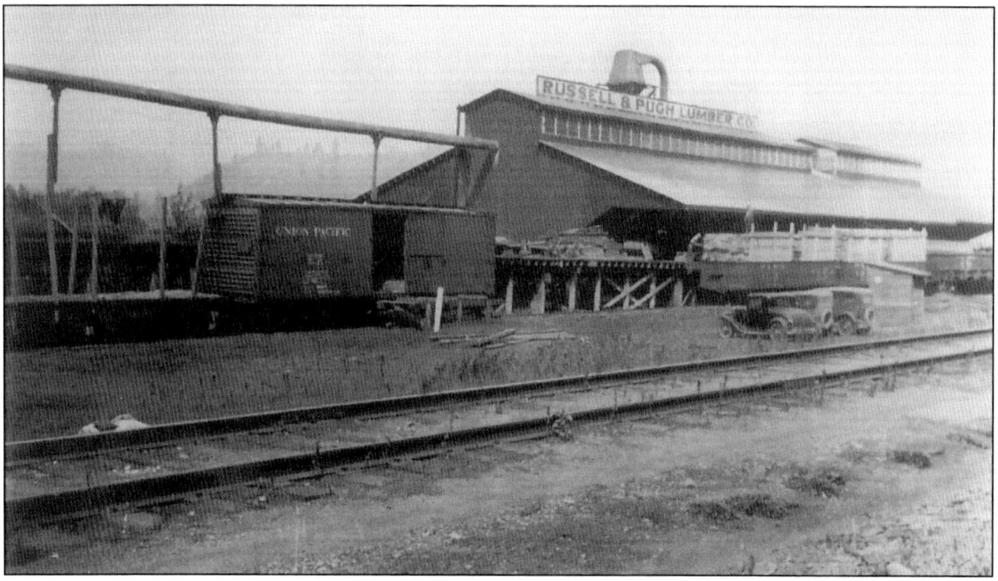

Lumber went from the carriage to the edger and then to the green chain, where it was stacked for drying. Dried lumber then went to the planer, where it was smoothed, preparing it for usage. As with all mill operations, feeding the boards through the planner was a dangerous occupation. Taken about 1934, this image is of the planer mill at the Russell and Pugh Lumber Company in Springston.

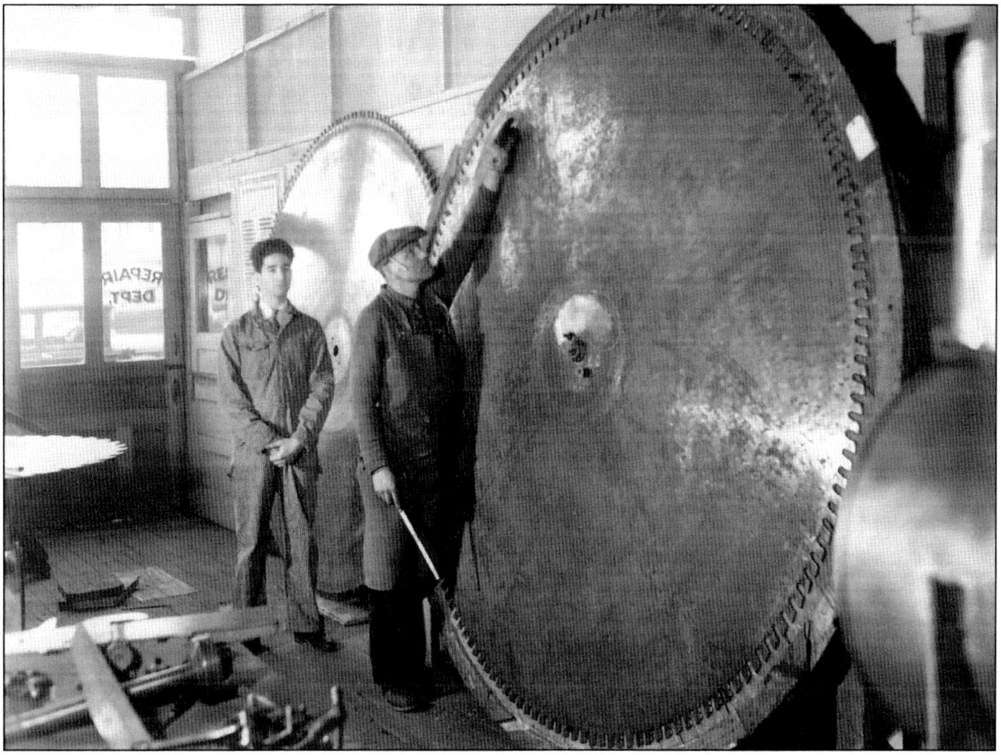

This 96-inch-diameter saw with a 9-inch crack was taken to Spokane, Washington, to be welded by Central Saw Works in the 1930s.

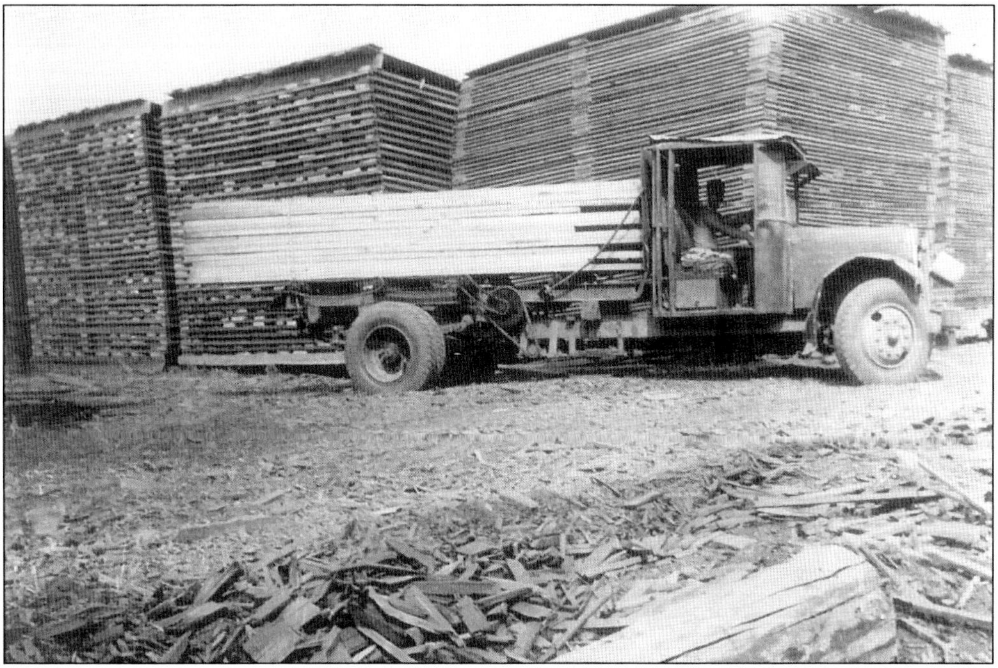

In 1934, this lumber truck is working in the yard of the Russell and Pugh mill at Springston. These lumber stacks will soon be shipped from the area by train.

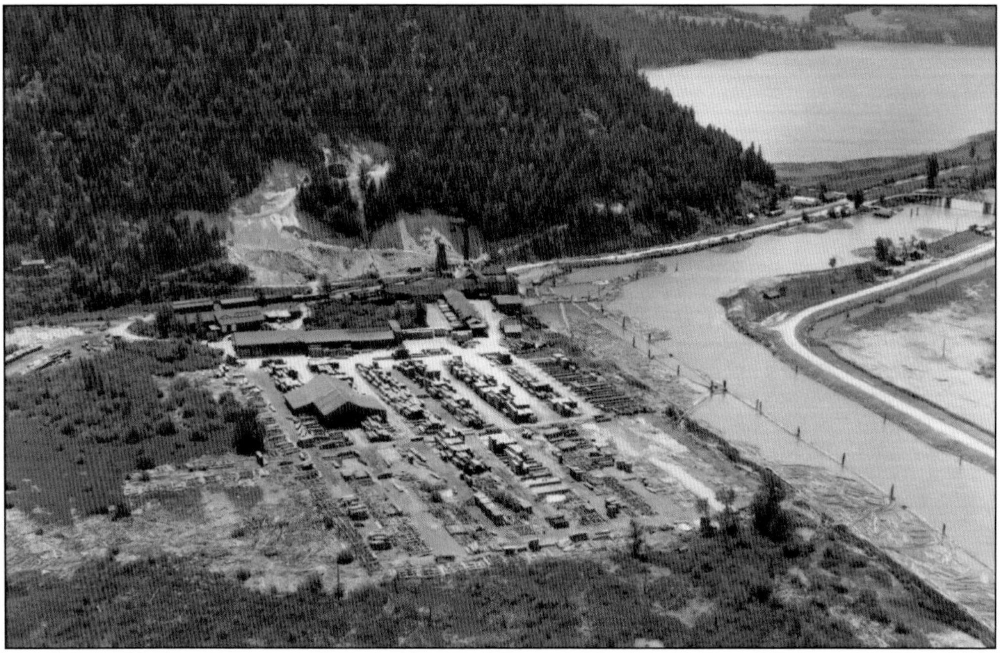

In 1951, John J. Pugh sold his interest in the Russell and Pugh Lumber Company. Operations continued as the Russell Lumber Company. In this 1952 aerial view of the company, Springston is at the upper-right corner between the Coeur d'Alene River and Anderson Lake. Note the piles of stacked lumber.

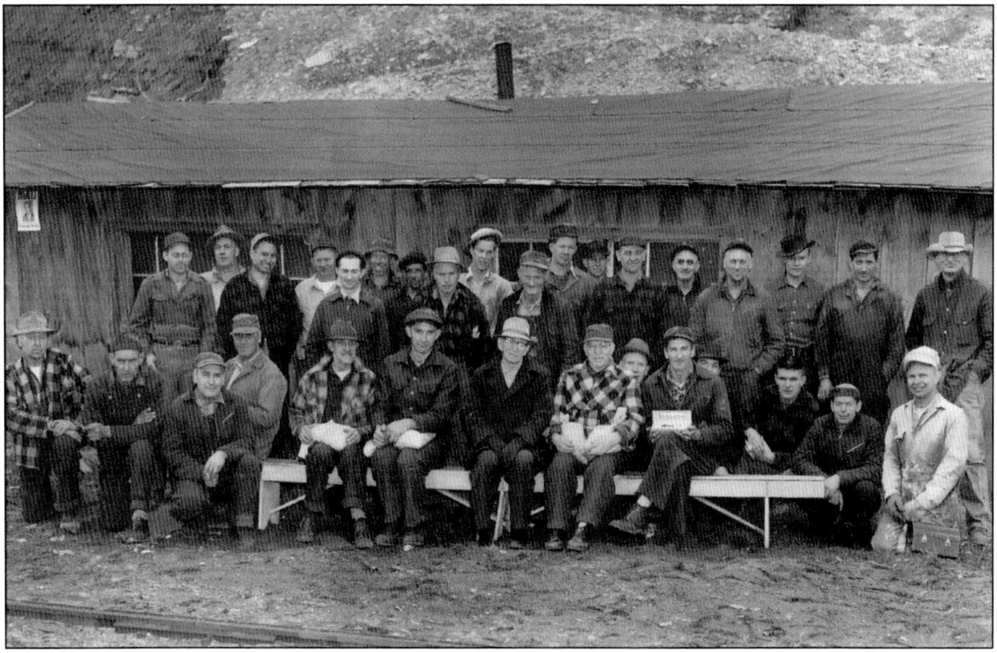

This photograph of the Russell Lumber Company sawmill crew was taken in 1955 as part of a ceremony honoring four employees who had worked for the company for more than 26 years. Seated on the bench are, from left to right, Axel Crantz, Clarence Asbury, company president W.B. Russell, Leo Chounard, and Bob VanBlaricom. When this last mill in the Harrison area closed in 1962, it was the longest operating mill in the state.

Three

Homesteads and Pioneers

The Homestead Act of 1862 was amended several times with different requirements, such as building a cabin and planting some fruit trees. Depending on the area, there were various other requirements. Families began settling the surrounding area in the 1890s, usually close to lakes and rivers that were used for transportation.

On Monday, August 9, 1909, in Coeur d'Alene, lucky winners were informed they had won 160 acres. Most of this acreage was timberland. Under this act, settlement could start near Harrison beginning on September 1, 1910. However, it was necessary to locate a piece of property on which to file. They did this by hiring a man called a locator. Knowledgeable about the homestead area, he would pick out a piece of ground that he thought would fit the person who had a winning number. His fee was usually $100, with half of it being paid immediately and the other half due when they were shown their acreage. Sometimes the locator selected more than one piece for a future landowner, which gave the settler options.

The homesteader was required to live on the property for a designated time, build a cabin, and clear one acre. They had to pay a small amount to be issued a patent or deed. Due to the way the regulations were written, some were kept a short time by the homesteader and then sold to lumber companies who logged the land. In a short time, these lumber companies harvested the timber and then moved out. Because there was a lot of fuel left on the ground, fires were a constant threat. Soon much of the beauty of the St. Joe River and Coeur d'Alene River valleys was gone. Miraculously, this area on the east side of Coeur d'Alene Lake was growing more timber. Native trees are hardy and germinate themselves. Eventually, mature forests emerged, proving that timber is a renewable resource. Beauty has returned to the area that newcomers and descendents of these original homesteaders and pioneers call home.

This chapter tells the story of some of the earliest pioneer settlers in the Harrison area.

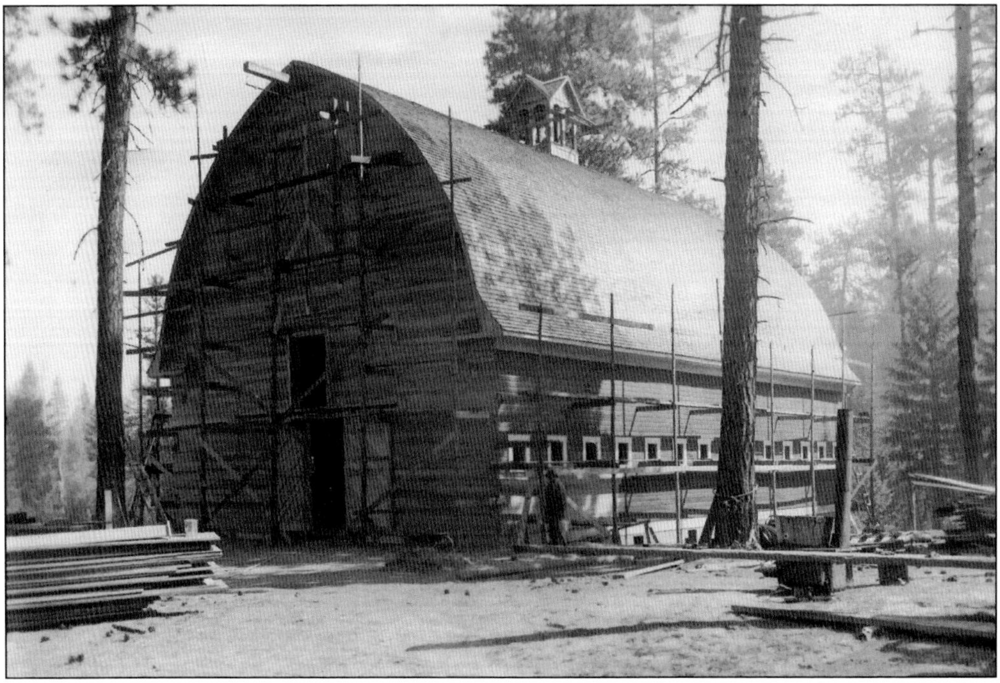

James and Alice Miller and their son Ralph moved to their new homestead on the Harrison Flats in the spring of 1910. They were homestead number 44 in Kootenai County. They lived in a tent through the summer until they could build a small cabin. The barn was under construction in 1912 when this picture was taken. The beams were hand-hewn logs that were 40 to 60 feet long.

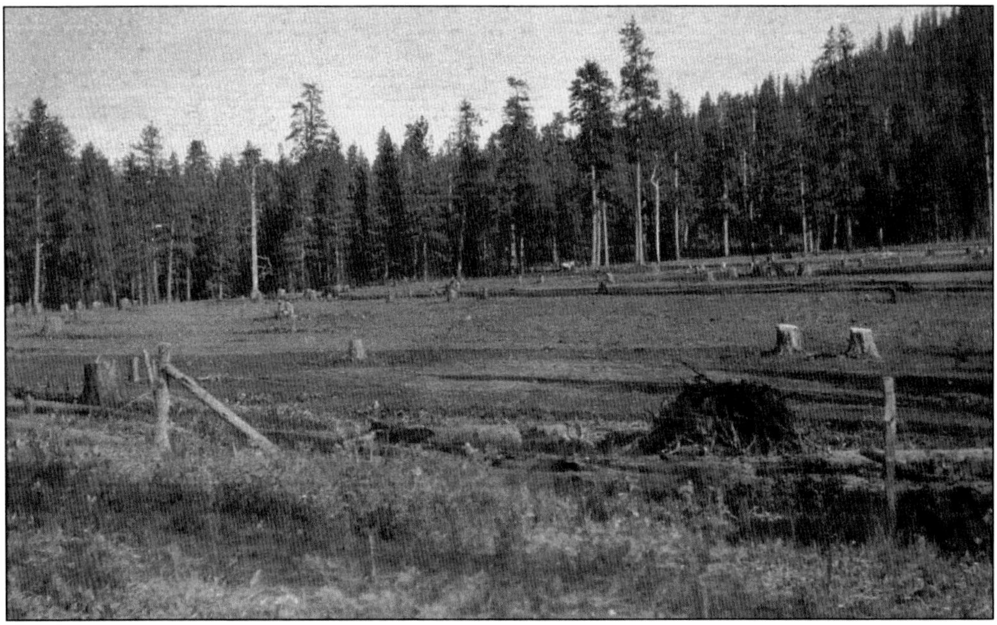

Part of the homestead requirements was to clear the land for production. After the trees were cut, stumps were removed with dynamite, a team of horses, and a lot of human muscle. Here the Miller property is in the process of being cleared.

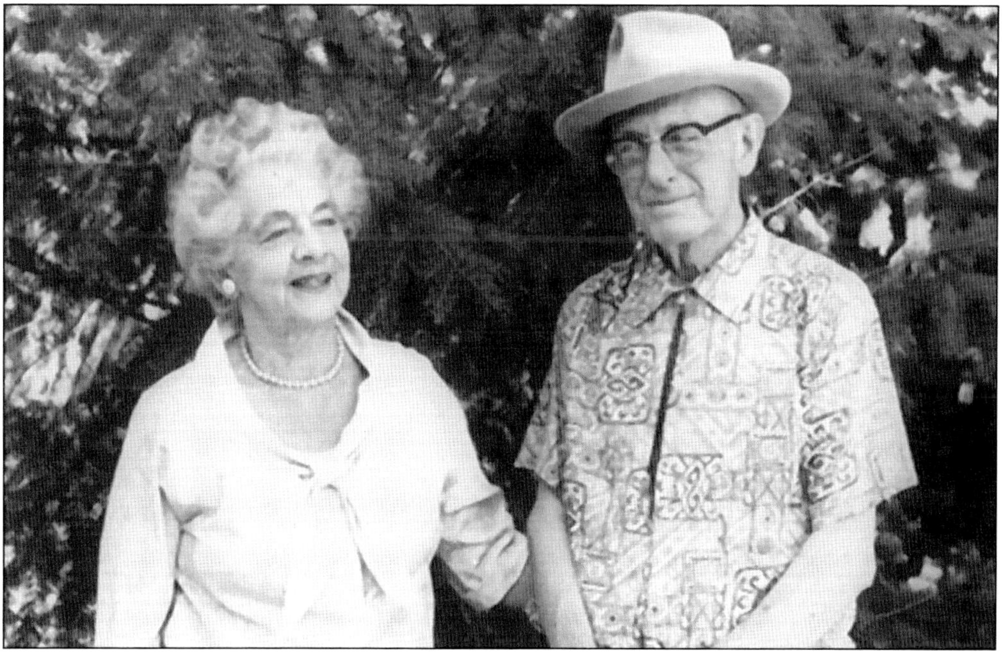

While he was in San Francisco practicing law, Albert E. Selby received word his homestead number had been drawn. In the spring, Albert and Hazel (Barrington) Selby left for Coeur d'Alene. The locator, hired for $100, selected three parcels and suggested they pick the one near the lake, which provided easier travel. Albert and Hazel posed for this picture on their 50th wedding anniversary.

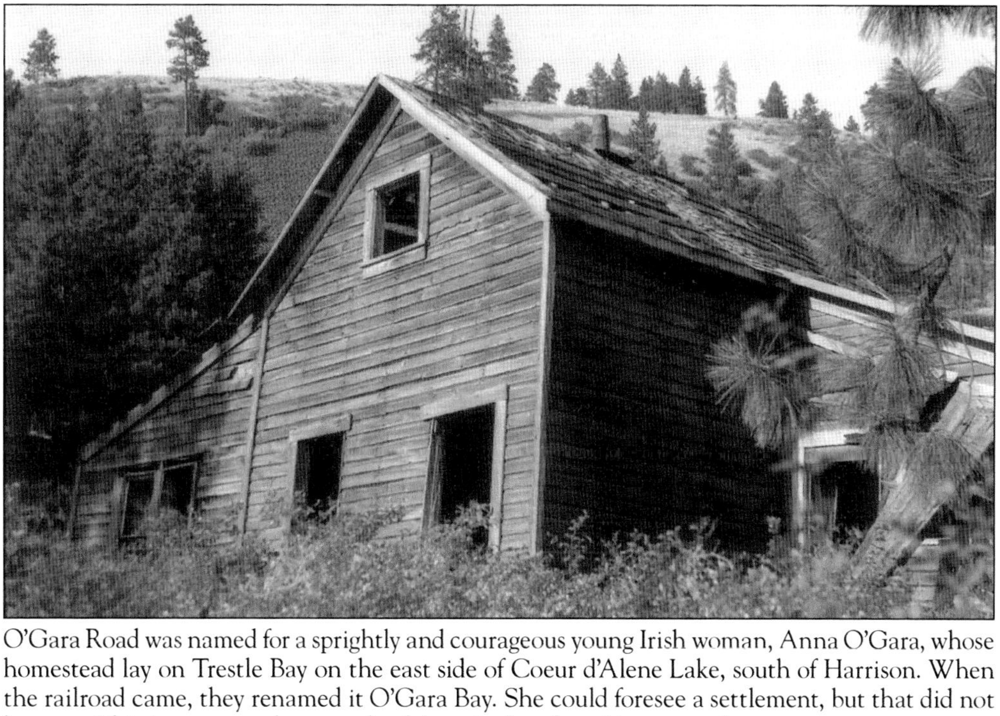

O'Gara Road was named for a sprightly and courageous young Irish woman, Anna O'Gara, whose homestead lay on Trestle Bay on the east side of Coeur d'Alene Lake, south of Harrison. When the railroad came, they renamed it O'Gara Bay. She could foresee a settlement, but that did not happen. This is a recent photograph of Anna's abandoned homestead.

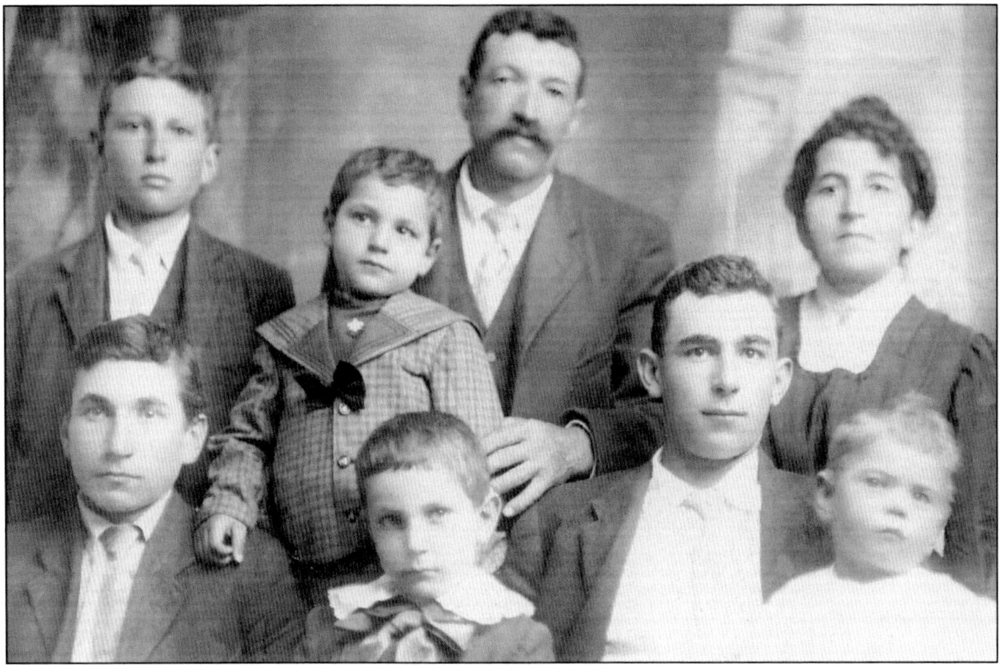

Battista and Guistina DeLuca came to the Harrison Flats from Italy in the early 1900s. Guistina's sister Olivia Sala had arrived a few years earlier, so they knew a little of what to expect in their new wilderness home. To receive their 160 acres, they were to build a cabin, clear some acreage, stay on the land, and further improve it. Like most families, they were supported by farming and logging. They are pictured above in 1908 when their family included six sons. In order of age, they were Emilio, Albert, Domenic, John, Ernest, and Victor. In the 1910 photograph below, the family poses in front of their new home.

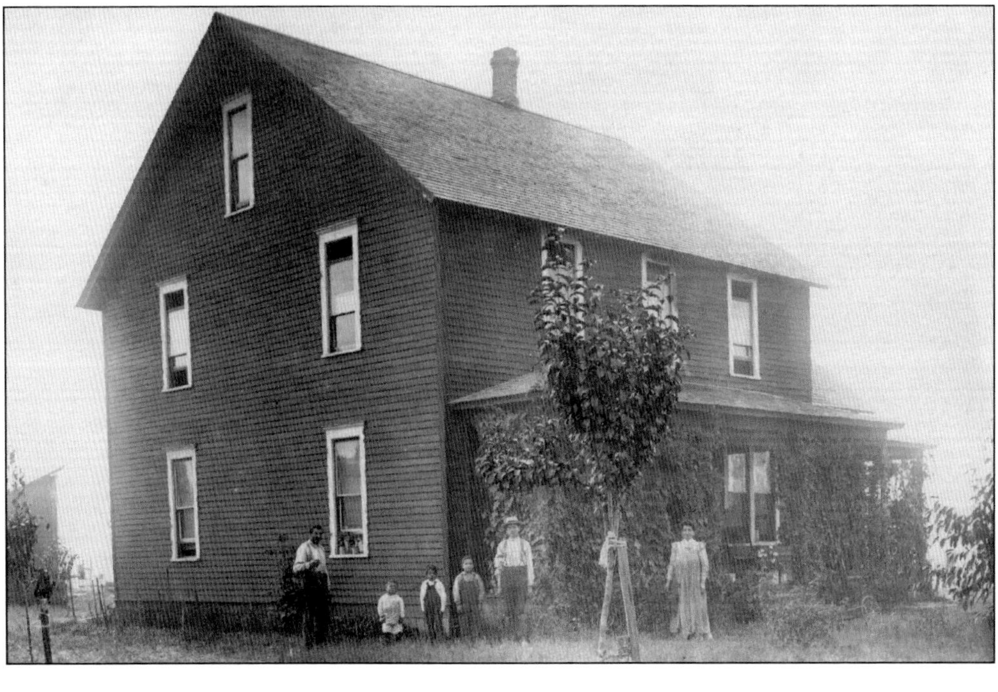

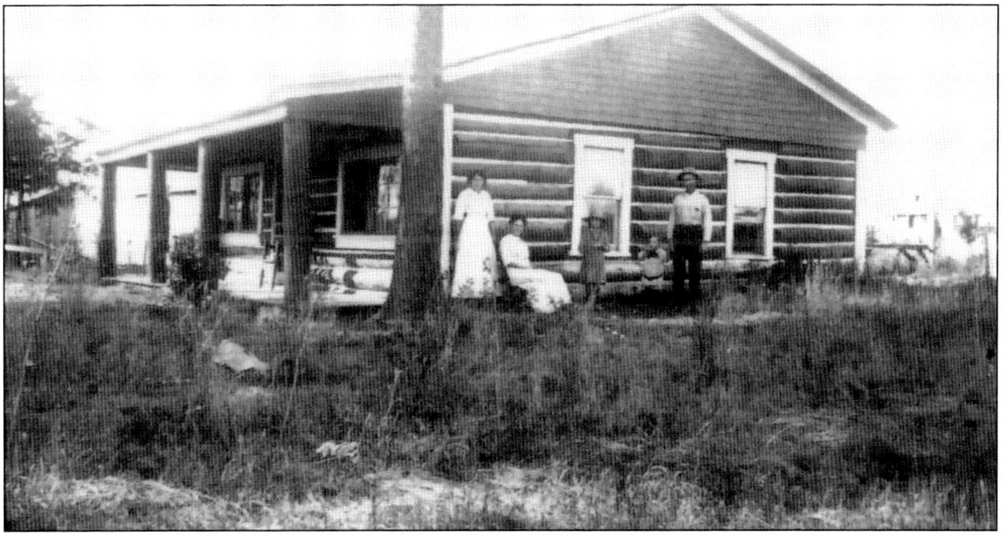

On August 9, 1909, at the drawings for the Harrison area homesteads, 105,000 applications were filed. The fifth number drawn belonged to Ella Maloney. A locator found a nice acreage for her and her brother, which had good timber, few rocks, was flat, and was located close to a wagon road. The locator, Charles Custer, visited several times. He married Ella in 1910. The Custers are pictured here at their homestead.

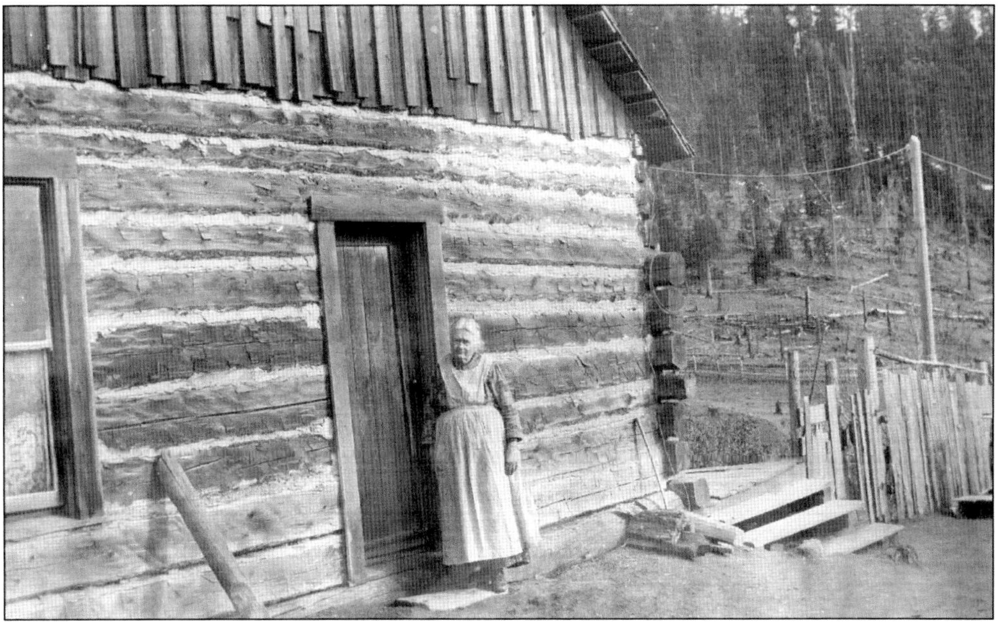

George Lamb and his brothers Thomas and Joseph arrived in 1900. They all had homesteads on the Harrison Flats and in the Bell Canyon area. Thomas and Joseph ran businesses in Harrison. George operated a sawmill at his homestead. Their mother Margaret "Grandma" Lamb is standing in front of the cabin built on George's property.

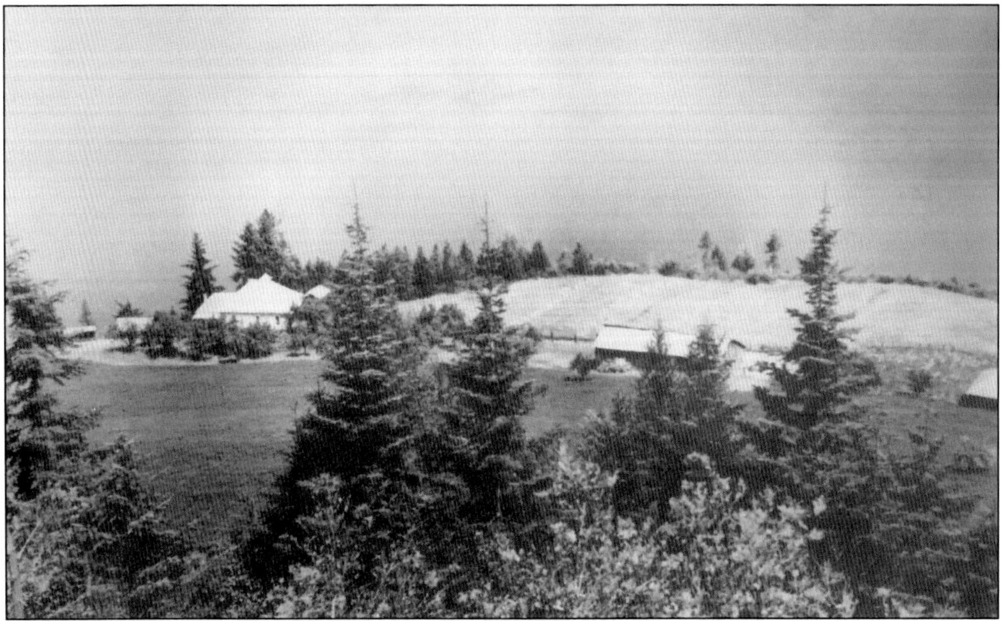

In 1890, Mathew "Matt" Sala arrived in Idaho. His homestead overlooked Anderson Lake, where he built a small cabin, raised cattle, hogs, and chickens, and had a large garden. He sent for his future wife, Olivia, in his home village in Italy. M.W. Frost, Harrison's justice of the peace, married them on August 26, 1896. At times, Matt worked at the mines for extra money for the family.

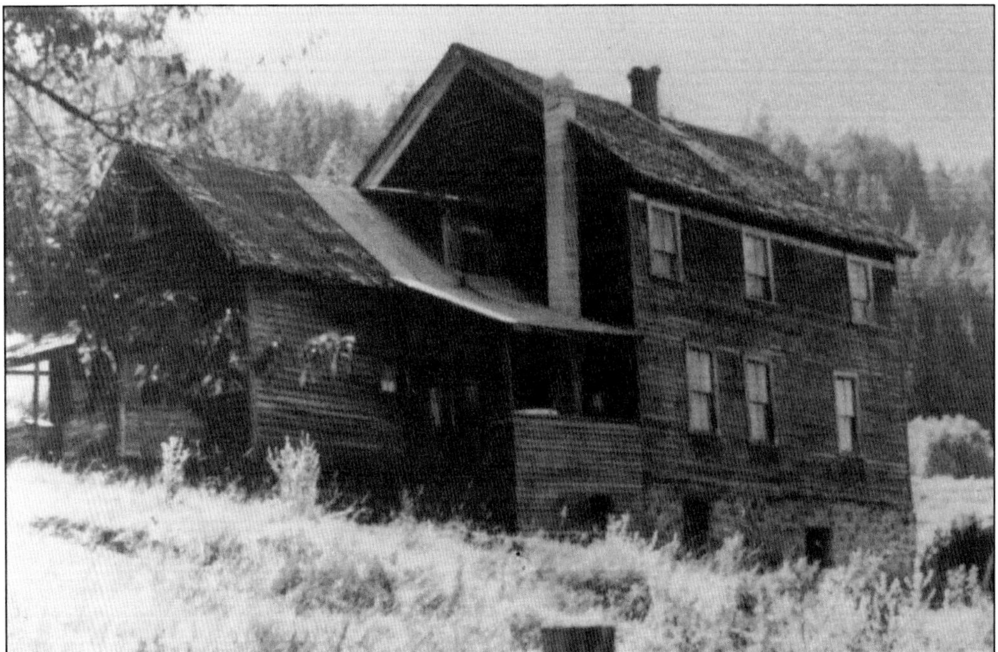

Antonio and Catherine (Tonti) Damiano arrived in the Harrison area in the 1890s. They cleared land and built this beautiful homestead house on Anderson Lake. Because jobs were available in the Silver Valley mines, Antonio worked there, occasionally getting home by walking 40 miles down the railroad track.

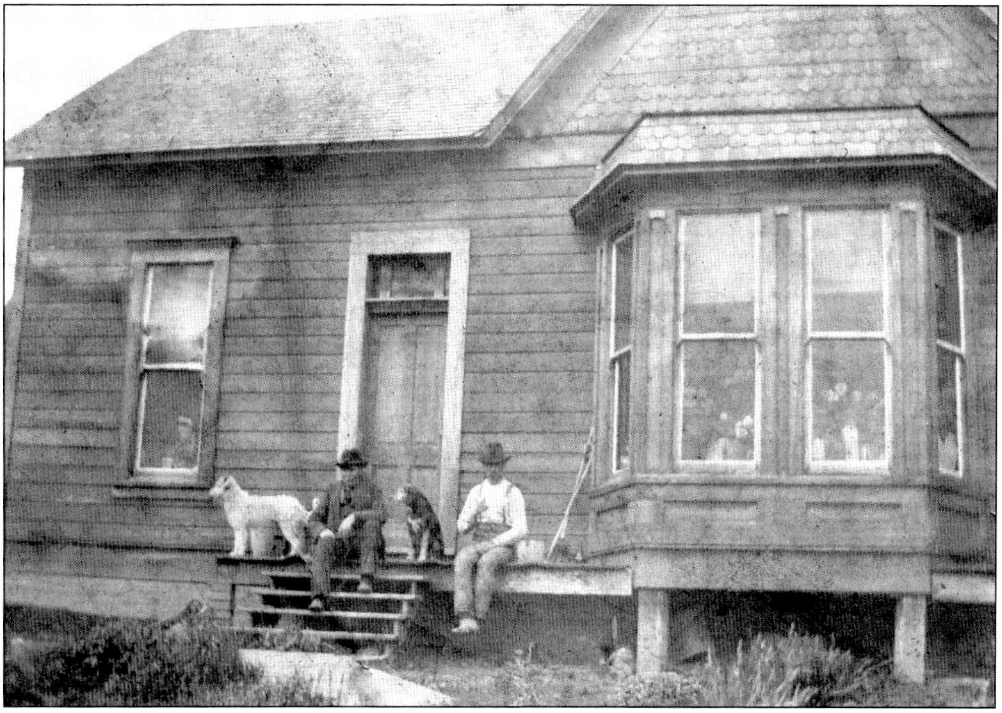

William J. and Sarah Thompson came west from St. Joseph, Missouri, in 1886. They homesteaded on Thompson Lake, which was named for the family, where they built a small log cabin. In 1893, they built this larger, lap-sided home. William and Benjamin, second of six children, are sitting on the steps. William's son Truman and his wife, Mary (Waldo) Thompson, also raised their four children in the same house.

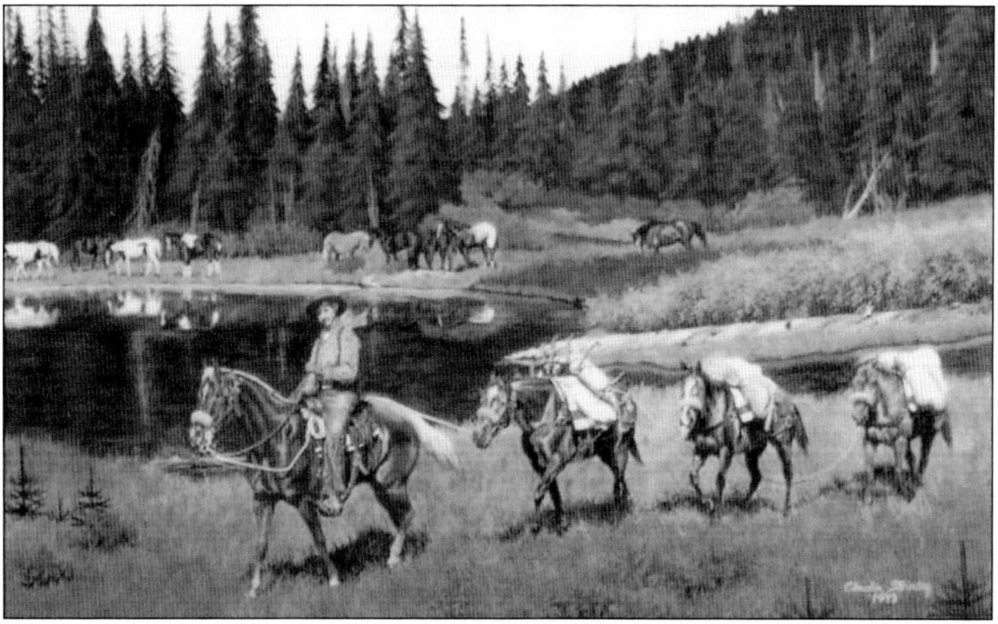

Truman and Mary Thompson's son Everett was a guide at a Mallard Lake hunting camp. Claudia Steinley painted this picture of Everett with a string of packhorses.

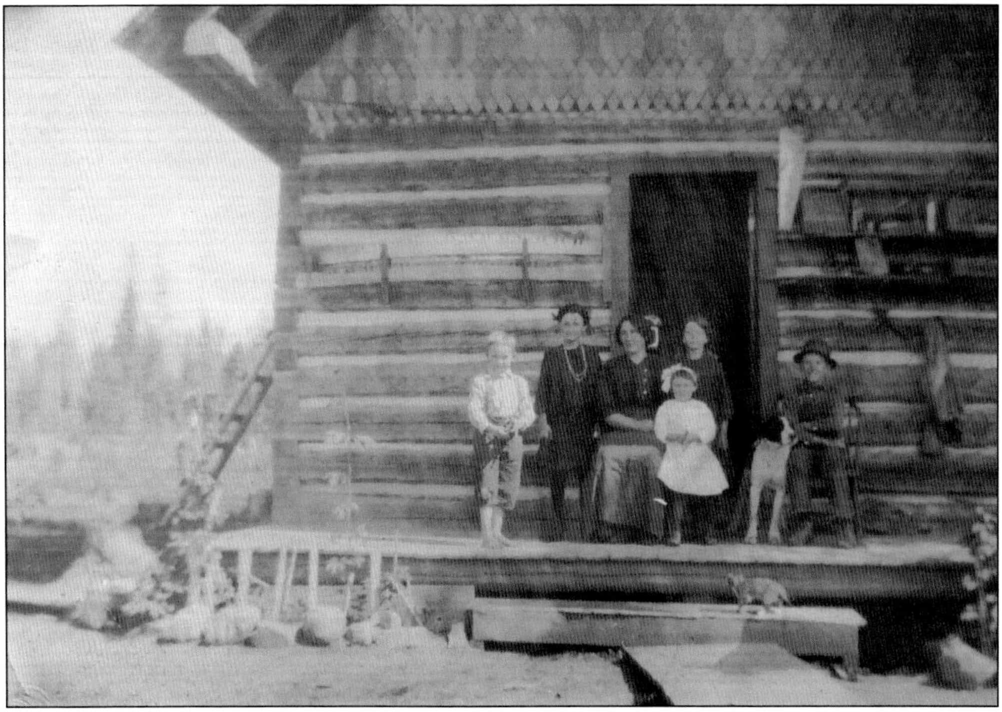

John and Minnie (Hollingsworth) Justus built this typical log cabin overlooking Thompson Lake, where they raised their family of seven children. On the porch are Charles, Hattie, Minnie, Ellen, Iness, and Chester. For entertainment, they participated in community picnics, dances, and school events and socialized in the homes of extended family and neighbors.

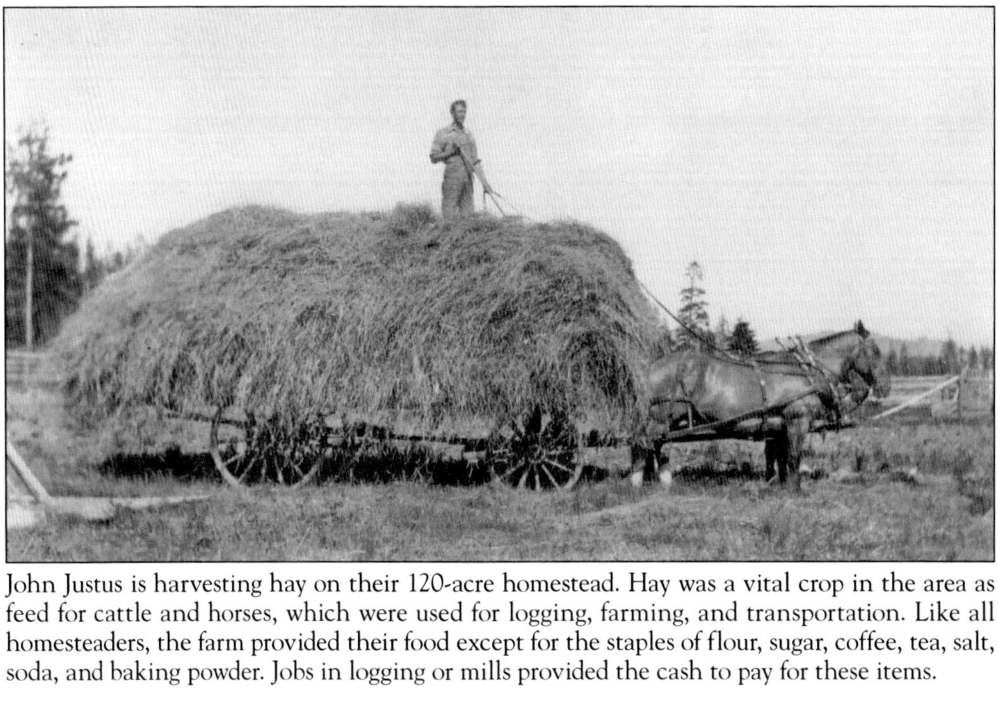

John Justus is harvesting hay on their 120-acre homestead. Hay was a vital crop in the area as feed for cattle and horses, which were used for logging, farming, and transportation. Like all homesteaders, the farm provided their food except for the staples of flour, sugar, coffee, tea, salt, soda, and baking powder. Jobs in logging or mills provided the cash to pay for these items.

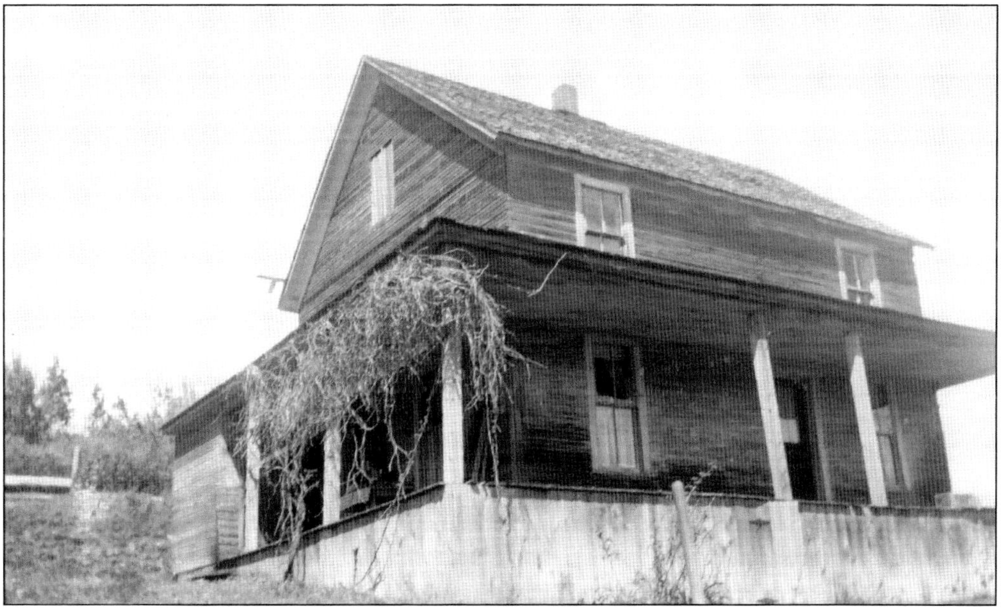

Pennsylvanians Willoughby and Louisa Yaxthemier settled on an 80-acre homestead near Thompson Lake in 1901. He built a large log house, pictured here, which he covered with lumber both outside and inside. In 1908, the family deeded an acre of their property for the Grandview School.

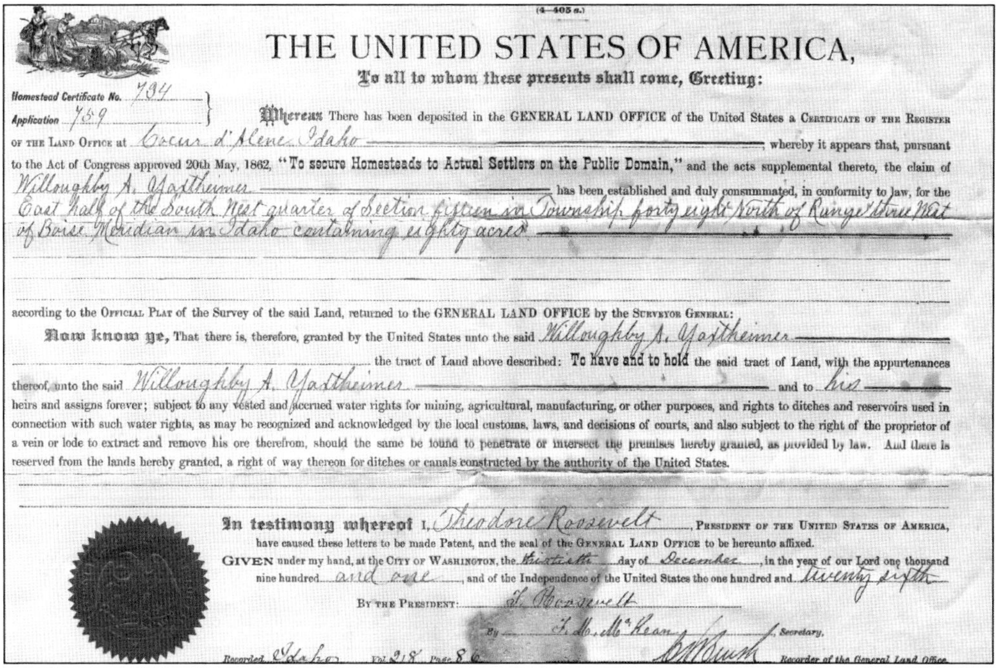

(4—405 a.)

THE UNITED STATES OF AMERICA,

To all to whom these presents shall come, Greeting:

Homestead Certificate No. 734

Application 759

Whereas There has been deposited in the GENERAL LAND OFFICE of the United States a Certificate of the Register of the Land Office at Coeur d'Alene Idaho whereby it appears that, pursuant to the Act of Congress approved 20th May, 1862, "To secure Homesteads to Actual Settlers on the Public Domain," and the acts supplemental thereto, the claim of Willoughby A. Yaxtheimer has been established and duly consummated, in conformity to law, for the East half of the South West quarter of Section fifteen in Township forty eight North of Range three West of Boise Meridian in Idaho containing eighty acres

according to the Official Plat of the Survey of the said Land, returned to the GENERAL LAND OFFICE by the Surveyor General:

Now know ye, That there is, therefore, granted by the United States unto the said Willoughby A. Yaxtheimer the tract of Land above described: To have and to hold the said tract of Land, with the appurtenances thereof, unto the said Willoughby A. Yaxtheimer and to his heirs and assigns forever; subject to any vested and accrued water rights for mining, agricultural, manufacturing, or other purposes, and rights to ditches and reservoirs used in connection with such water rights, as may be recognized and acknowledged by the local customs, laws, and decisions of courts, and also subject to the right of the proprietor of a vein or lode to extract and remove his ore therefrom, should the same be found to penetrate or intersect the premises hereby granted, as provided by law. And there is reserved from the lands hereby granted, a right of way thereon for ditches or canals constructed by the authority of the United States.

In testimony whereof I, Theodore Roosevelt, President of the United States of America, have caused these letters to be made Patent, and the seal of the General Land Office to be hereunto affixed.

GIVEN under my hand, at the City of Washington, the thirteenth day of December, in the year of our Lord one thousand nine hundred and one, and of the Independence of the United States the one hundred and twenty sixth.

By the President: T. Roosevelt

By F. M. McKean, Secretary.

[illegible], Recorder of the General Land Office.

Recorded Idaho Vol. 218 Page 8[illegible]

This document, an original homestead paper dated December 13, 1901, is from the estate of Willoughby and Louisa Yaxthemier.

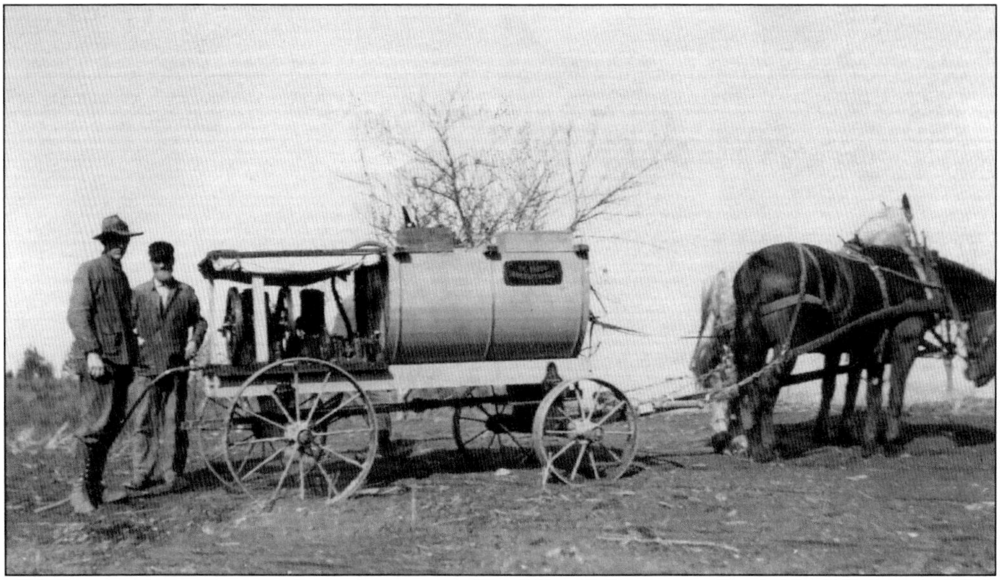

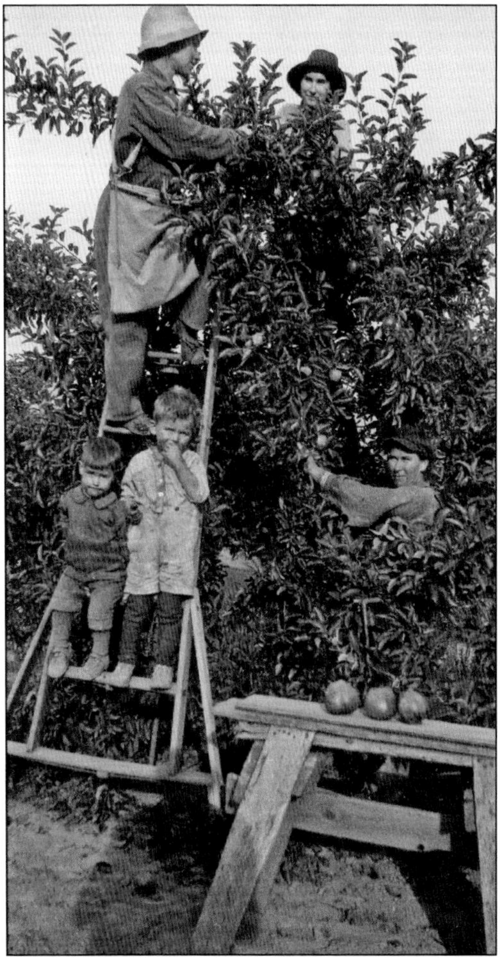

Isaac "Ike" and Martha Hollingsworth arrived in the Carlin Bay area in 1903. Ike built a large barn of hand-hewn logs and a two-story house. Because they had a good source of water, they were able to have a commercial orchard. Paul Hyde and Ike are shown with Paul's horse-drawn sprayer used in area orchards. Isaac Hollingsworth brought his mother Sarah, wife Martha, their seven children, son-in-law John Justus, and a grandson by train from Missouri to Carlin Bay in 1903.

Picking apples in the Hollingsworth orchard are, counterclockwise from bottom right, Ora (Hollingsworth) Chadbourne, Max Chadbourne, James Leslie Carns, Dolly (Cunningham) Love, and Iva (Hollingsworth) Carns. The apples were packed in wooden boxes and shipped by boat to Coeur d'Alene, where they were transferred to trains and sent to market.

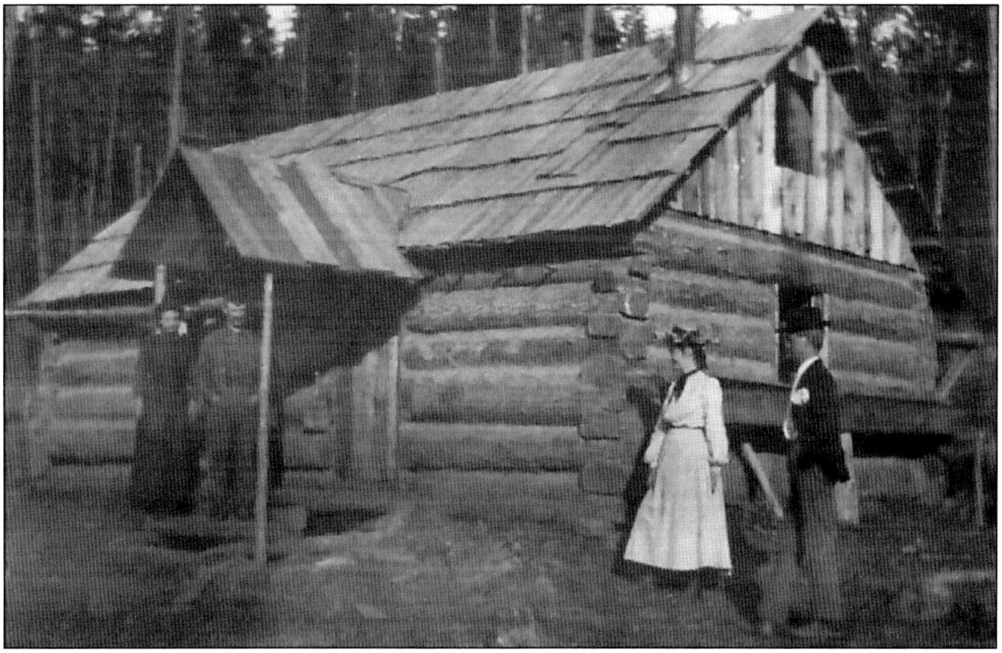

It took the physical strength, courage, and optimism of the young to be pioneers. George and Abby (Cogswell) Lemon were newlyweds when they came to Harrison in 1901. Their homestead was about five miles west of Harrison, at the end of what is now Stott Road. In this 1902 photograph, George and Abby are at their front door welcoming neighbors Dolly and Roy Slayton.

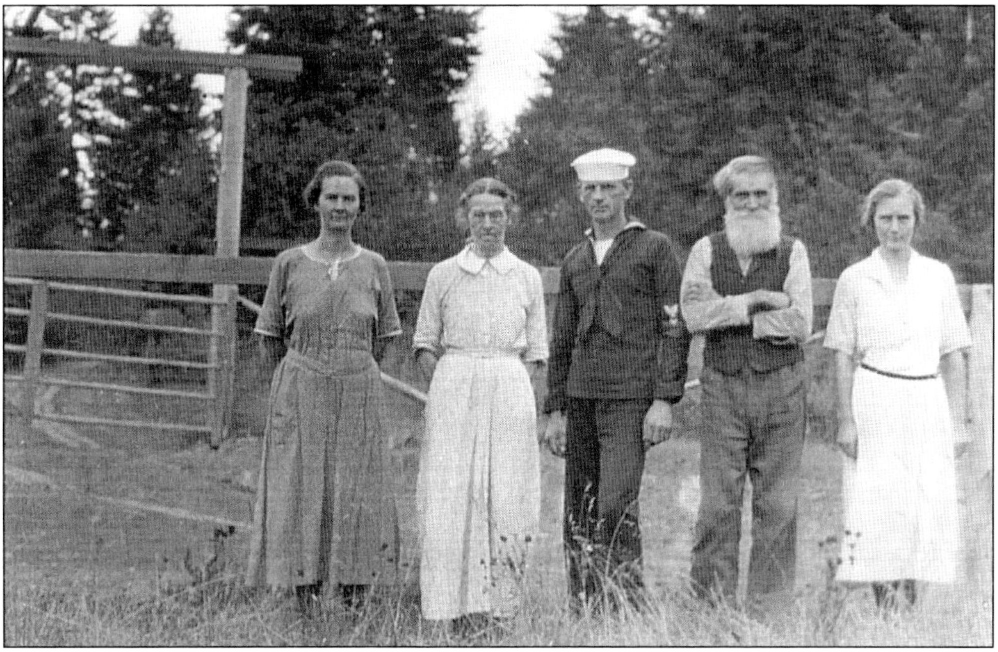

In the late 1890s, William and Julia Slayton homesteaded about five miles from Harrison on the north side of the Coeur d'Alene River. The timber was so thick, they could only see straight up. William had to move their log cabin twice to be sure it was on his property. Pictured in the early 1920s are, from left to right, Dolly, mother Julia, Roy, father William and Doris Slayton.

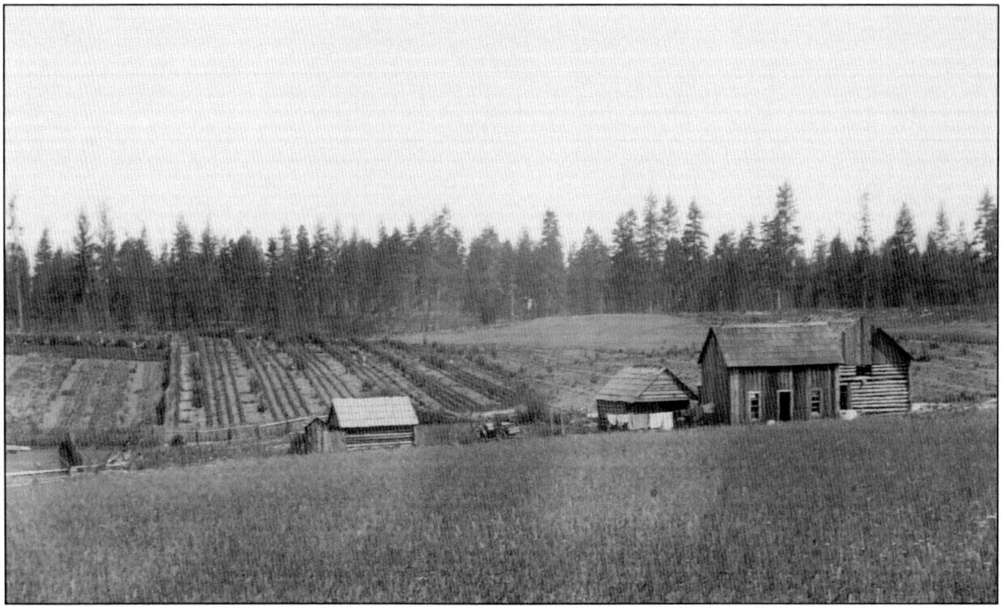

Newlyweds John E. and Ida M. Fisher arrived in Harrison in 1890. They first lived near Blue Lake, and in 1894, moved to this farm on East Point, where the land was level and the soil rich. They grew vegetables and fruit, transporting the produce by rail to the Silver Valley to supply the miners.

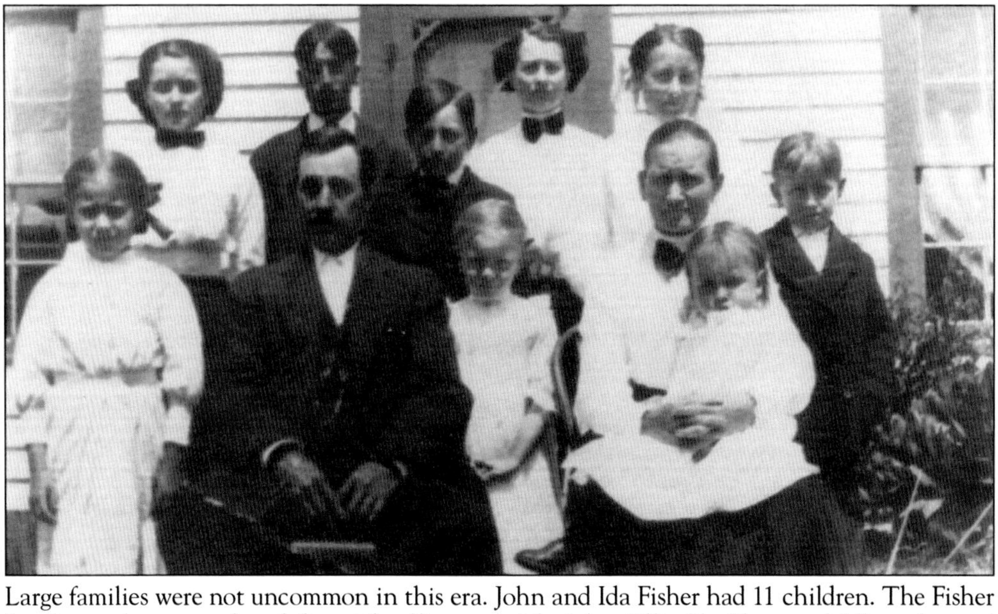

Large families were not uncommon in this era. John and Ida Fisher had 11 children. The Fisher family members were, from left to right, (first row) Ada, John, Effie, Ida, Flora, and Albert; (second row) Maude, Charlie, Henry, Stella, and Gladys. Gertrude was born after the picture was taken, and Agnes had passed away young.

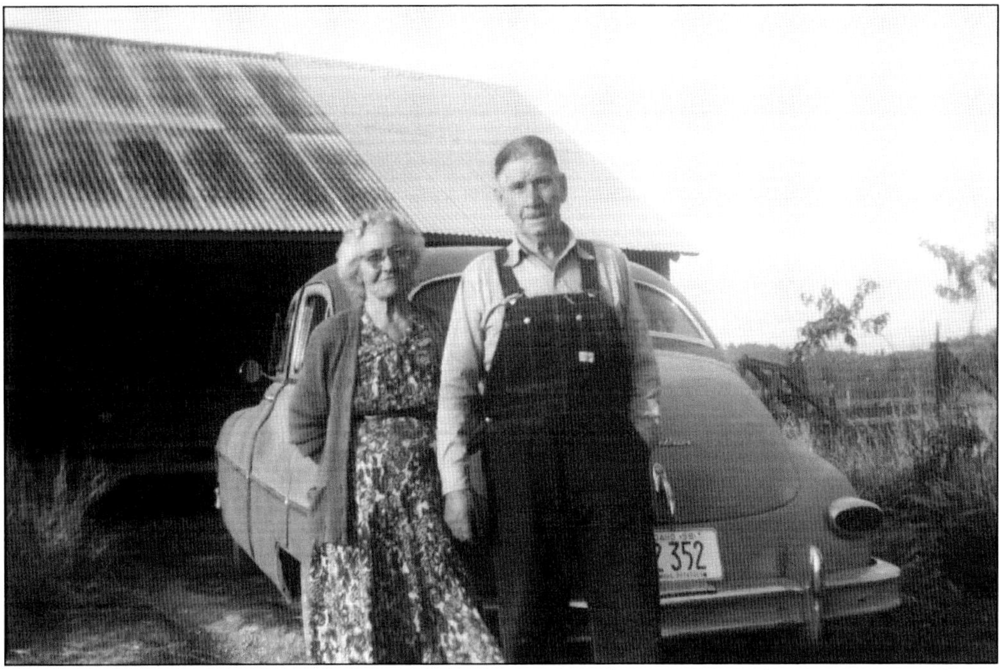

In 1908, Swedish immigrants Eric and Kirstina Lund arrived in Harrison where Eric was employed as a lumber grader at Grant Lumber Company. In 1914, they moved to East Point, which was where they farmed and operated a dairy. This picture of Kirstina and Eric was taken in the mid-1940s.

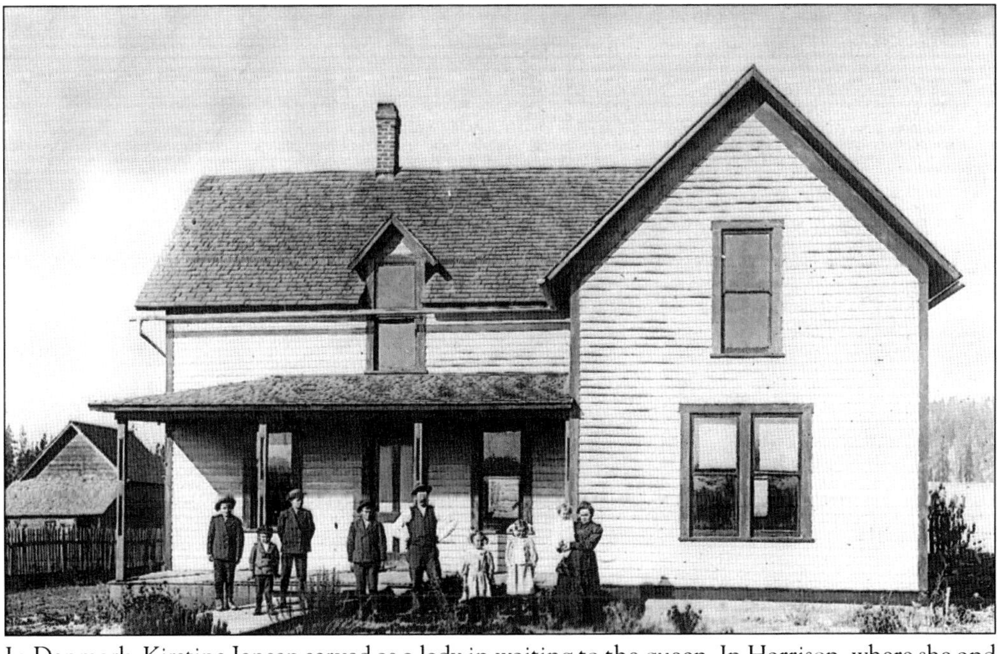

In Denmark, Kirstine Jensen served as a lady in waiting to the queen. In Harrison, where she and her husband, Peter, homesteaded on East Point in 1902, she was a homemaker. She purchased raw wool, and washed, carded, and spun her own yarn. She often shared work with close friend and neighbor Kirstina Lund. Peter and Kirstine are shown here in front of their home with seven of their nine children.

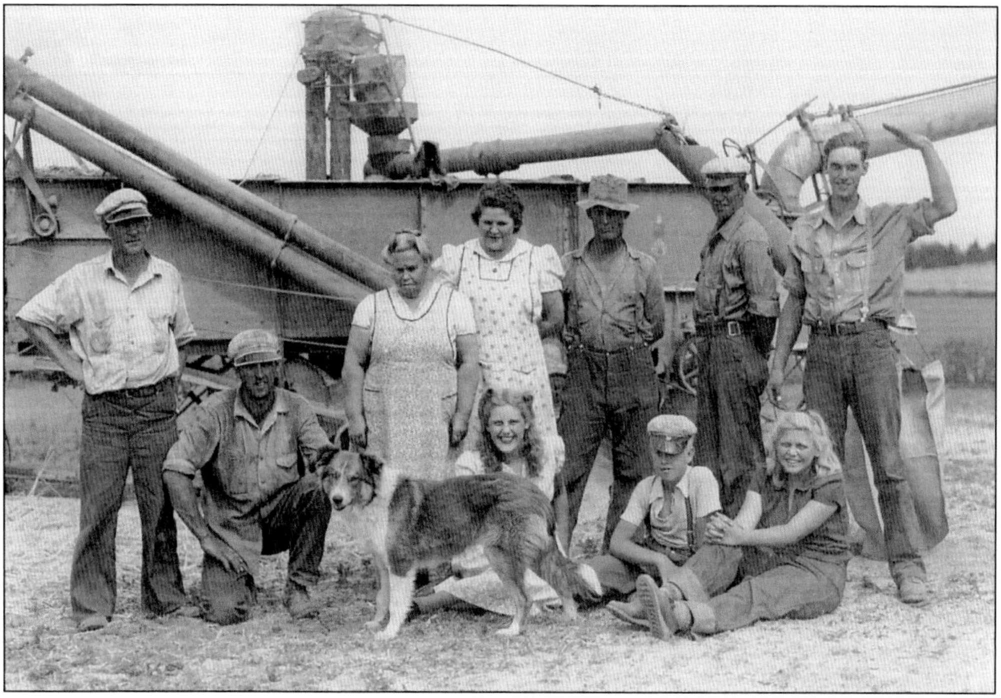

Grain was essential for nourishing hard working farm and logging animals. Threshing machines were expensive, prohibiting farmers from owning their own equipment. As a result, the Jensens threshed grain for the surrounding farms. On threshing day, the farmer's wife prepared the noon meal for the entire crew, aided by Kirstine, who is third from the left in this photograph of the threshing crew.

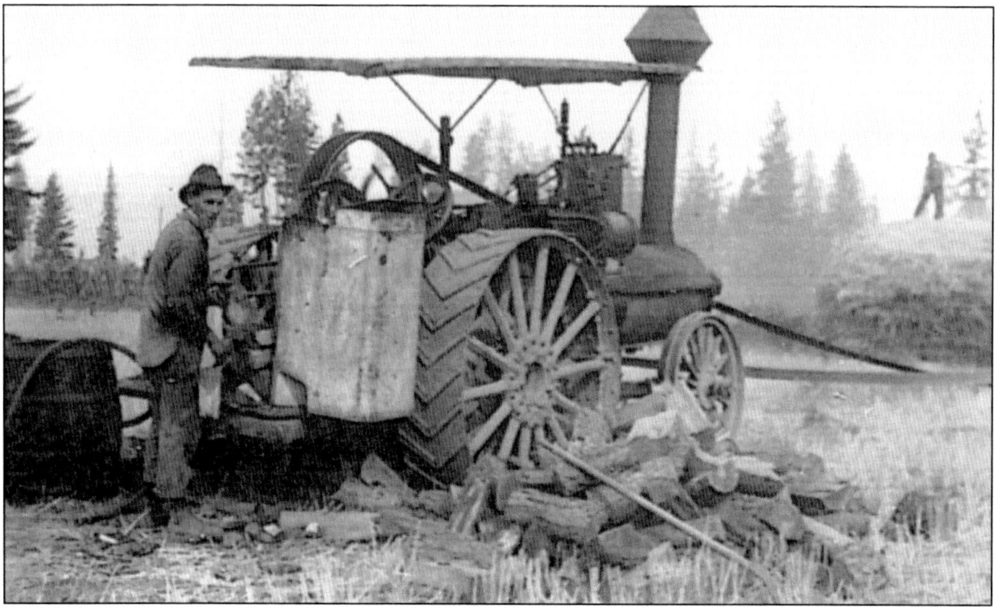

Harry Jensen's steam-operated tractor is providing the power to run the threshing machine. The pile of wood in the front is used to fire the engine. The belt to the thresher is on the right side of the picture.

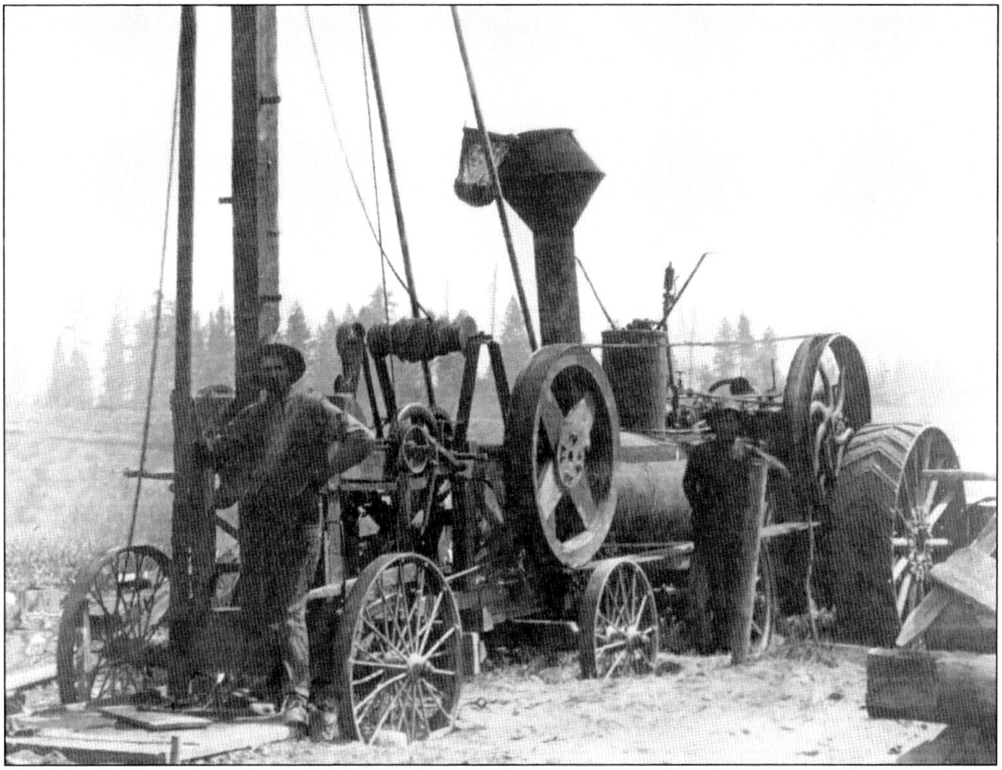

Early families who located along lakes, rivers, or streams used these natural water sources, took water from springs, or dug shallow wells by hand. When Harrison Flats and East Point were settled, deeper wells necessitated the use of well drilling equipment. Peter and Jim Jensen are drilling for water on East Point about 1912.

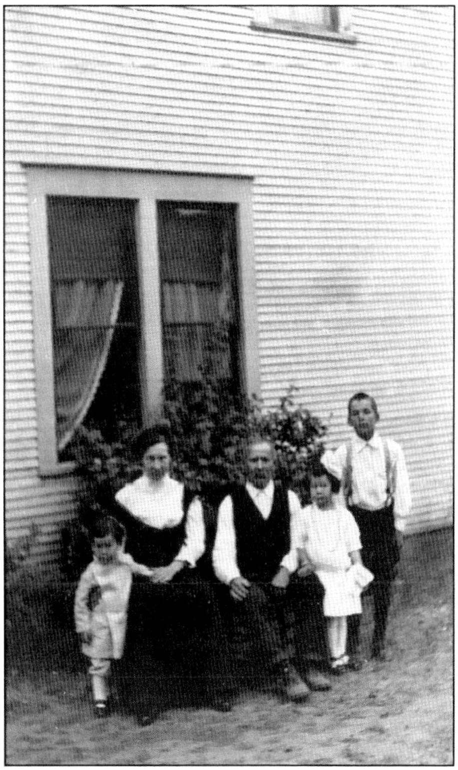

George Roberts came from Missouri to Harrison around 1898. He married and had a son, George. After he was widowed in 1907, he remarried. George farmed, ran a tavern in town, and cut wood for the large boats on the lake. Members of the Roberts family are, from left to right, John, George's second wife Minnie (Rasor) Roberts, George Sr., Minnie, and George Jr.

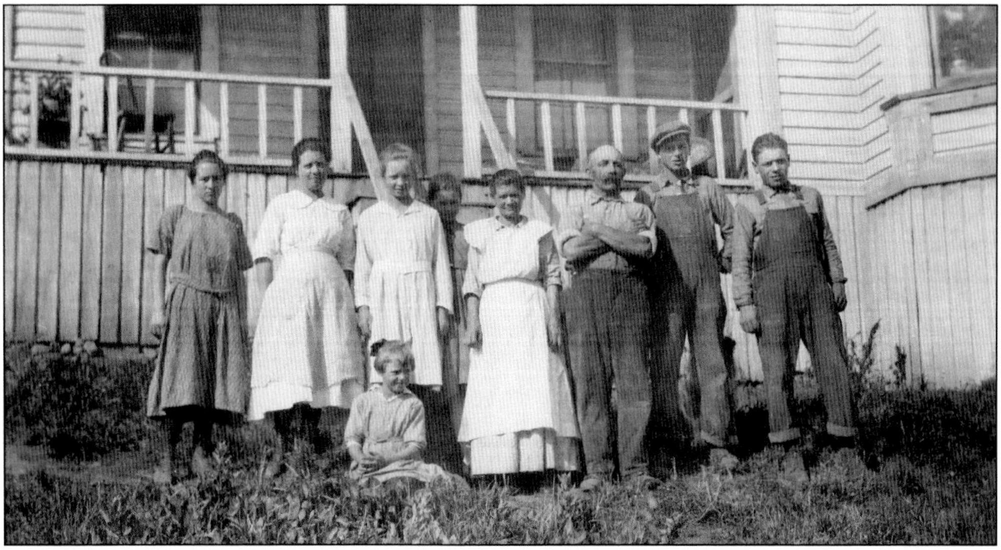

In 1903, Hans and Ellen Fabricius paid $1,500 for 80 acres and a herd of dairy cows. They later added acreage and built a new home. The Fabricius family sold fruit and milk in Harrison, their primary market. By herself, the Fabricius's 14-year-old daughter, Anna, delivered the milk before going to school. Those pictured are, from left to right, Mary, Anna, Ida, Emma, Ellen, Hans Sr., Hans Jr., and Peter. Amanda is sitting in front.

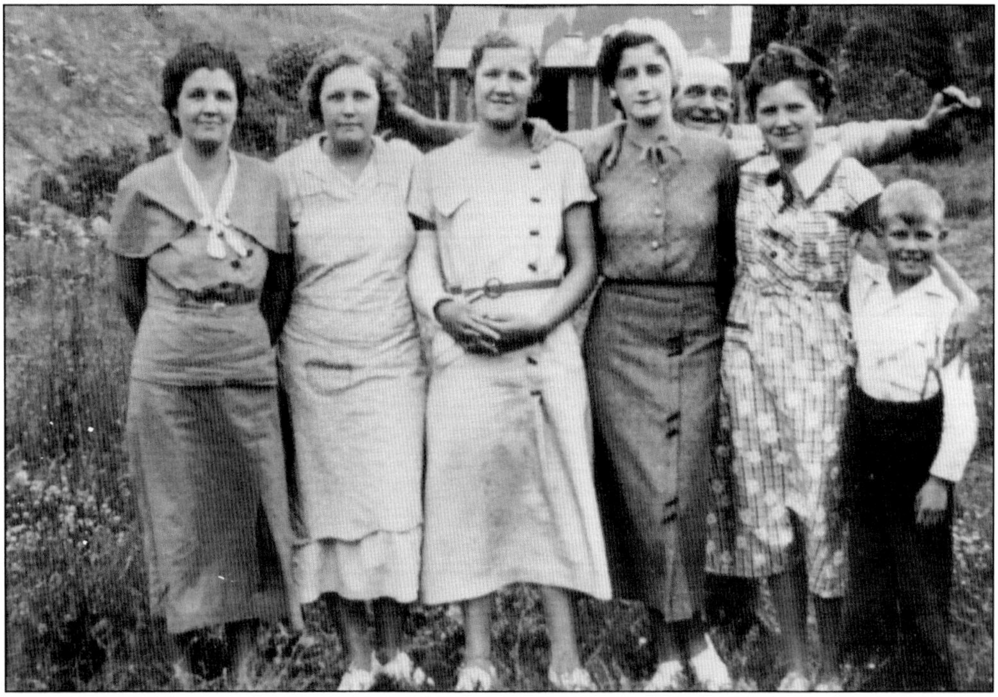

Like many others, Josiah and Artie (Holstein) Cunningham came west in the 1890s looking for work they had read about in a newspaper. Settling in Harrison in 1907, Josiah worked in logging, construction, and harvesting. Those pictured are, from left to right, daughters Freda, Beulah, Reba, Virginia, and Marjorie, and son Donald. Greta and Dolly are not shown in this image from the 1930s. Josiah is peeking from the back. Freda married Donald Rose and they opened the Rose Café in Harrison.

Four

Transportation

In 1883, gold was discovered, and in 1885, a silver claim was filed in the Silver Valley. The rush was on. The only means of transporting supplies, workers, and ore was pack mules or horse-drawn freight wagons. Trails were rugged; in bad weather, roads, such as they were, would become impassable.

The transportation plan proposed by Montana entrepreneur Daniel C. Corbin incorporated a network utilizing trains and steamboats. Train tracks were laid to the docks in the city of Coeur d'Alene at the north end of the lake. Steamships met the trains and provided transport up the Coeur d'Alene River to Cataldo. From there, trains continued to points east. In 1886, the Northern Pacific Railroad assumed control.

In the same year, the Washington and Idaho Railroad, later the Oregon Railroad and Navigation (OR&N), began a line from Washington state, crossing the water by bridge at Chatcolet, following the lake and the Coeur d'Alene River to the Silver Valley. By 1890, there was a rail line that went into the mining country. The Union Pacific Railway acquired ownership in May 1888. The history of railroads is complex, as there were six or eight lines involved—with subsidiaries there were 12—but all were controlled by either the Union Pacific or the Northern Pacific.

The history of steamboat names, builders, and ownership is no less confusing. In spite of partnerships, mergers, sales, and name changes, two major steamboat lines stand out, the White Star and the Red Collar. Needless to say, rivalries between the Northern Pacific and Union Pacific railways and between the White Star and Red Collar lines were often heated.

When Harrison was founded in 1891, the transfer station between boat and train moved from Cataldo. With the timber and excursion-boat booms, Harrison became the hub for traffic entering and leaving the St. Joe River.

With highways, the need for lake and river travel ended. When the highway was built through the Fourth of July Canyon, it was a faster route between the Silver Valley and Coeur d'Alene than the train through Harrison. Travel became easier and faster, but not as romantic.

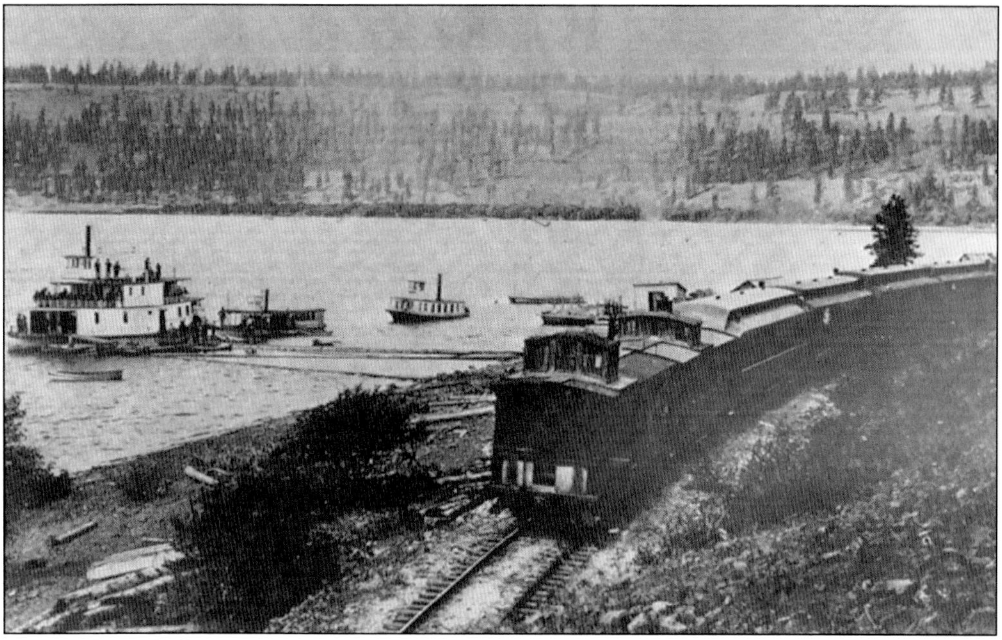

In 1880, Peter C. Sorenson, a Norwegian immigrant, was commissioned to build a boat for hauling hay to feed the cavalry animals at Fort Sherman in Coeur d'Alene. The *Amelia Wheaton*, the first steamer on the lake, is shown here around 1890, just before the City of Harrison was founded.

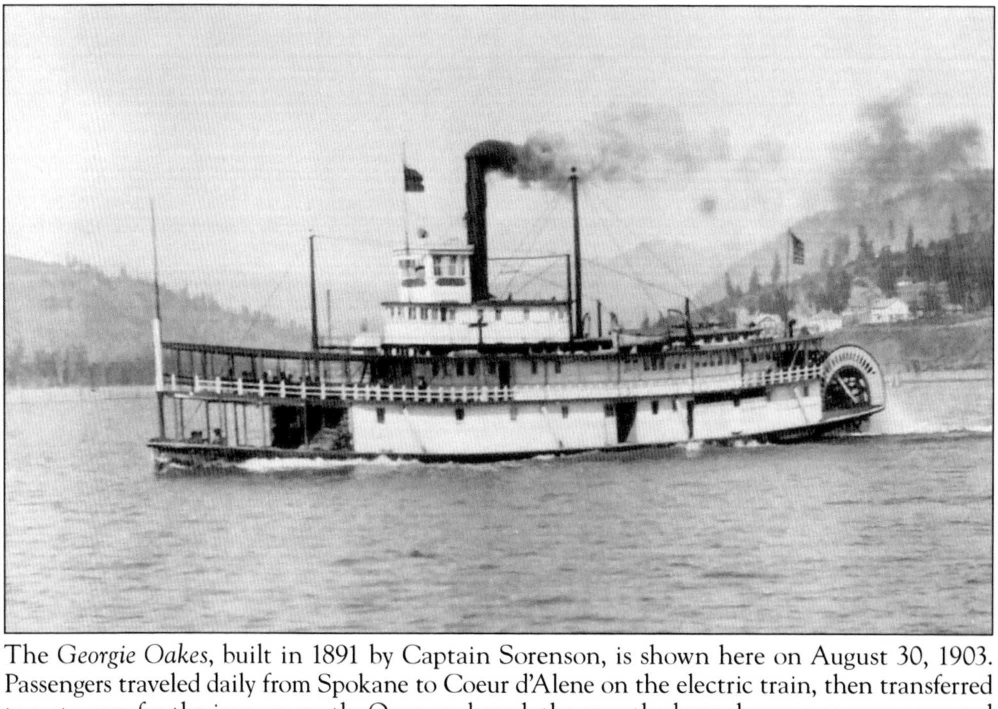

The *Georgie Oakes*, built in 1891 by Captain Sorenson, is shown here on August 30, 1903. Passengers traveled daily from Spokane to Coeur d'Alene on the electric train, then transferred to a steamer for the journey south. Once on board, the smartly dressed passengers were treated to plush lounges, fine food, drink, and music. The round trip from Coeur d'Alene to St. Maries cost the princely sum of $1.25.

A gang of rustlers operating between Montana and Washington used Harrison as their headquarters. It was 1906 when they got the idea to hire the *Georgie Oakes* (shown here) to take a load of horses across the lake rather than swimming the St. Joe River. Word reached the authorities, and a shootout on the pass at the Idaho-Montana border later stopped the gang.

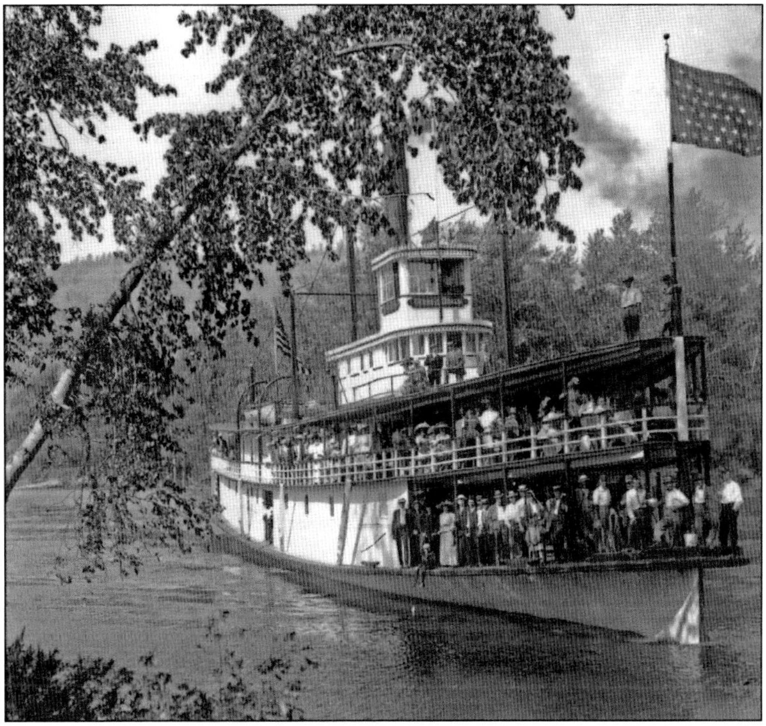

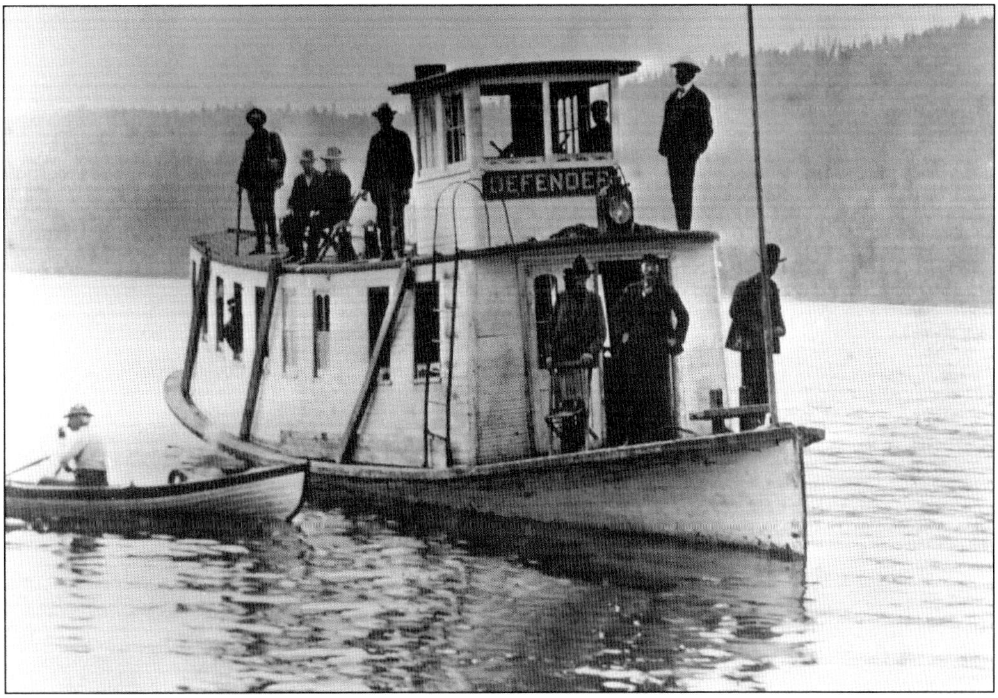

The former *Laura Lyons* became the *Defender* in 1892. Ike Turner, owner and operator of the *Defender*, was the first to supply passenger service to the numerous bays beginning in 1904. This photograph was taken in 1908. The *Biddie*, owned by Carl Searles, offered the last passenger service by boat after the road was completed in 1933.

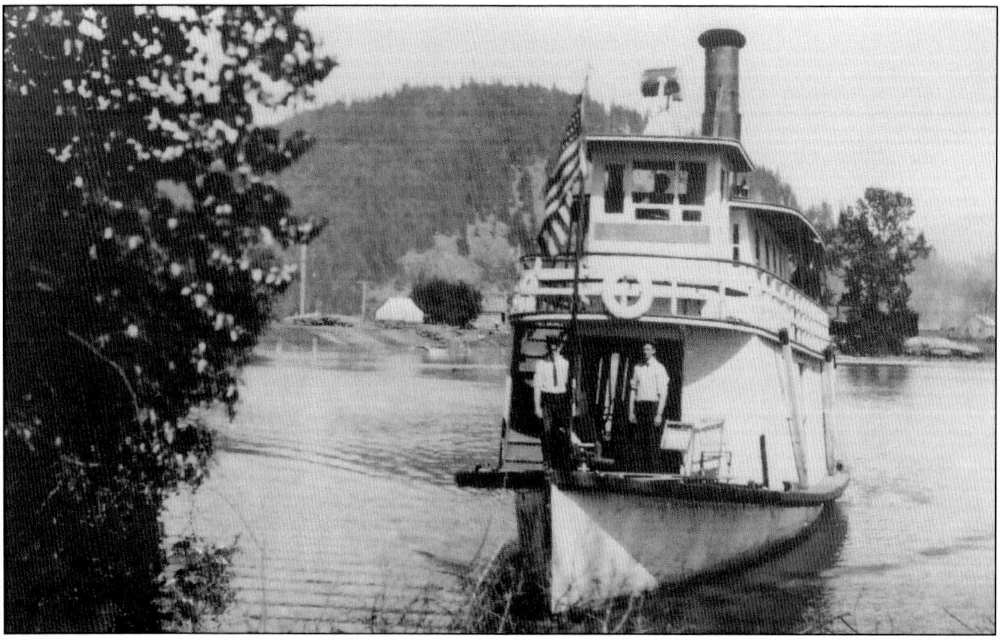

Many boats were rebuilt and renamed, and parts were taken from one and put in another, which called for a name change. This undated photograph is of the *Milwaukee*. It was originally built by the Blackwell Lumber Company for hauling freight and passengers for the company. It was later used as a tugboat and eventually rebuilt as the *Bonnie Doon* in 1900.

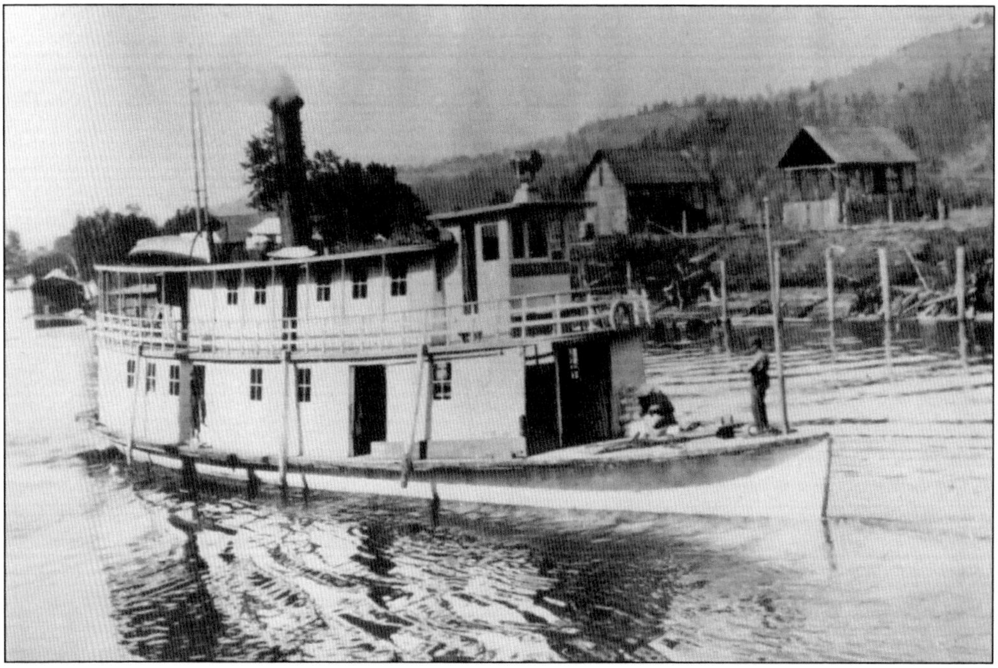

The *Bonnie Doon* was a small passenger boat that had a daily route following the lakeshore, in addition to traveling the rivers. The lower deck was for freight; the upper deck for passengers. The *Bonnie Doon*, shown in this undated photograph, was built by Peter W. Johnson for H.M. Strathern's Lumber Company in Post Falls.

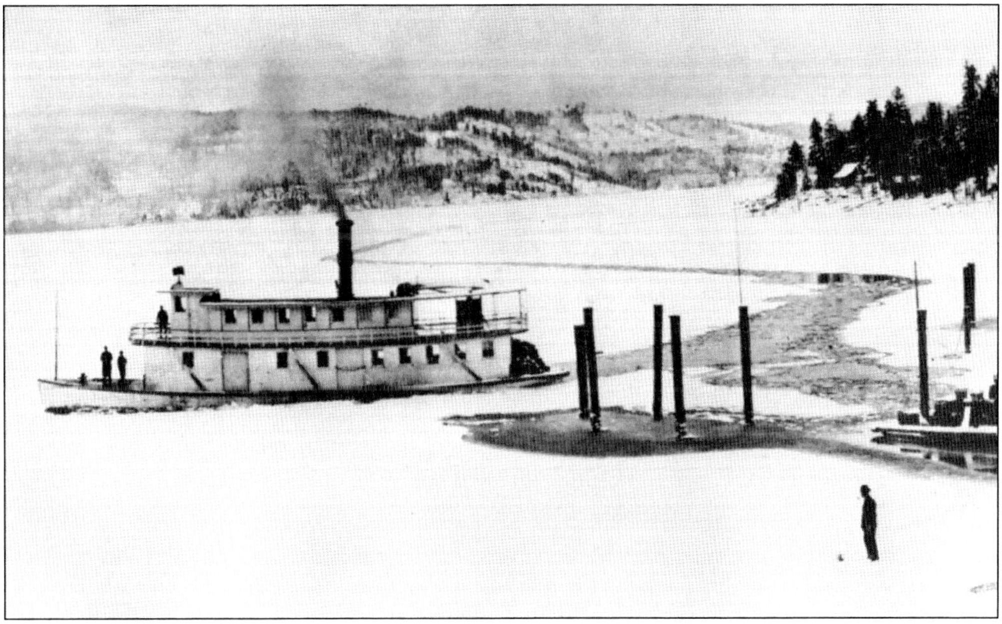

This is an undated photograph of the *Bonnie Doon* breaking ice on Coeur d'Alene Lake. It probably could not match the ice-breaking capabilities of the earlier *Kootenai*. Built in 1887, the *Kootenai* was made of heavy planking and boiler plating. It could break ice 10 inches thick and still make good time, or 20 inches at a slower pace.

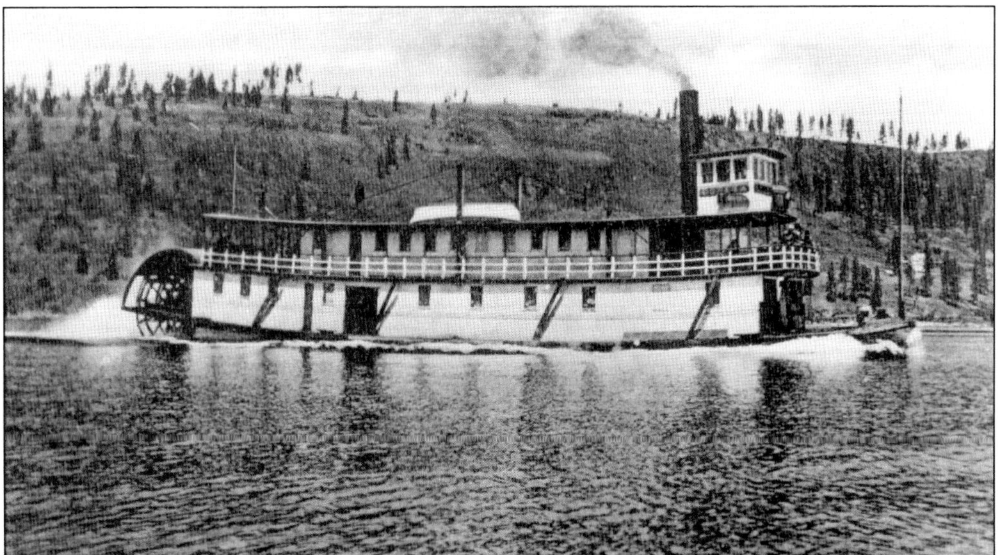

The *Boneta*, built in 1900 by Peter W. Johnson, belonged to George Reynolds and E. Daniel McDonald, of the White Star Line. On July 22, 1905, the *Coeur d'Alene Press* reported there had been an accident involving the *Boneta* and the *Idaho*, belonging to the Red Collar Line. The much larger *Idaho* struck the *Boneta*. No one was killed or injured, but the *Boneta* sank in a matter of minutes.

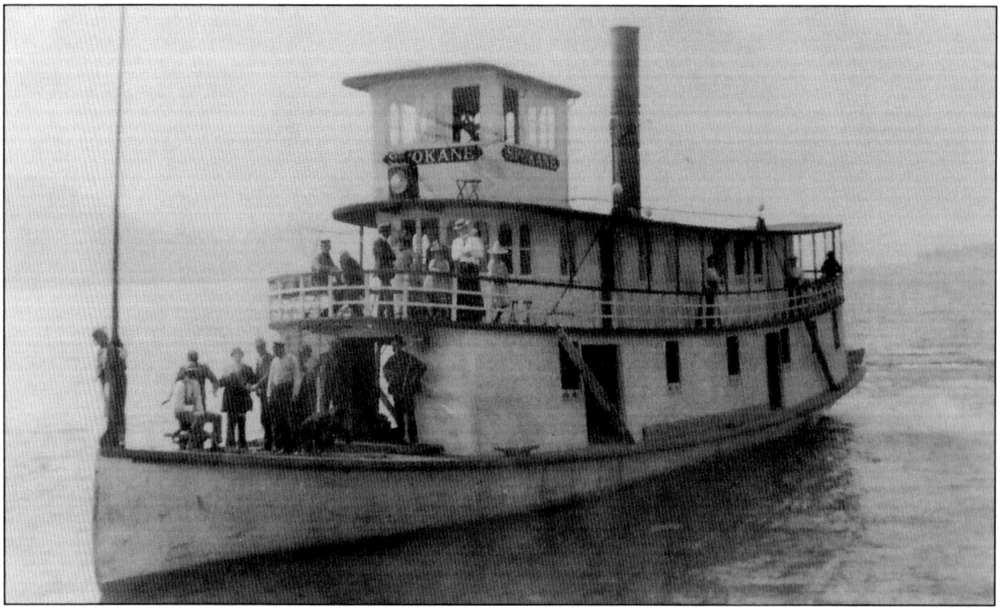

Unlike other steamers that were built to carry freight on the lower level and passengers on the upper deck, the *Spokane* was built in 1901 as a speedy excursion boat. The *Spokane* was propeller driven, not a stern-wheeler like the *Idaho* or the *Georgie Oakes*. There were two staterooms and a smoking room on the lower deck and steam-heated, well-furnished women's and gentlemen's lounges on the upper deck. This boat, like many others, was built by Captain Sorenson and his partner P.W. Johnson, also a Scandinavian immigrant. The *Spokane* met her end by being set on fire as part of the 1914 Fourth of July celebration.

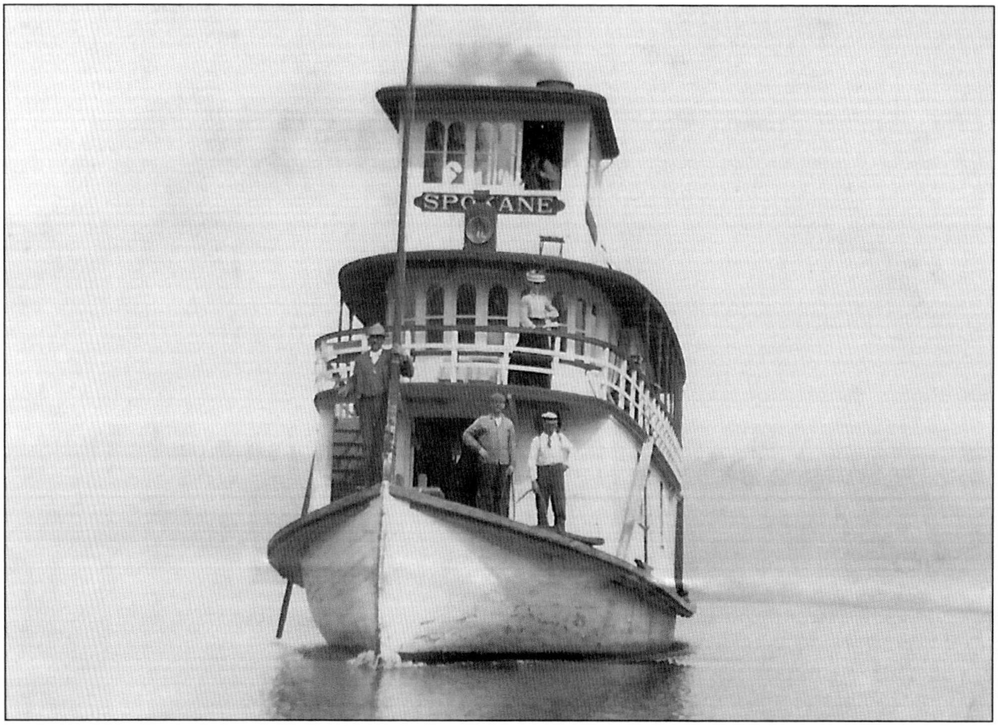

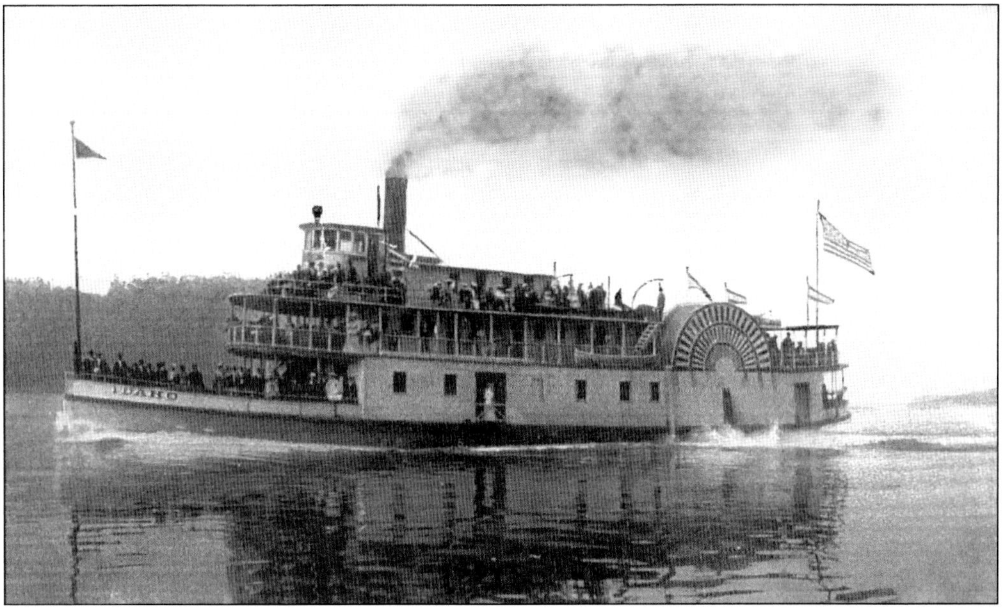

The *St. Maries Courier* reported that on August 23, 1903, the *Idaho*, carrying 300 passengers plus freight, made its first run from Coeur d'Alene to St. Joe City, a 48-mile trip, in three hours and ten minutes, which included a stopover in Harrison. According to the *Spokane Daily Chronicle*, "The boat is said to be the largest, finest, and fastest boat on the lake."

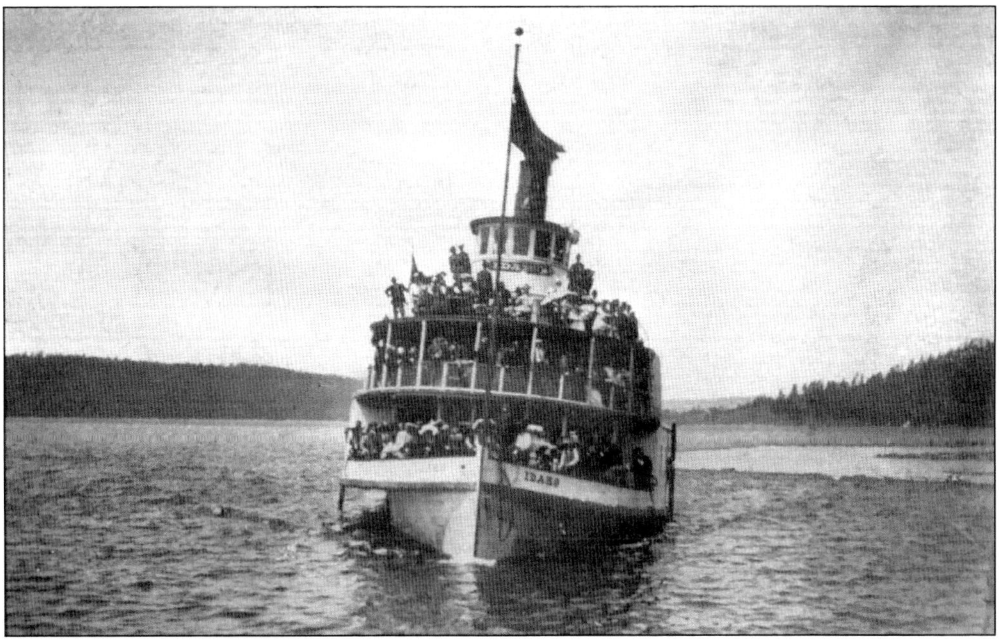

The *Idaho* was one of the largest steamboats on the lake. At 147 feet long and 23 feet wide, the *Idaho* had the capacity to hold 1,000 passengers. It had a wheel on each side rather than a stern wheel. Each wheel was 21 feet in diameter.

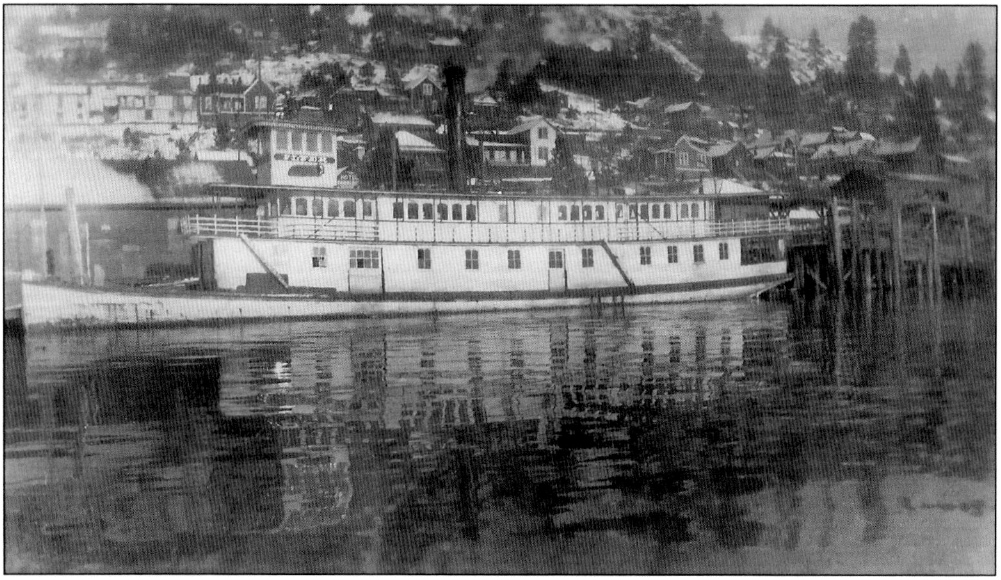

The *Flyer*, launched in 1906, was the masterpiece of shipbuilder Peter W. Johnson. The *Flyer* had a steam-operated propeller with a capacity of 700 passengers plus freight. For 30 years, it made passenger runs from Coeur d'Alene through Harrison to St. Maries. In this undated photograph, the *Flyer* is docked in Harrison.

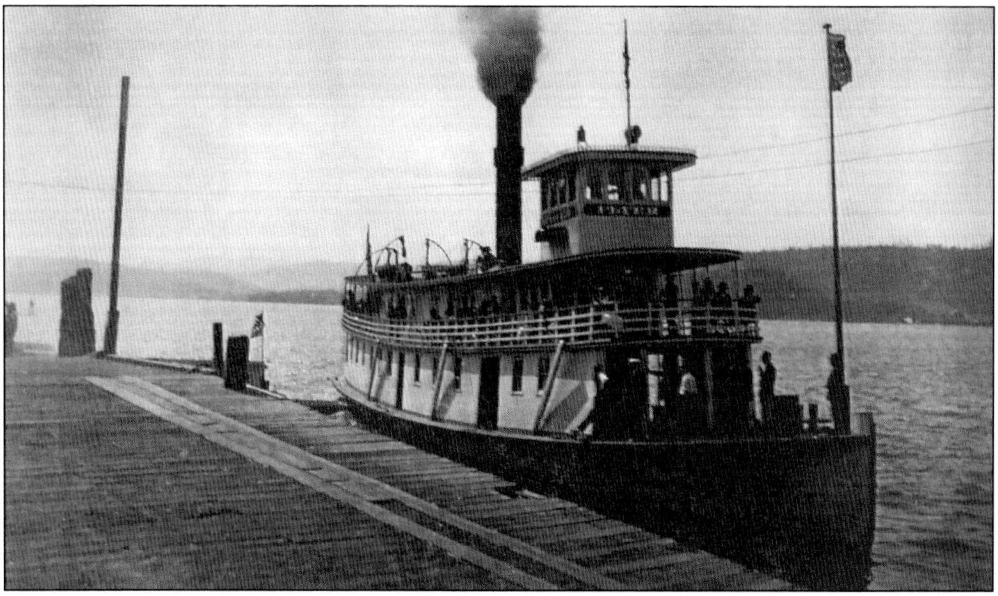

Here is another undated picture of the steamer *Flyer* docked at Harrison. Unfortunately, the steamers had fates unbecoming their glorious beginnings. When age or a poor economic climate took their toll, they became barges, were sunk, or were burned as a part of Fourth of July festivities. The *Flyer* was sold to the Potlatch Corporation and in 1938, when she was no longer useful, was set afire.

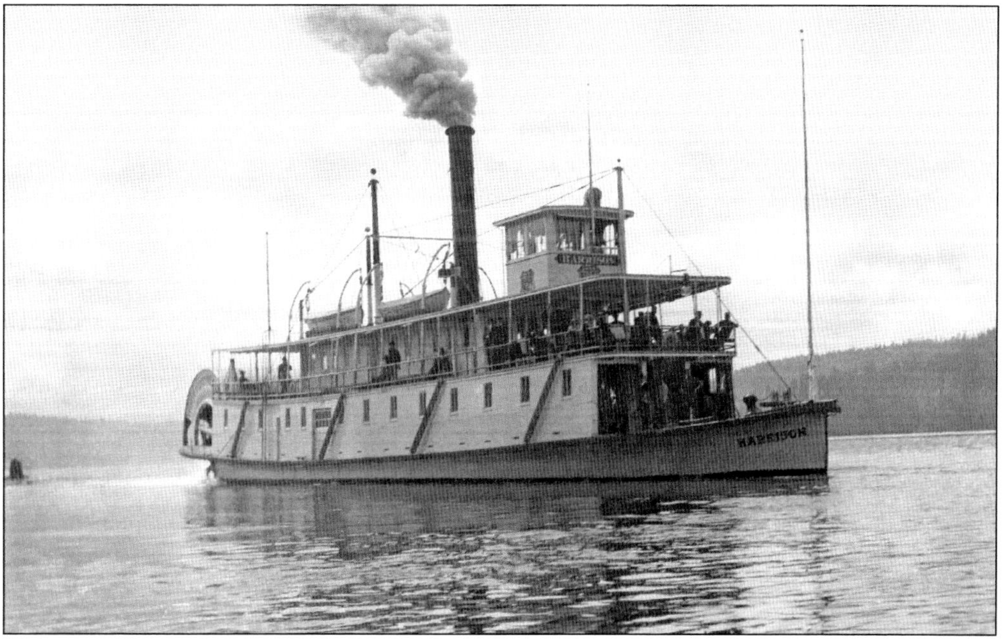

Before 1912, passengers traveled by boat from Harrison to Coeur d'Alene to catch the train to Spokane. That year, the *Harrison* was built to take passengers from Harrison to Amwaco at the entrance to Windy Bay, across the lake. There, they could catch a train to Spokane. This cut 30 minutes from the travel time. This undated photograph is of the steamer *Harrison*.

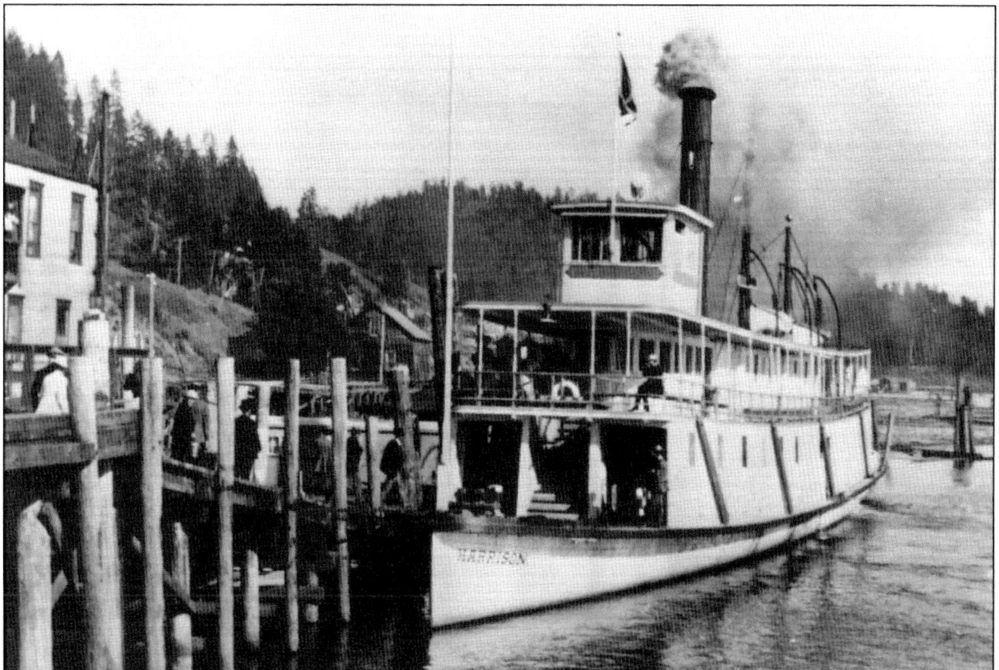

The *Harrison* and the *Georgie Oakes* were the two fastest sternwheelers on the lake. They would often race from Harrison to Coeur d'Alene. The streamer *Harrison* is docked in Harrison around 1920. Pete the Greek's Café is the building on the left.

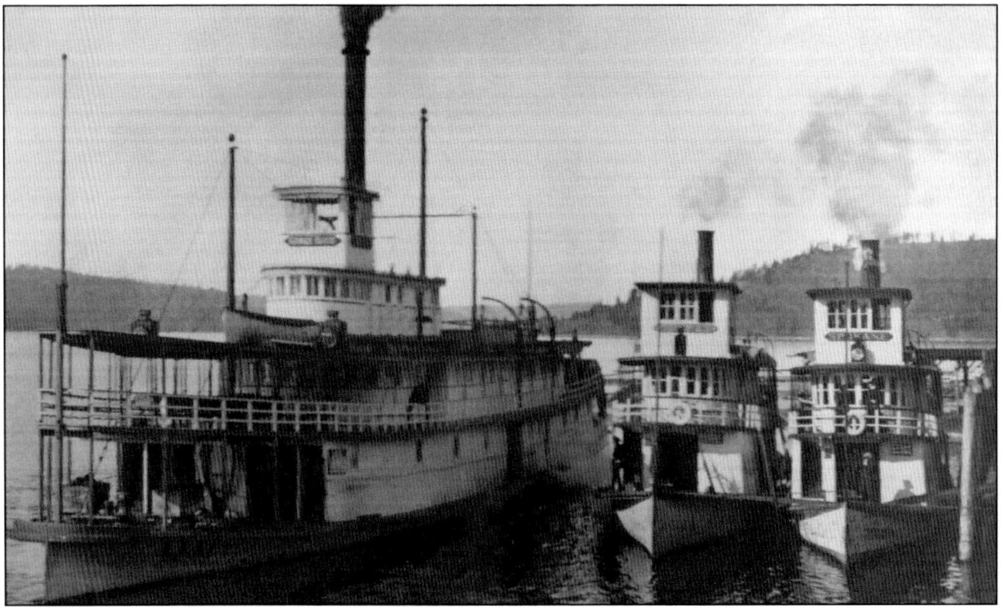

Three grand steamers owned by the Red Collar Line are docked in Harrison. They are, from left to right, the *Georgie Oakes*, the *Colfax*, and the *Spokane*.

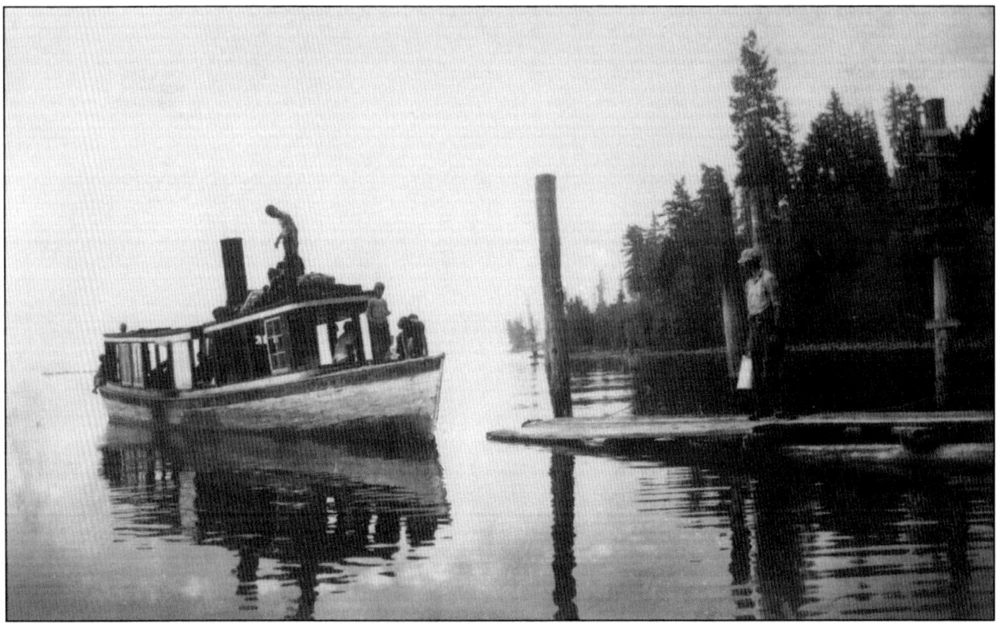

Coming into the dock at Ben Martin Bay is a boatload of Boy Scouts heading for a campout. Dairyman Conly Wilkinson is waiting with a cream can to be sent to a creamery in Coeur d'Alene. The *Sly*, pictured here, is only one example of how the lakes and rivers were used by everyone for transportation.

Tugboats were the workhorses on the lake. Most lumber companies owned two or three. Besides hauling freight and supplies, they towed brails of logs to the mills. It took 28 to 40 hours, non-stop, to haul logs from the holding area at Conkling to Coeur d'Alene. The job of a tugboat captain was hard, dangerous, and required great skill.

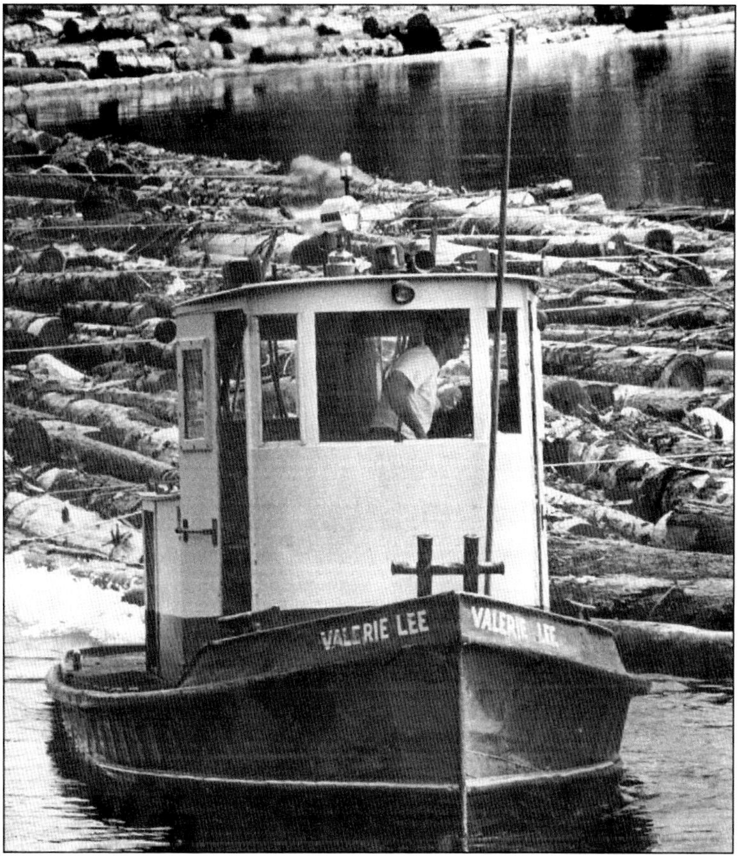

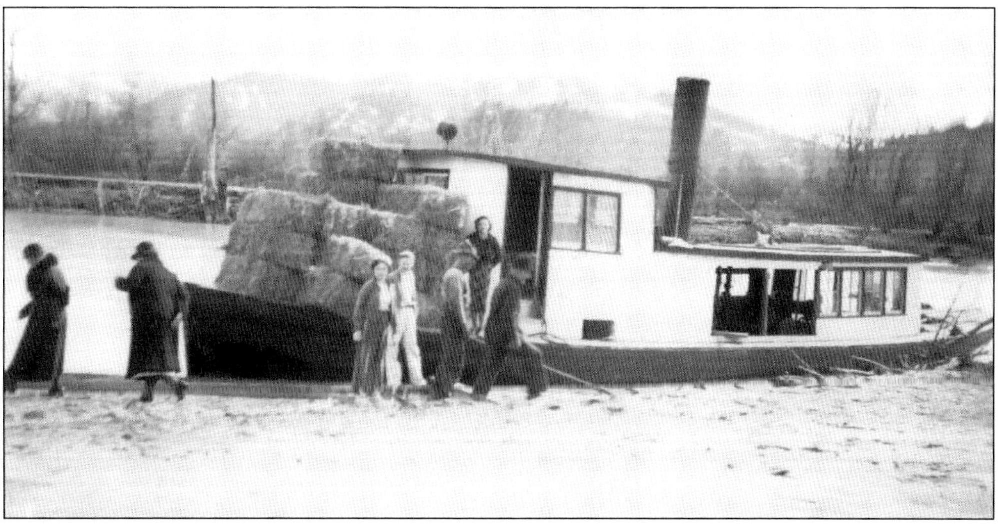

The tugboat *Golden Star* was built in 1936 by Andrew Knutsen for the Russell and Pugh Lumber Company. On her first run, she hauled hay and supplies for the Sandie Baillie and Frank Smith logging camp, located near Medimont. Two unidentified ladies are leaving on the left. The hay crew included Geraldine and Howard "Bubs" Russell, Lee Porter, Sandie Baillie, and one unidentified man.

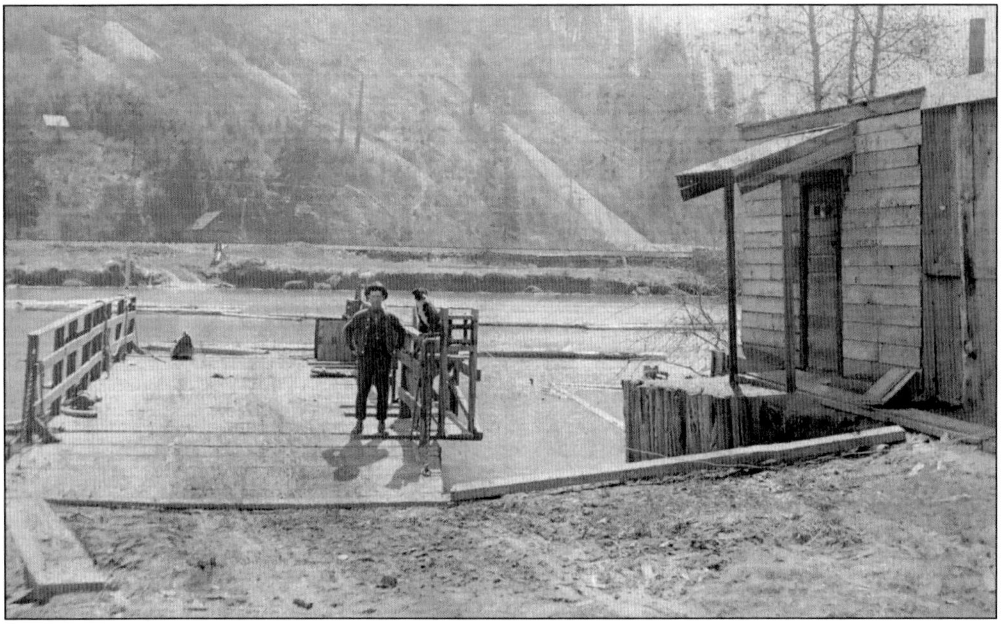

Prior to roads or bridges, passengers, animals, and supplies were transferred across the rivers by ferries. The county maintained the Springston Ferry, paying the operator $30 a month. It crossed the Coeur d'Alene River approximately three miles east of Harrison. (John V. Wood collection.)

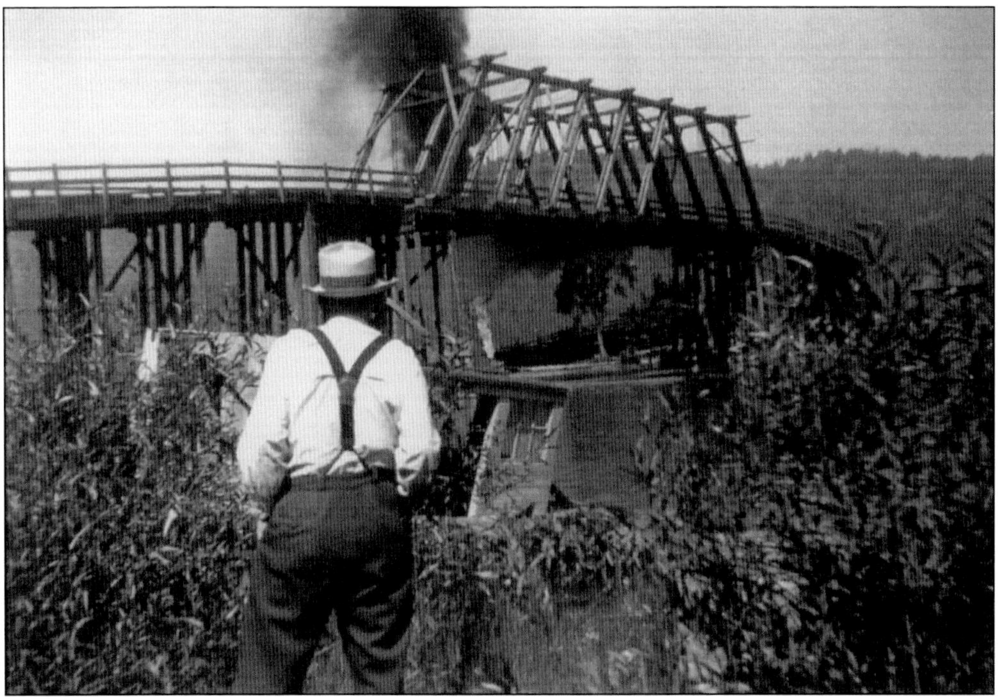

When the Russell and Pugh Lumber Company moved its operations from Harrison to Springston in 1919, a bridge was constructed. The original Springston Bridge, shown here, was made entirely of wood. It was replaced by a steel bridge in 1955.

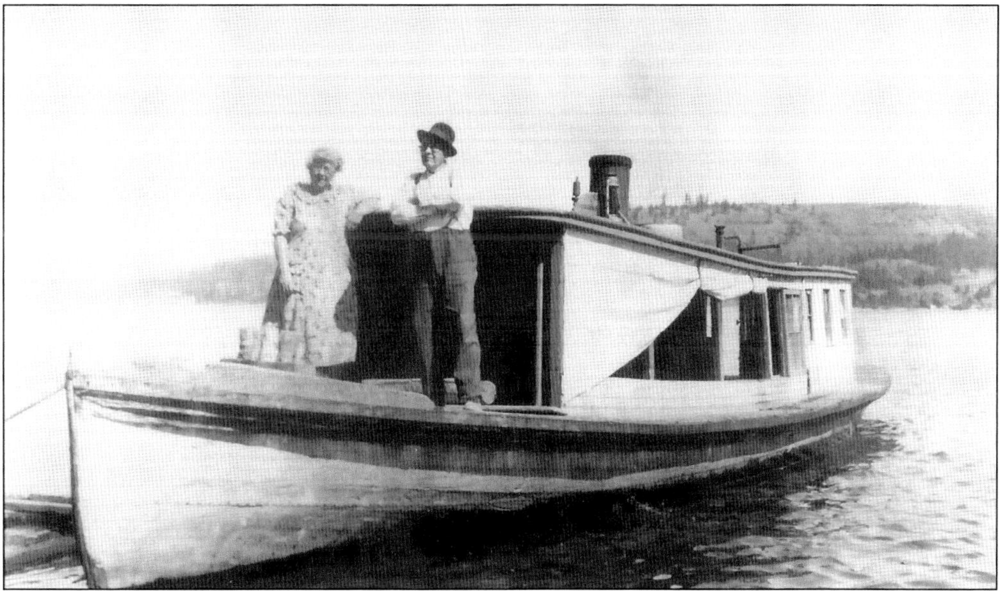

By the 1930s, roads were being built, and the steamers were going out of service. However, it was an arduous two-day trip from Harrison to Coeur d'Alene or Spokane. The choice was between the winding lake road or the road following the Coeur d'Alene River from Harrison to the old Mullan Road at Rose Lake. Matilda and Franklin Ketchum, owners of the Harrison Hotel, began a ferry service between Harrison on the east side of the lake and Ferry Landing (now Spokane Point) on the west. Above, the Ketchums are on the ferry *Pissant* in 1934. Below, the Ketchum ferry passengers on July 19, 1935, included, from left to right, Matilda Ketchum, Bob Patterson, Beryl Berg, Margaret Berg, Lela Berg, and Ralph Berg Jr.

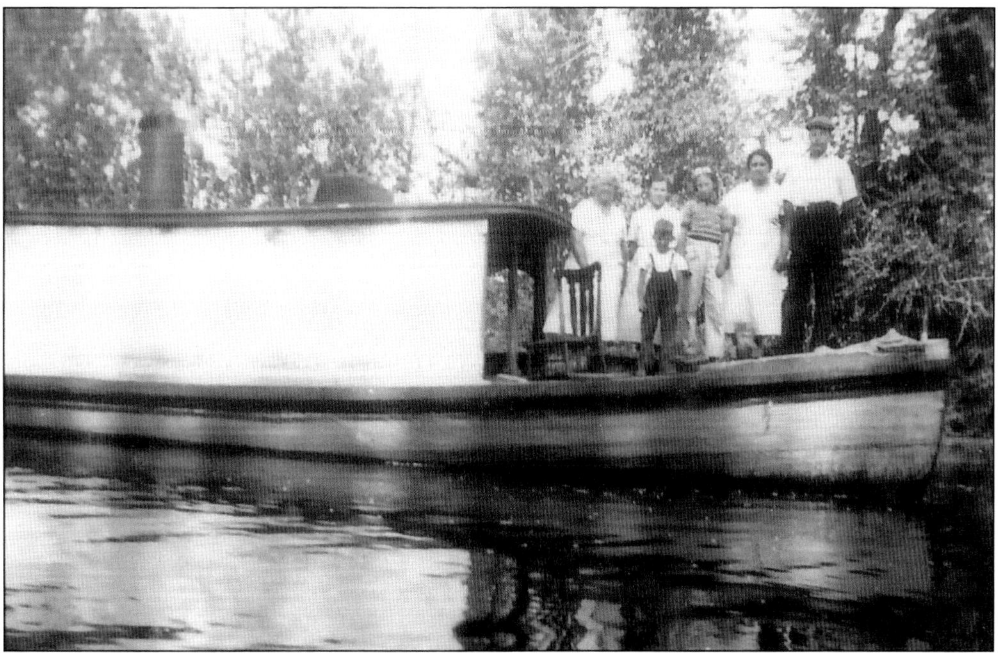

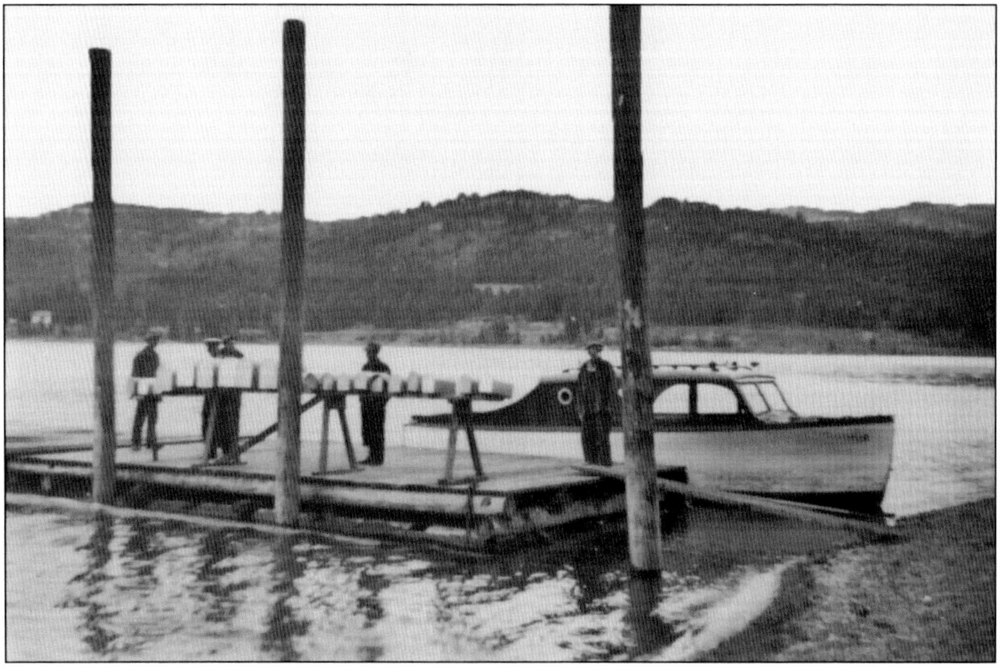

The first marine mail route west of the Mississippi was granted for Coeur D'Alene Lake to Lester C. Shadduck in 1908. The steamers made stops along the shores of the lake to Harrison and up the St. Joe River to St. Maries. When the steamers were phased out, smaller powerboats still made deliveries. This photograph is of a boat delivering mail to the Carlin Bay docks around 1933.

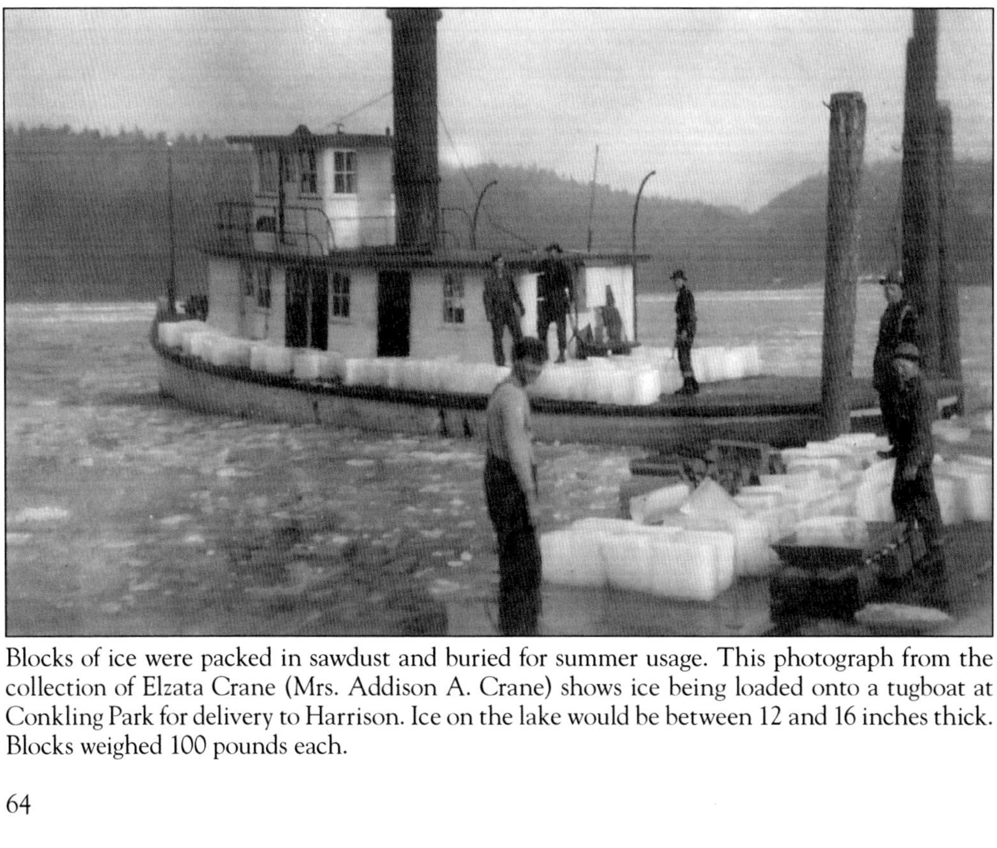

Blocks of ice were packed in sawdust and buried for summer usage. This photograph from the collection of Elzata Crane (Mrs. Addison A. Crane) shows ice being loaded onto a tugboat at Conkling Park for delivery to Harrison. Ice on the lake would be between 12 and 16 inches thick. Blocks weighed 100 pounds each.

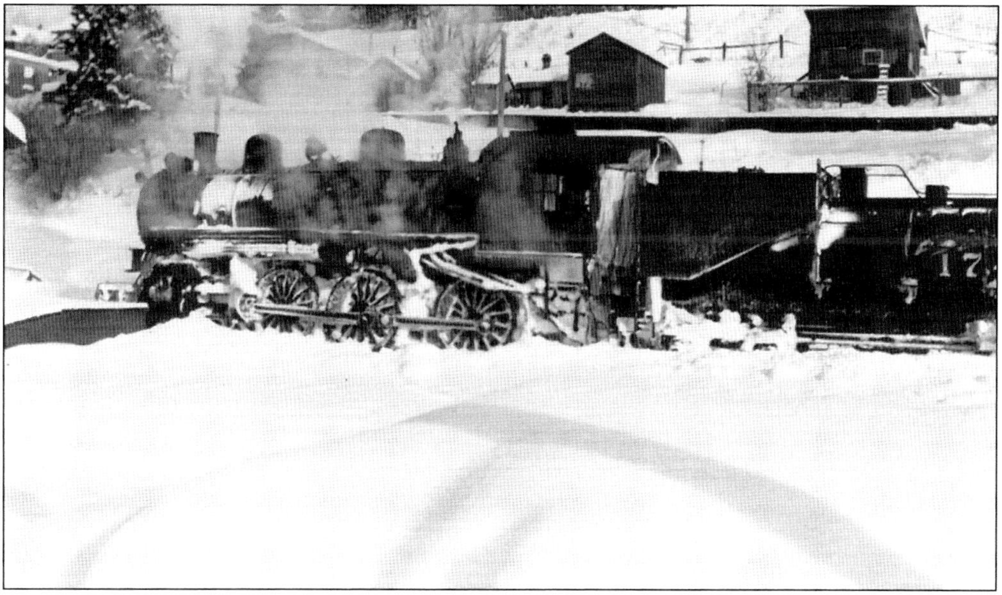

Here is the Oregon Washington Railroad and Navigation (OWR&N) train arriving in Harrison about 1900. The last train trip was made on April 29, 1993.

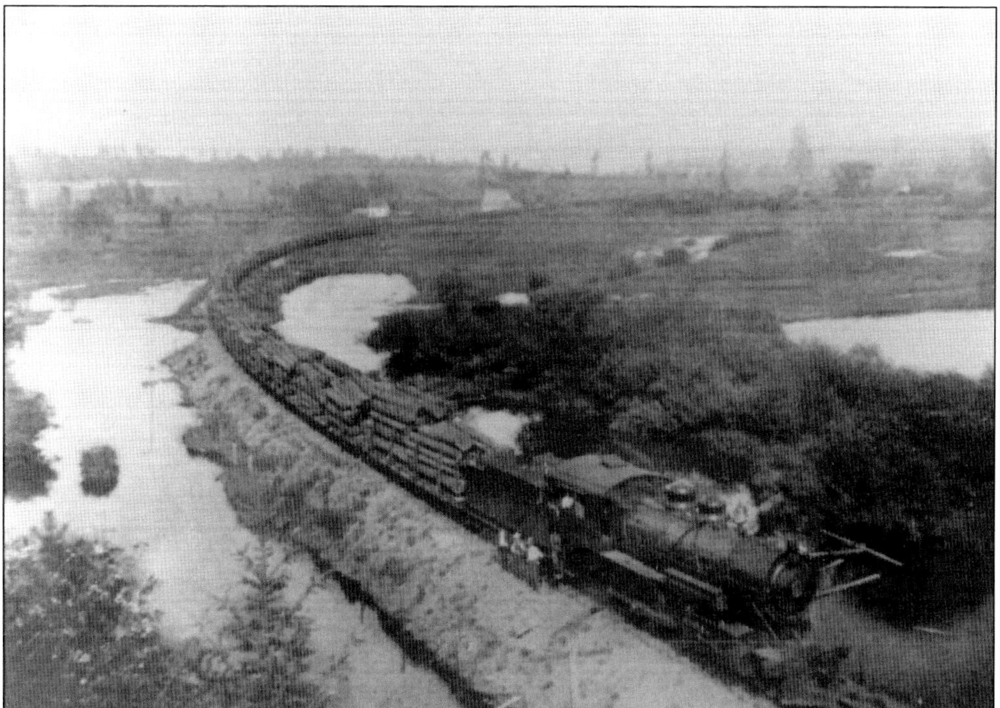

Trains were invaluable for hauling freight and logs, as well as passengers. A Washington Idaho and Montana Railway Company train is carrying a load of logs to Potlatch. There are 104 "flats," or flat cars, carrying 1,300,000 board feet.

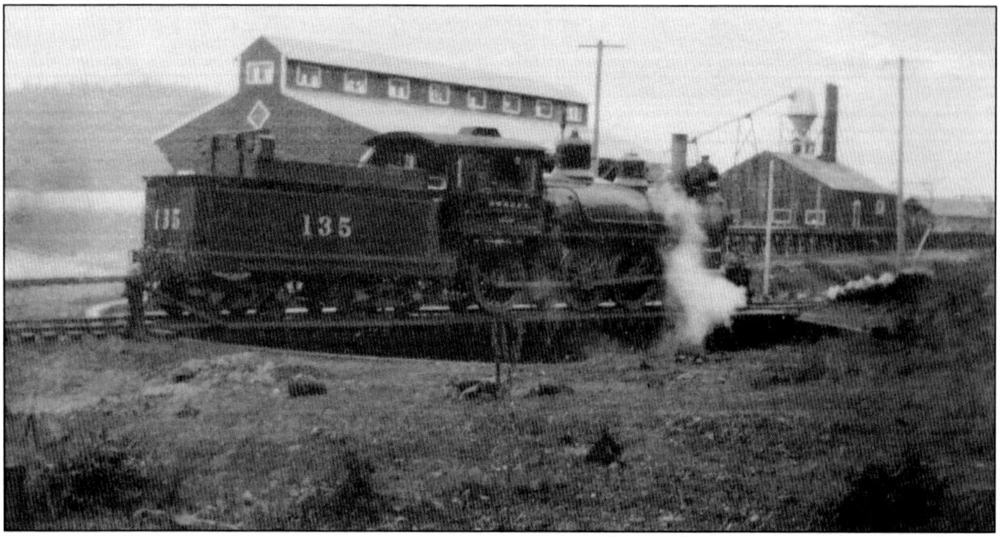

The *Harrison* could carry 600 passengers, and the *Georgie Oakes* could have 1,000 passengers. It required two to four trains per day to transfer passengers from Harrison to Wallace. A turntable was needed. In this photograph, taken about 1924, a train is on the turntable, which was located close to the Harrison Box Factory on the south end of town.

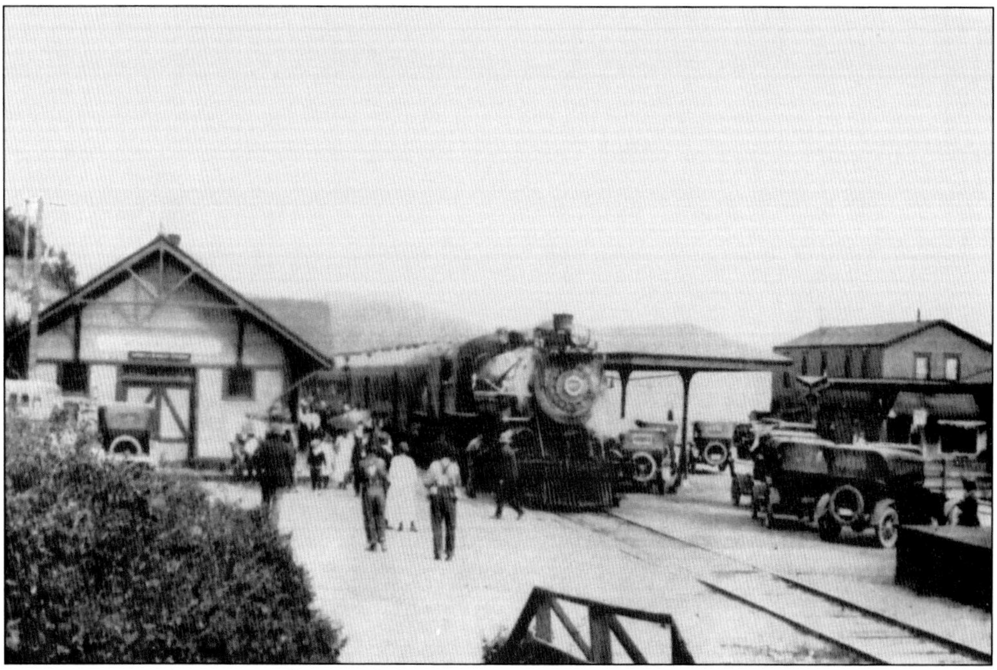

Here is a scene from around 1921 of the train depot on the docks where trains, cars, and boats converged. The first station was built in 1899 and was moved to become a freight house when this new station was built in 1903.

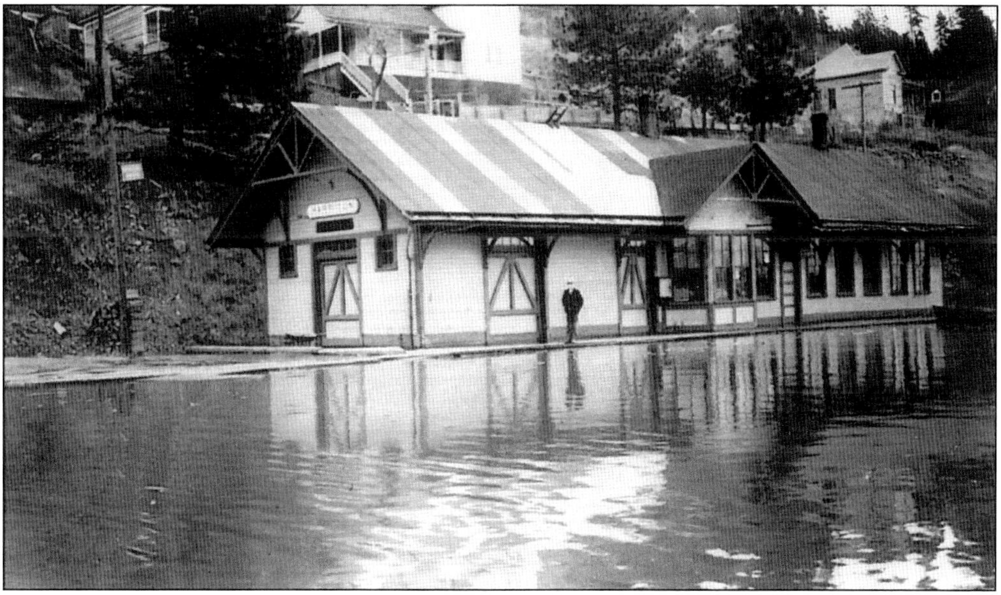

Train travel was not without difficulties, including flooding. This picture was taken on Christmas Day 1933. For 17 days, no trains operated from Harrison to Kellogg and Wallace. Two private cars of railroad officials from Omaha were trapped in Harrison.

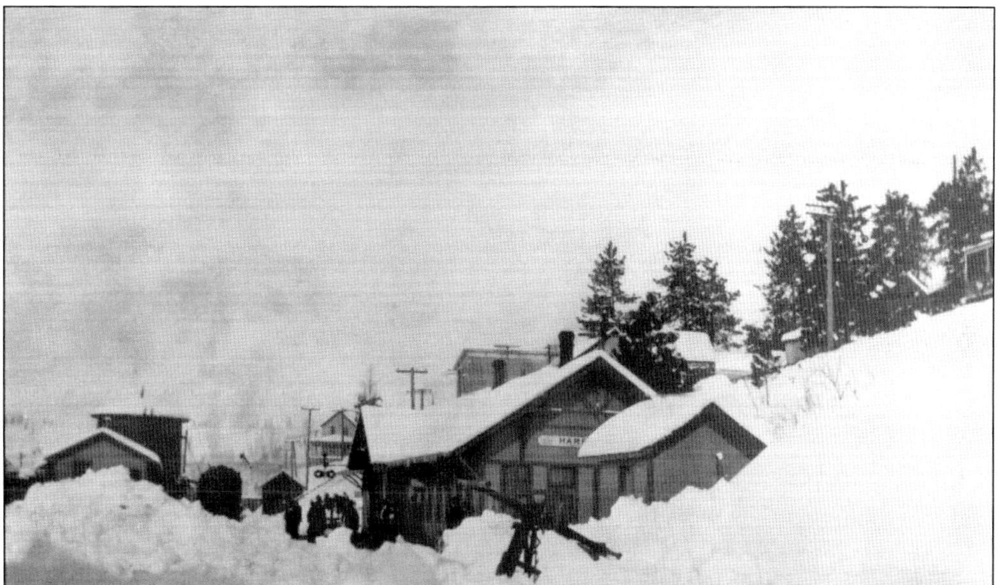

Heavy snowfall blankets the train depot. This undated photograph could easily depict a snowy day in most winters.

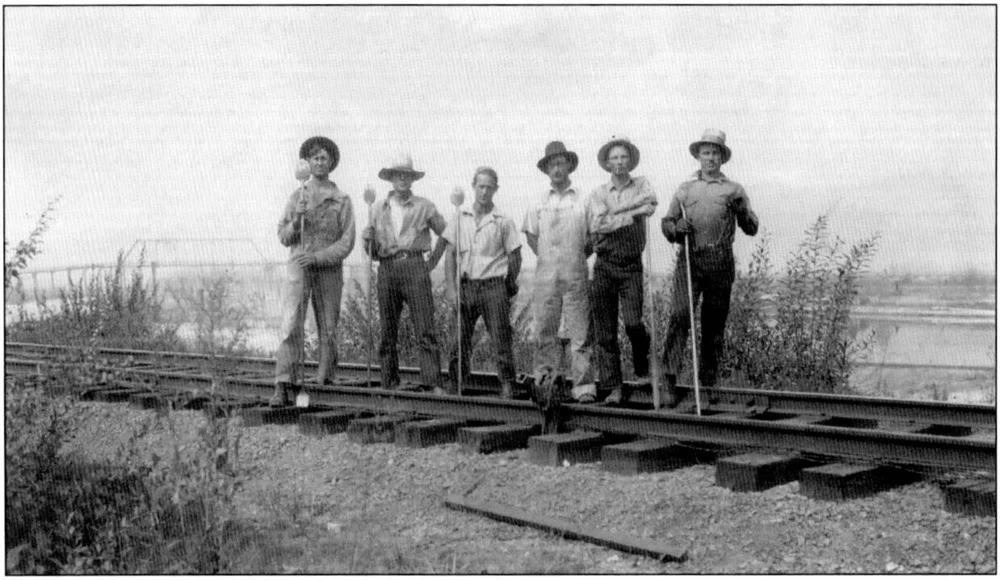

The Union Pacific gang that worked on the Springston to Lacon section between 1935 and 1938 included, from left to right, Everett Thompson, Robert McKaslin, Mr. Botts, Robert Van Blaricom, and two unidentified workers.

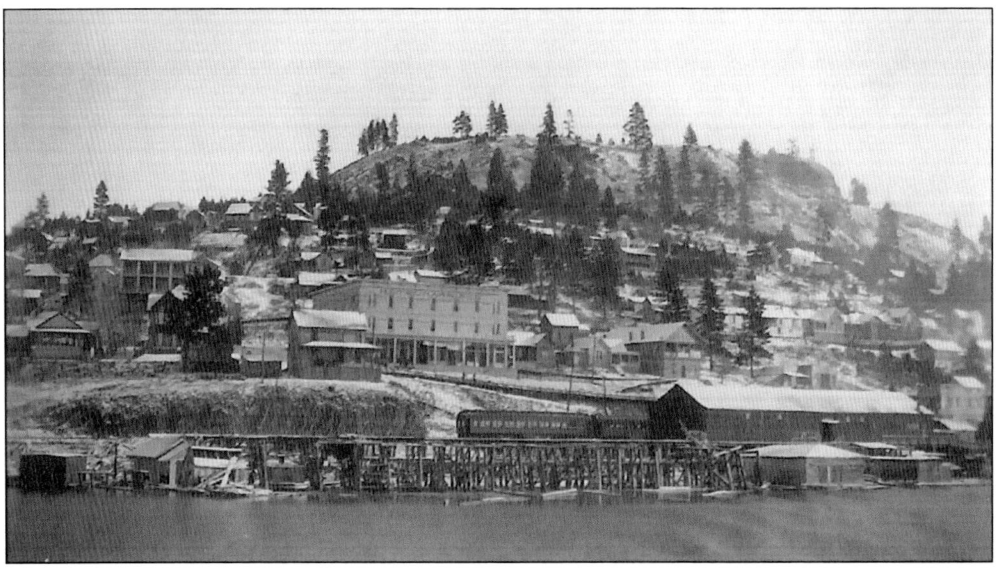

This photograph, taken sometime prior to 1917, shows a train at the Harrison dock area. The large building in the center is Hotel Harrison. Passenger service through Harrison ended in 1957.

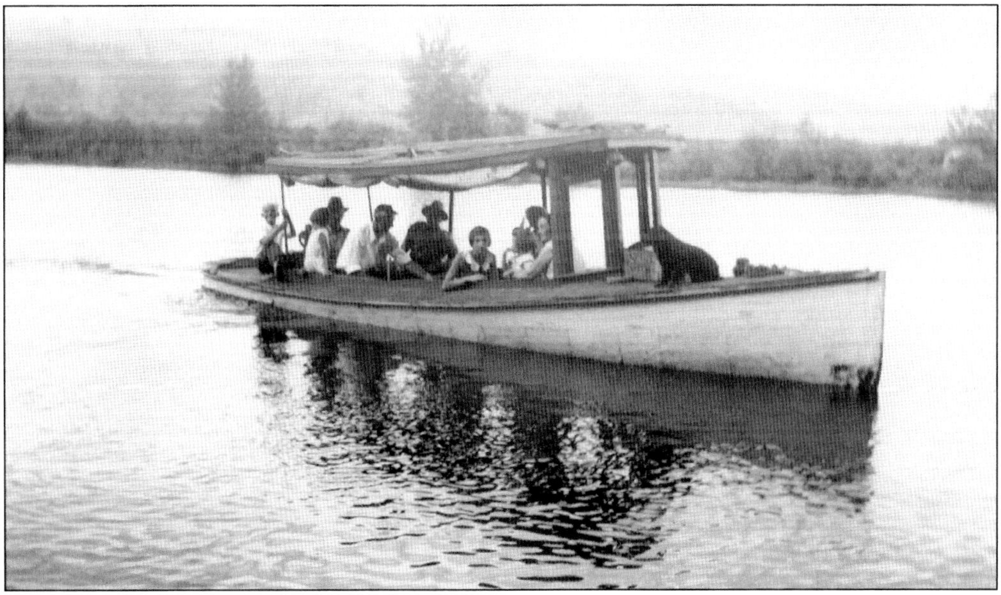

Private launches, like this one owned by the Connelly and Kroetch Company, as well as steamboats, tugboats, and barges, filled the lake with traffic. Smaller launches were used for family picnics and outings.

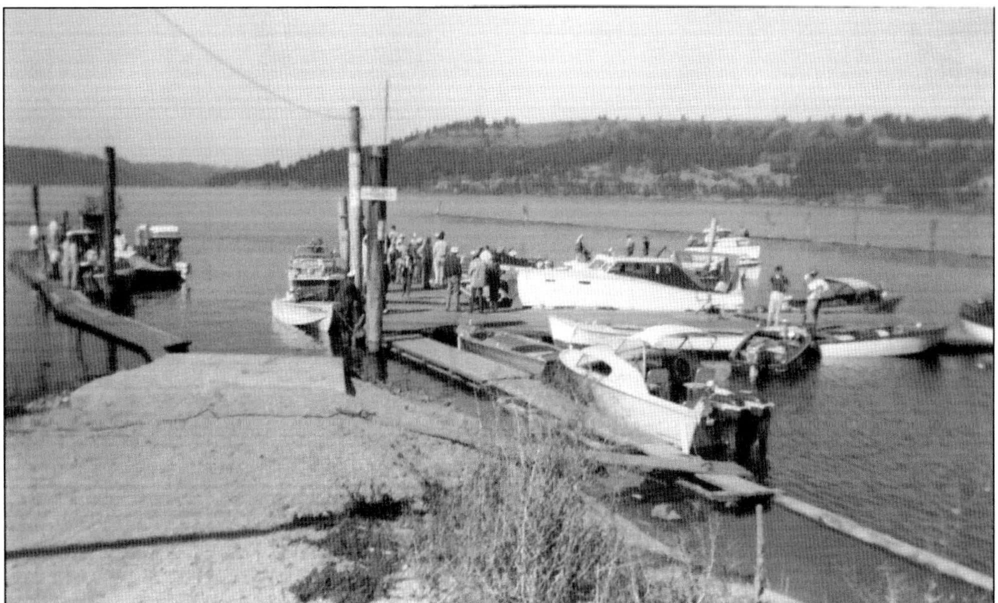

After the mills and steamships were gone, the shoreline took on a different look. Here are pleasure boats at the Harrison docks in 1958, on the site of the former Grant Mill shown on page 26. Boating continues to be a major form of recreation in the area today.

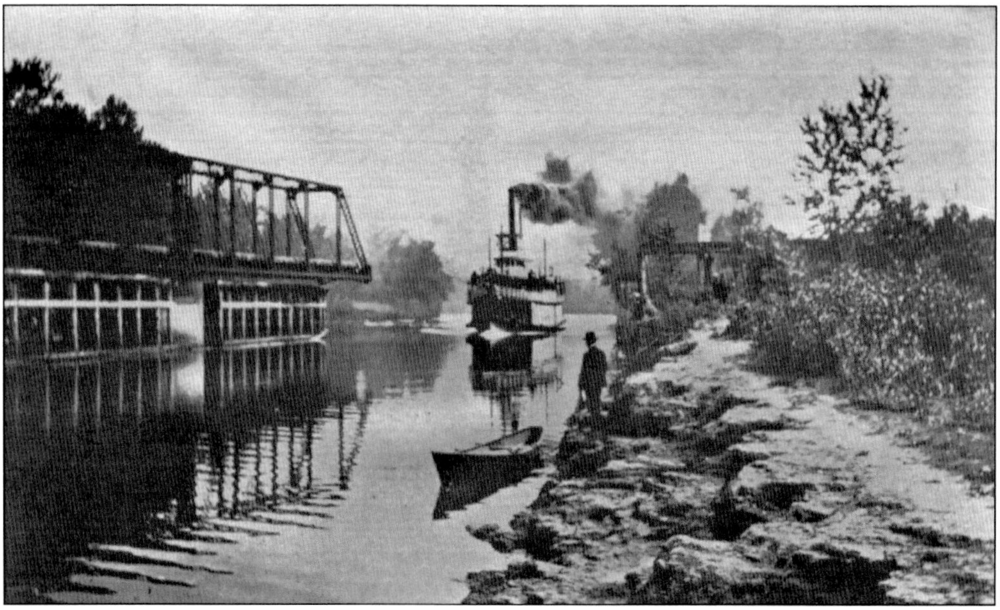

The first train from Spokane Falls, Washington, to Wallace, Idaho, in 1889 would have used this hand-operated, wooden swinging bridge, built in 1884, over the St. Joe River. Four blasts from the boat whistle signaled the operator to open the bridge. In 1921, this bridge was replaced by a steel bridge, operated by a gas engine.

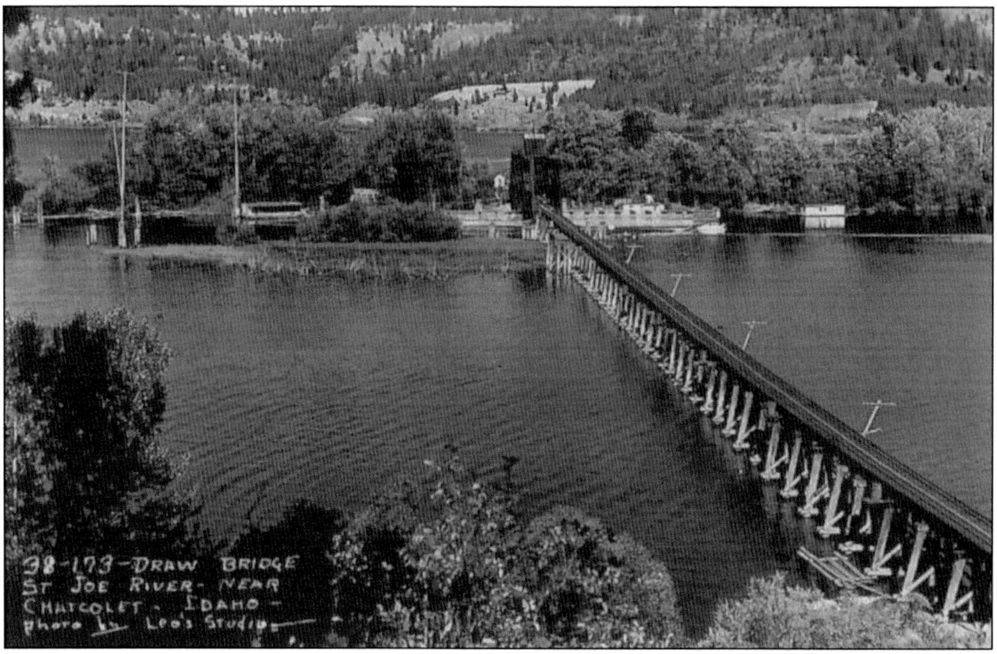

The trestle to the swinging bridge is shown here. A boat is passing through the bridge, which is in the upper-center of the picture. An identical approach goes from the bridge to the bank on the other side. One of the last remaining swinging bridges in the country, it was raised and became part of the national Rails to Trails bicycle trail system. This photograph was taken after 1921.

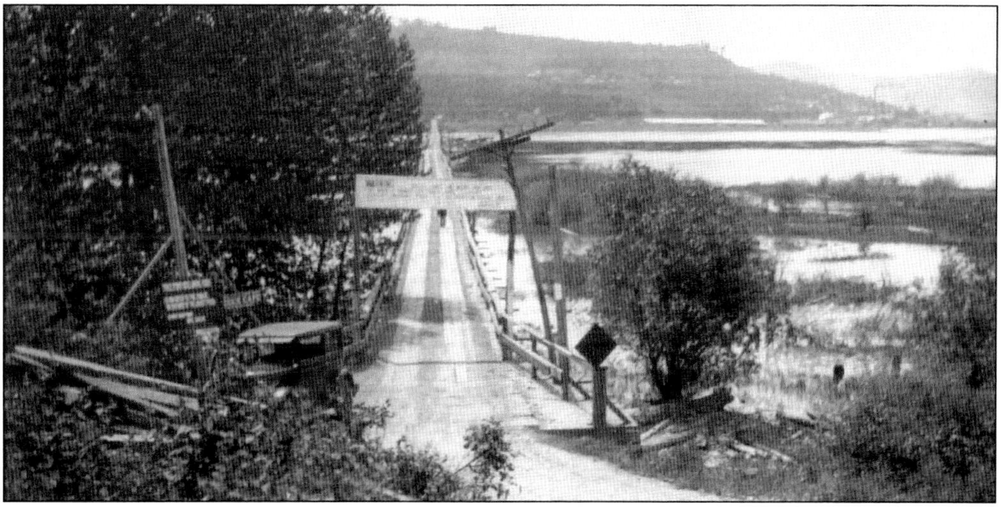

Originally, the only way across the Coeur d'Alene River north of town was by boat or a self-operated barge attached to a cable system. Seeing the need for a bridge, settlers donated teams, labor, and pilings to build this trestle bridge. The pilings were brought by water from Half Round Bay and Carlin Bay to Harrison. This undated photograph shows the north approach facing south toward the city of Harrison.

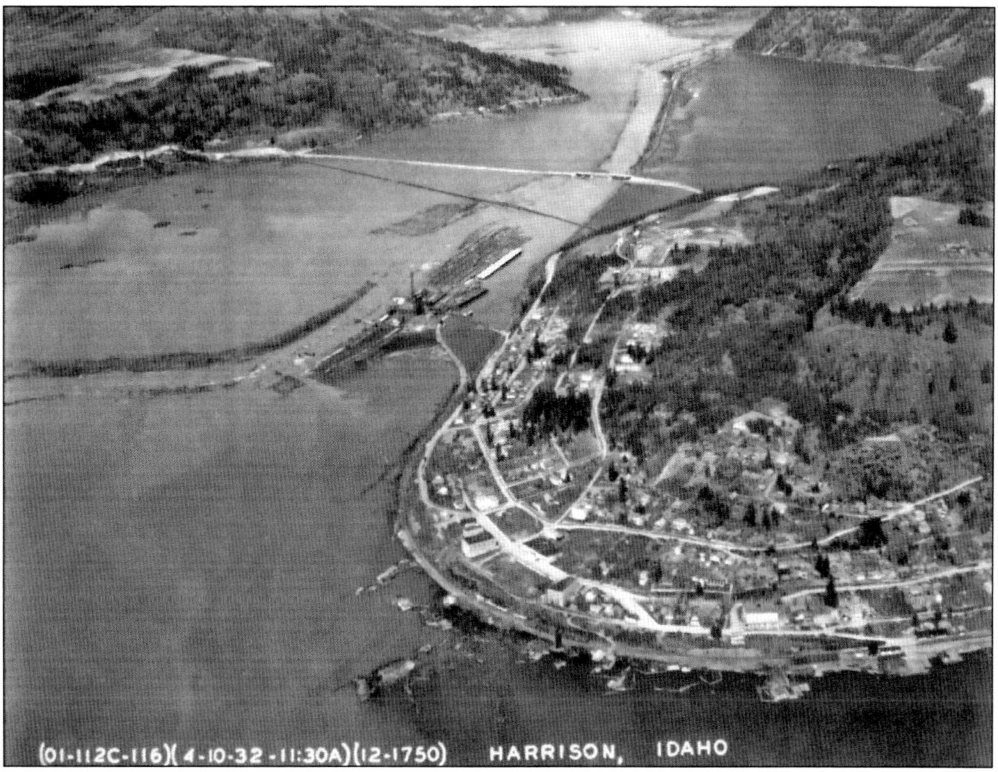

This aerial view of Harrison, taken in the early 1930s, shows the location of the new steel bridge and causeway across the Coeur d'Alene River. Just below that bridge and to the west is the original trestle bridge shown in the upper image. In low water, some of the pilings are still visible. The Export Lumber Company lies in the center of the picture.

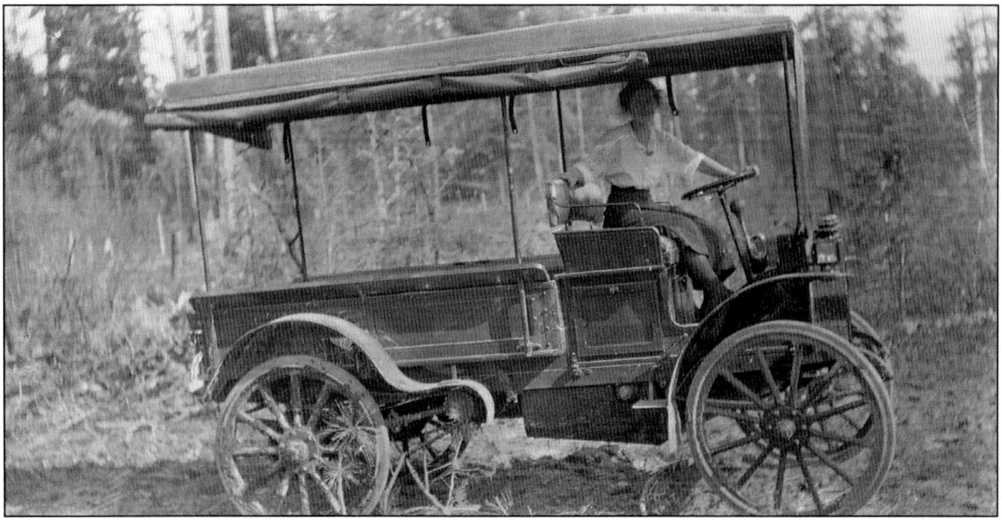

An unidentified woman sits behind the wheel of this 1907 International chain-drive two-cylinder truck. She is possibly delivering lunches to logging crews.

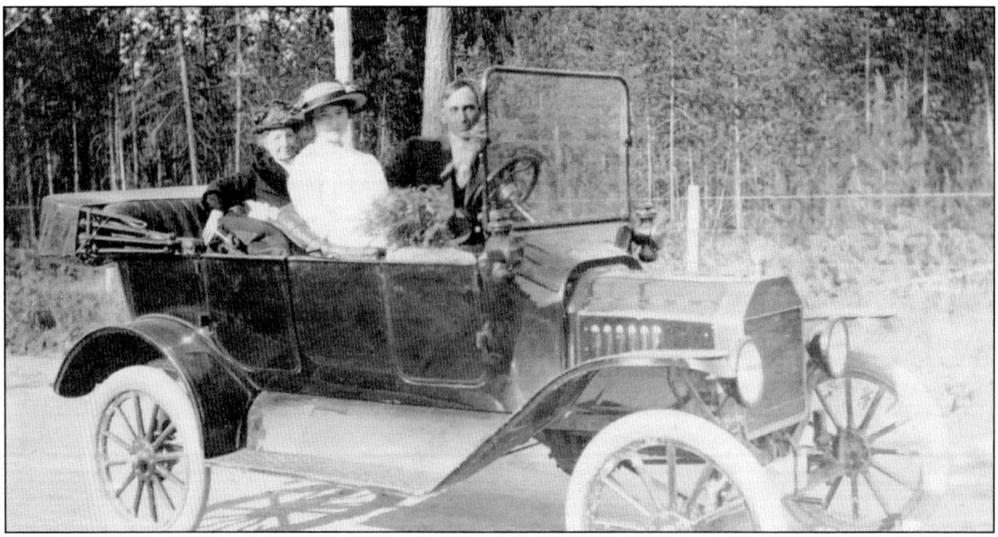

The first automobile in town was a Model T Ford purchased by Dr. John M. Finney. Before that, he traveled by foot, horseback, or boat. The second automobile was also a Model T Ford but was owned by John E. Fisher, who drove from his farm on East Point to his jewelry store in town. Soon others were riding in Model Ts, as are Susie Russell, Mamie Russell Thibault, and Al Thibault in this photograph.

Five

Churches and Schools

Much is made of the wild, untamed West, with stories including high-fliers looking to get rich quick, saloons, drunken fights, and ladies of the night. But in truth, most of the settlers were solid citizens looking for jobs in forests or mines; men looking to build homes and businesses. They brought their customs, religions, and families from the Midwest, the East, and overseas. After a home, the first building erected would often be a multi-purpose church/school. This served until the congregation could build a church and the number of students demanded a larger school.

Harrison's first home was built in 1891. By 1893, the school was under construction. Methodists built the first church in 1895–1896.

The Baptist church was built in 1900 and dedicated in 1902. The Presbyterian church was constructed in 1901. Catholic Mass was held in the Adventist's building and later in the vacant hall above Greiner's store until the early 1920s, when a local residence was converted into a chapel. There is no record of a building used by the German Lutheran congregation in Carlin Bay, so it is presumed to have been the school. Services in German (translated to English) were led by a preacher from Spokane.

In addition to the large three-story school in Harrison, there were small one-room schools scattered throughout the countryside. In any given year, a school's student body size varied from 7 to 70. A country school consisted of one main room heated by a wood stove. A shed on the back stored wood. There was no indoor plumbing or electricity. The teacher or students hauled water in buckets from a nearby well or spring, kept the fire burning, and did the janitorial work.

As primitive as that may appear today, the curriculum was well rounded. In addition to "readin' 'ritin' and 'rithmatic,' " one teacher covered spelling, geography, history, grammar, composition, government, Idaho history, civics, art, and music. The highlight of the school year was the Christmas program.

With school consolidation, the one-room schools were closed. The vacant buildings had a second life as community centers or farm sheds, but eventually most became dilapidated through lack of use and were demolished.

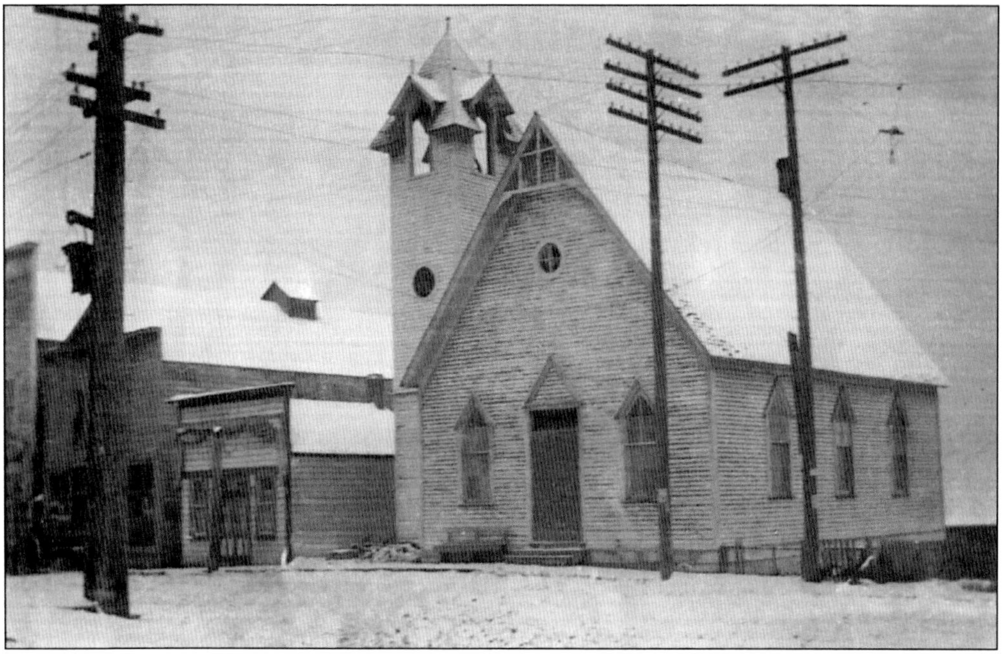

The Grace Methodist Episcopal Church, built in 1895, was the first church building in the city. In addition to church services, school was held here for a short time while the school building was under construction. After this building was destroyed in the 1917 fire, they immediately built a new church a block away. The new building was later purchased by the Masons.

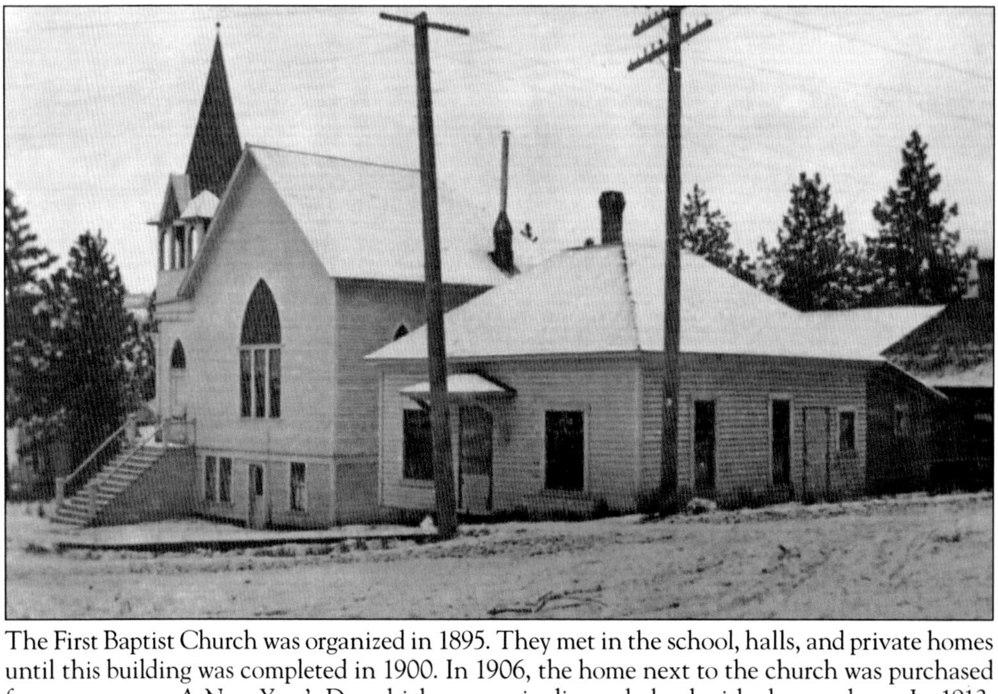

The First Baptist Church was organized in 1895. They met in the school, halls, and private homes until this building was completed in 1900. In 1906, the home next to the church was purchased for a parsonage. A New Year's Day chicken pot pie dinner helped with the purchase. In 1913, Addison A. Crane donated the bell from the old schoolhouse.

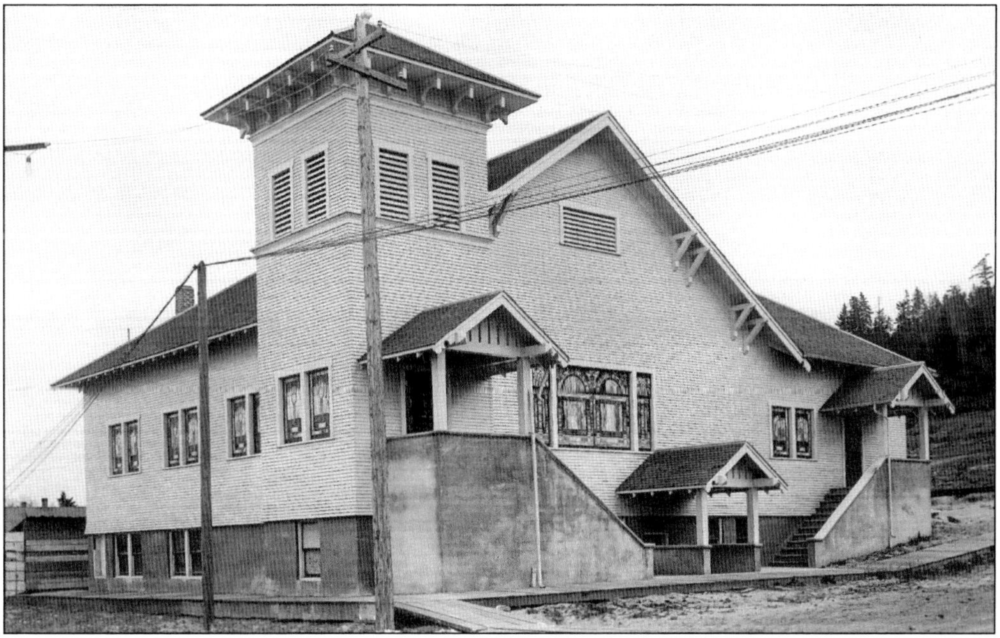

After the 1917 fire, united services with the Baptists, Presbyterians, and Methodists were held in a tent. This new Baptist church was built in 1920. The church piano, rescued from the fire, is still in use. The varnish was scorched on one side, but the playing action remains excellent.

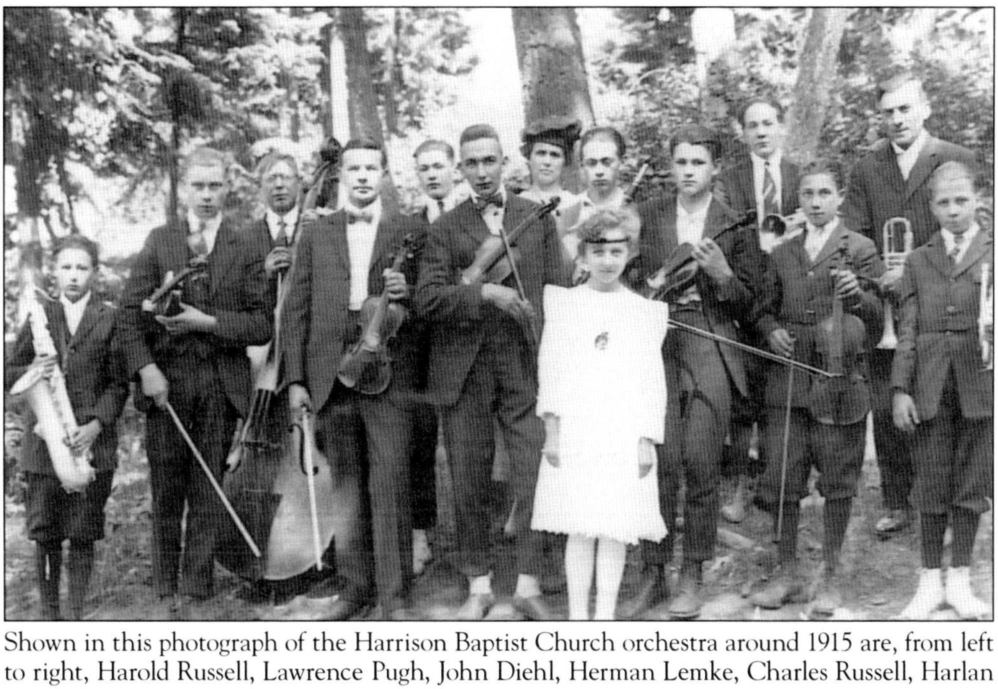

Shown in this photograph of the Harrison Baptist Church orchestra around 1915 are, from left to right, Harold Russell, Lawrence Pugh, John Diehl, Herman Lemke, Charles Russell, Harlan Kimmel, Martha Russell, Lynn Russell, Frances Pugh, Floyd Russell, Joe Wark, Clyde York, Otto Mavies, and Bernard York.

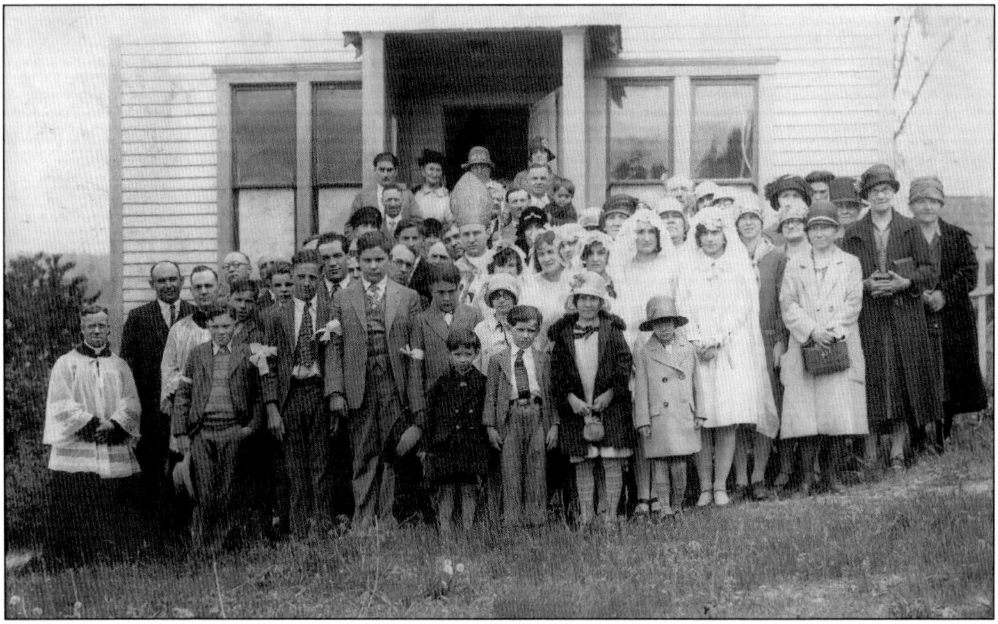

Father Purcell obtained a small store on the main street in 1906 and remodeled it in 1908 to become the first Catholic church. When this church was burned in the 1917 fire, Father Daly bought a house and remodeled it as a church. In 1959, a new church was built on the site. This photograph of the congregation was taken at Confirmation Mass on May 28, 1929.

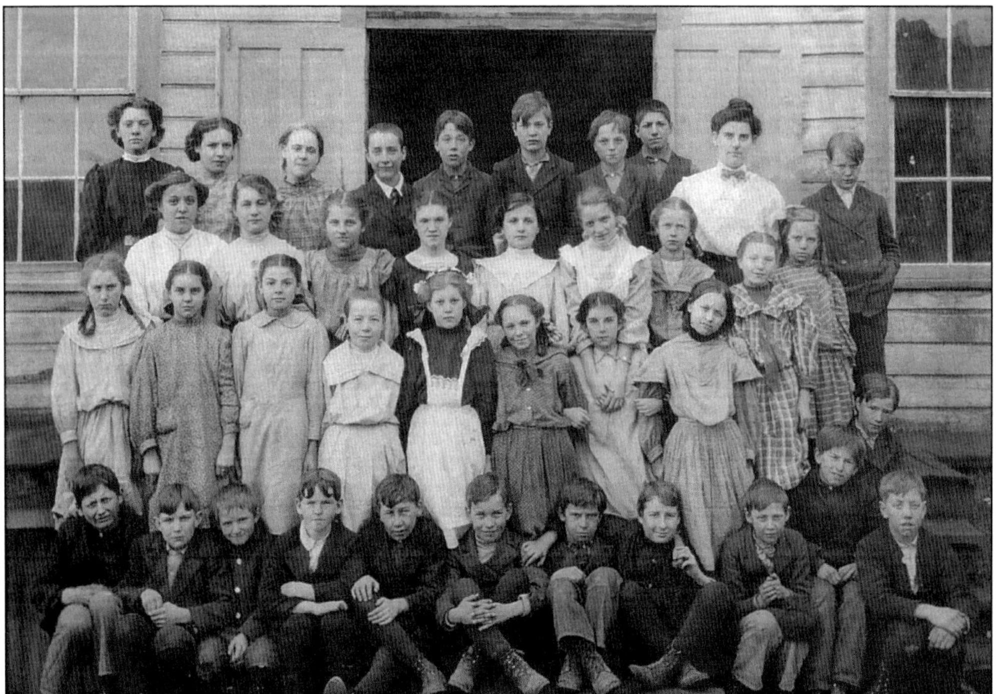

This picture was taken outside the newly completed Grace Methodist Episcopal Church around 1895. School was held in the church while the Harrison City School was still under construction.

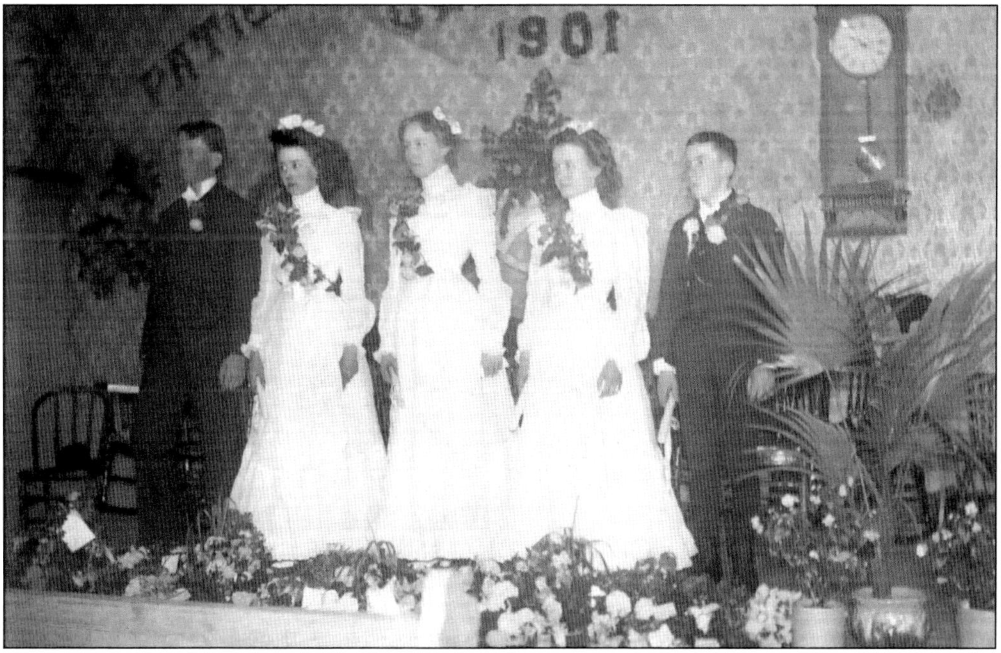

The fourth graduating class of Harrison High School included, from left to right, Joel Gilman Beeler, Claire Helene Crane (Kroetch), Bessie Wanda Turnbow, Julia Josephine Moe (Palmer), and Harry Daniel Manning. Dr. Samuel Avery, of the University of Idaho, issued the address at the commencement on June 1, 1901.

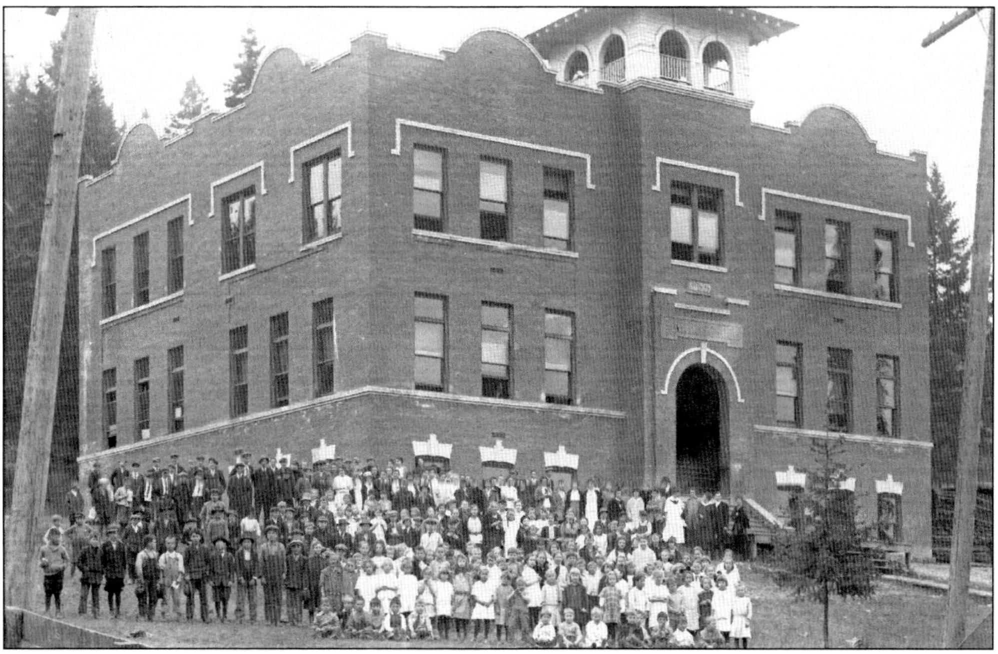

No sooner was the Harrison City School erected than additions were made to accommodate the student body, which had grown to 225. By 1906, four separate buildings scattered throughout the city were used to accommodate the students. The large brick school building was completed in 1909. This picture was taken prior to 1928, before the bell tower was removed.

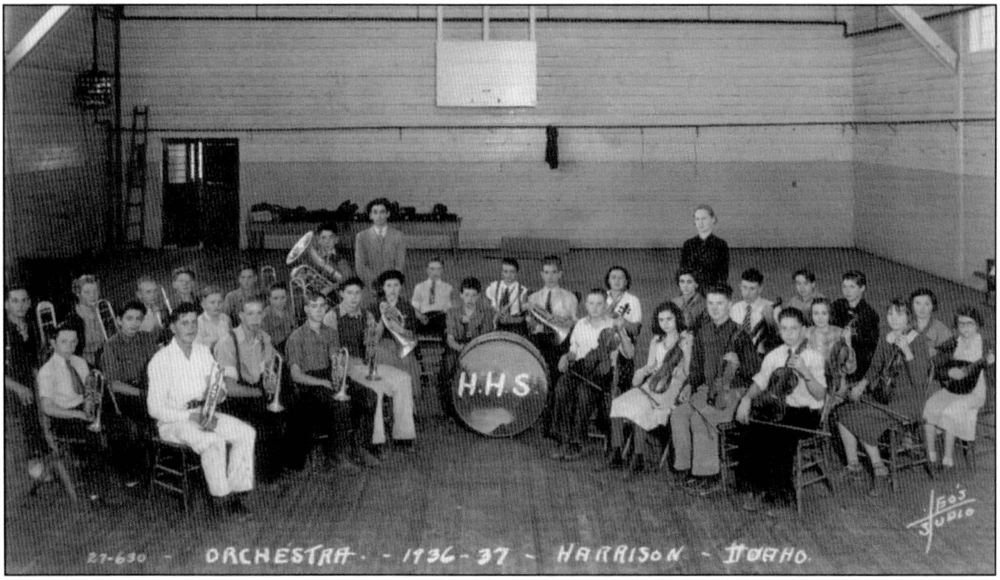

Built in 1929, the gymnasium was home to the basketball team, which was organized in 1925. The first basketball games were played in the school basement. The ceiling was lower, so the home team had an advantage over the visiting team. The gymnasium also made an excellent practice room for the Harrison High School orchestra, pictured here in 1936–1937.

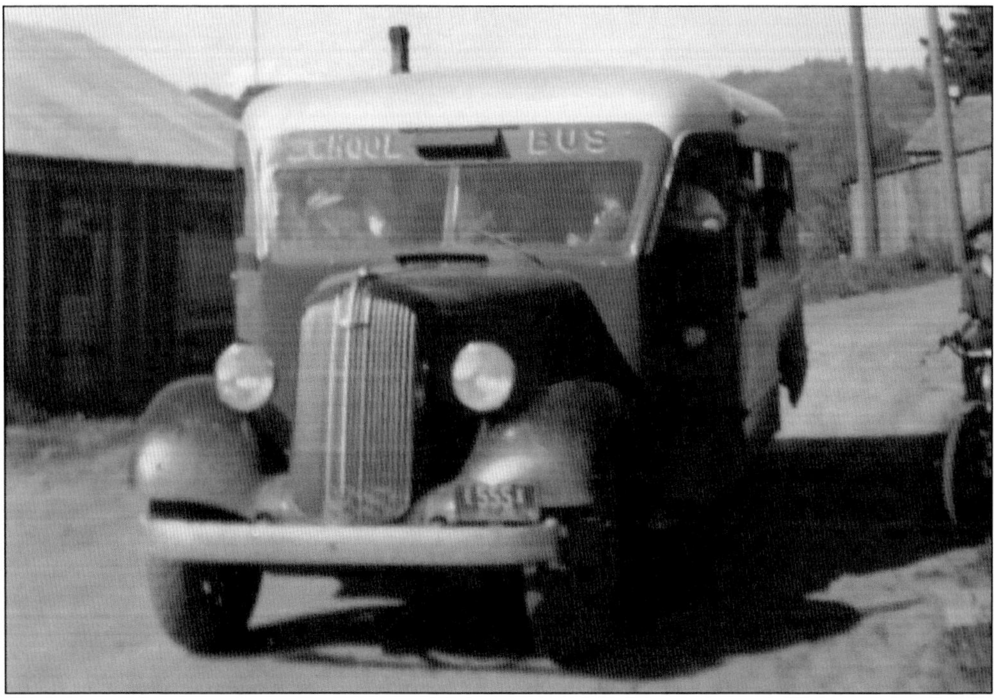

In the 1920s and 1930s, roads and motorized buses brought about consolidation of schools. Earlier modes of transportation were by foot, horseback, or boat, so country one-room schools were usually spaced no more than five miles apart. Even then, many children, some as young as six, had to walk two to three miles to school. Longer distances or inclement weather might find a parent providing a buggy ride.

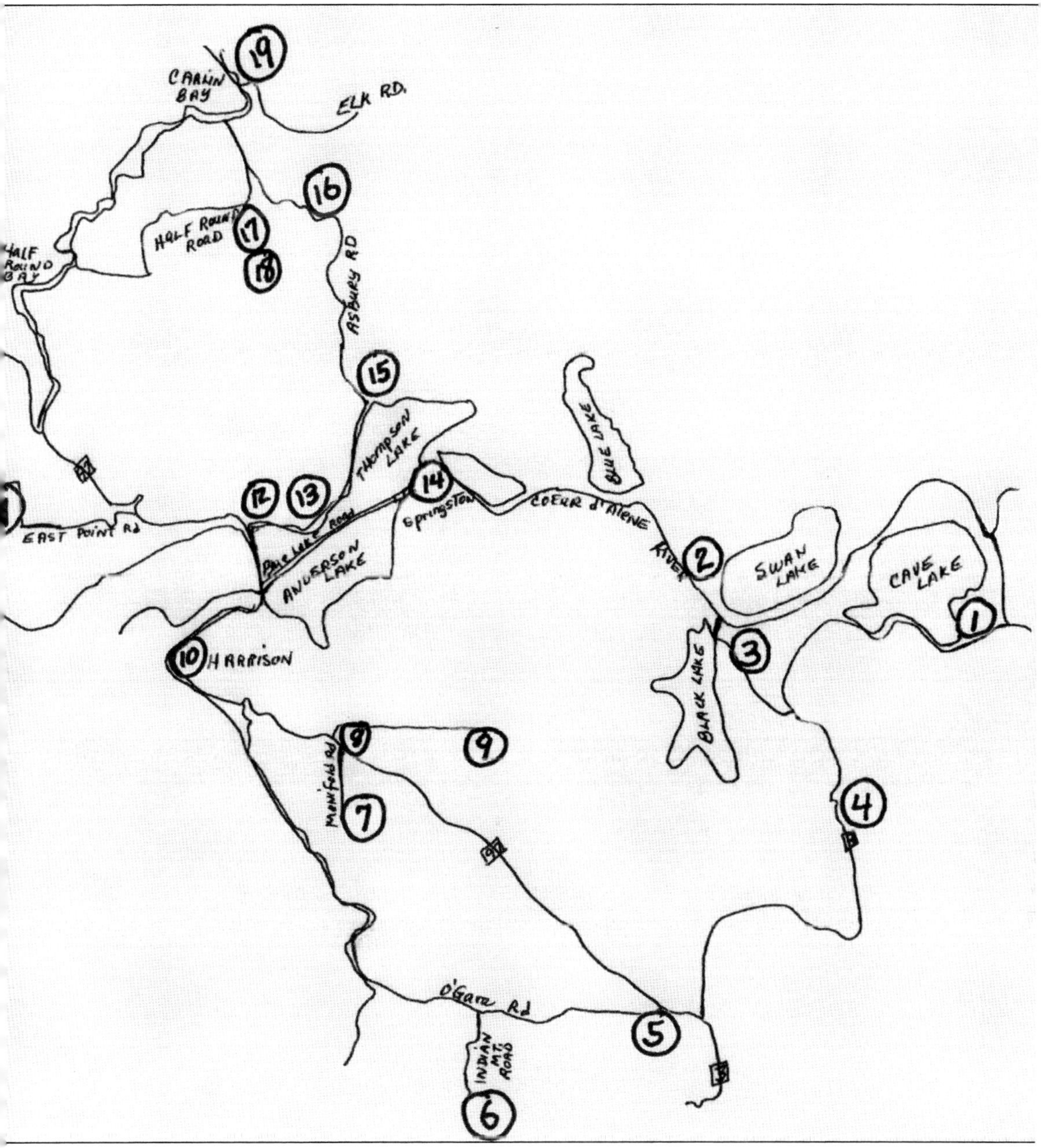

This map shows the locations of the following schools: Cave Lake (1), Swan Lake (2), Black Lake (3), Indian Springs (4), Powerline (5), Walters (6), Manifold (7), Brown Jug (8), Van Dusen (9), Harrison (10), East Point (11), Fairview (12), Doty (13), Springston (14), Grandview (15), Gilfoil (16), Upper Carlin Bay (17), Skyline (18), and Lower Carlin Bay (19).

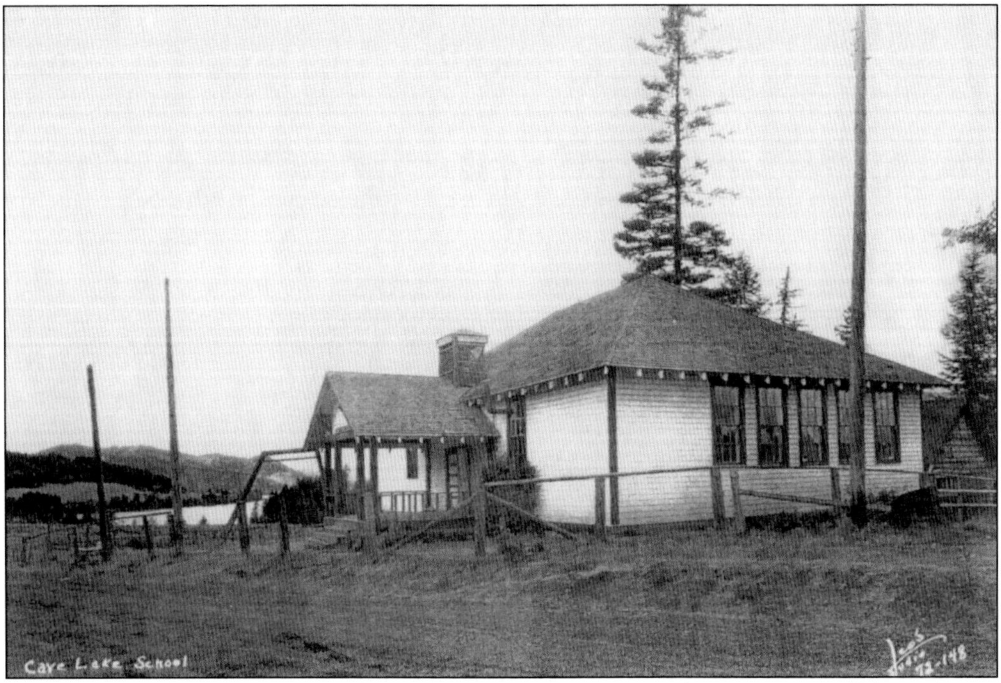

This two-room, wood-frame school on Cave Lake was constructed in 1913. A small frame home, called the teacherage, was built for the teacher's residence. After closure in 1951, the building was used for hay storage until it burned.

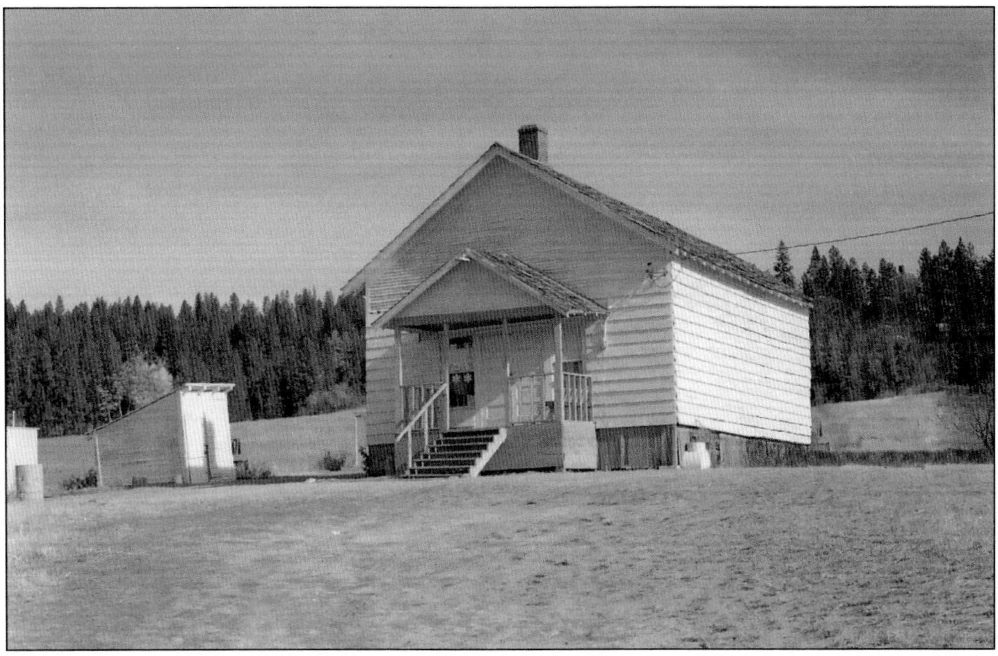
The original Indian Springs School was a lean-to. The building shown here was erected in 1915. As many as 46 students were enrolled. Unusual for the area, the students wore a cape-type, dark blue uniform lined in red. In addition to the general curriculum, they were taught tap dancing and had a rhythm band. The school was closed in 1952 and for a time was used as a community center.

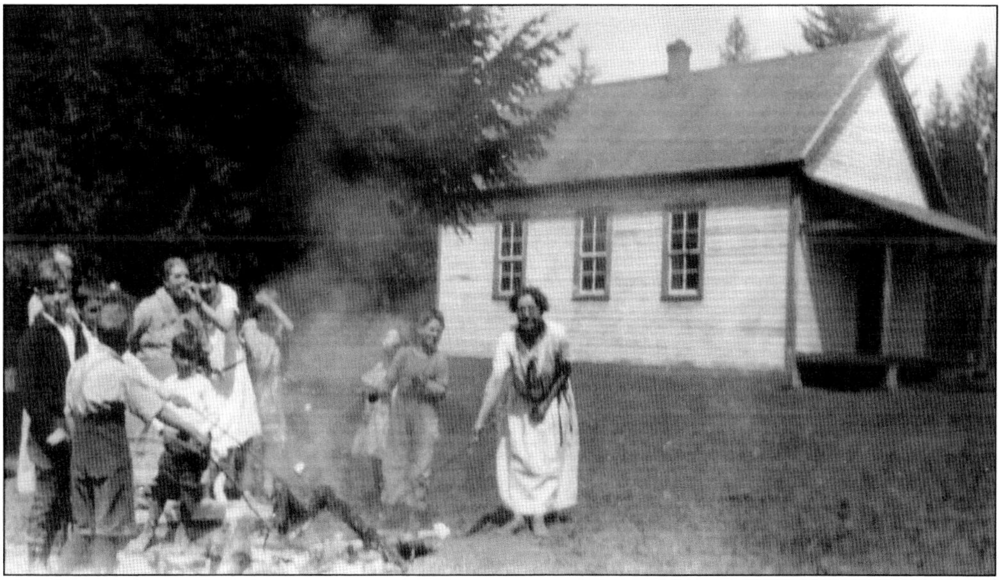

Teacher Iness Justus (fifth from the left) with her students and their families are preparing lunch on the last day of the school year at Black Lake School sometime around 1926–1930. Lunch would consist of what was available, which probably included potatoes that were placed in ashes and roasted.

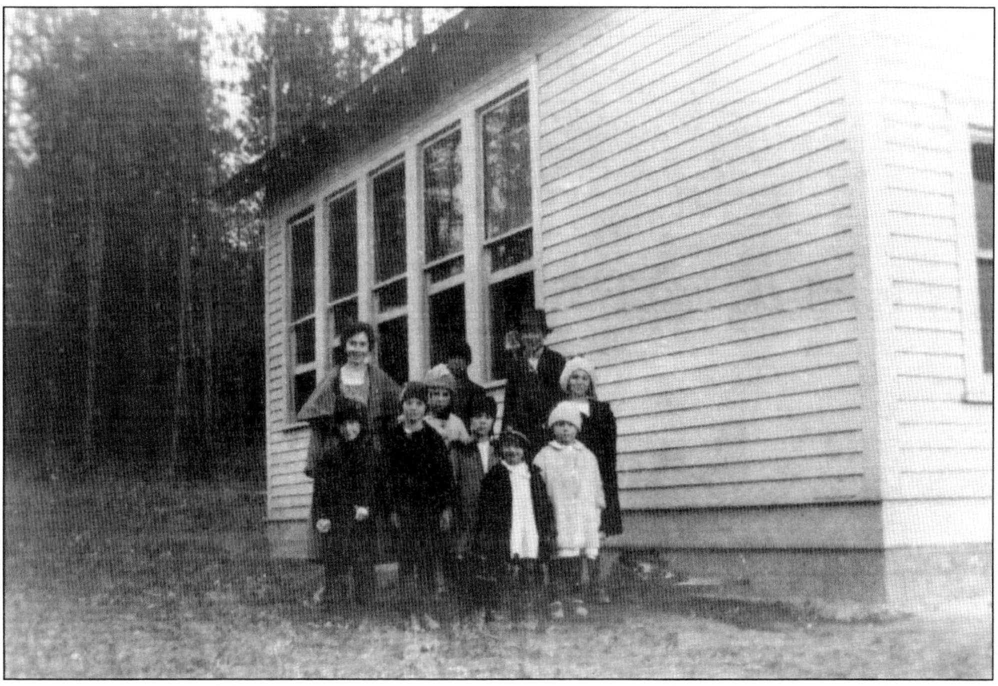

Powerline School was built in 1917 and closed in 1939. Former student Marcella (Lavigne) Gunter remembers the blackboard across the front and inkwells in the desks. Stews were cooked on the wood stove from ingredients the students brought to school. In this photograph, taken about 1920, teacher Kate Murray (left rear) is shown with nine unidentified students, except for Arlie Walters (center rear) and Ralph Miller (right rear).

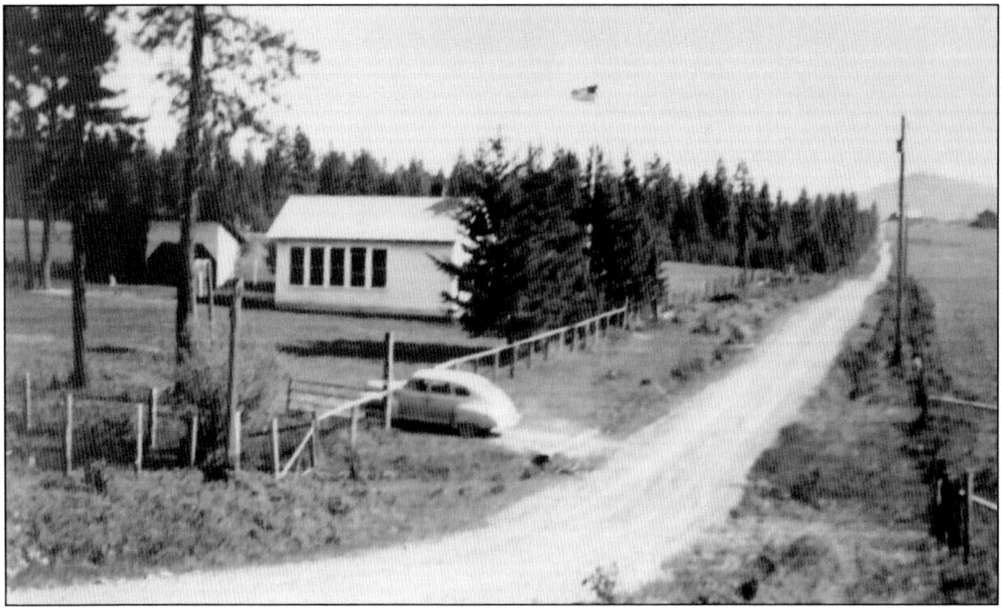

The Walters School on Indian Mountain Road operated from 1920 to 1947. After closing, the building was used as a tool shed and machine shop.

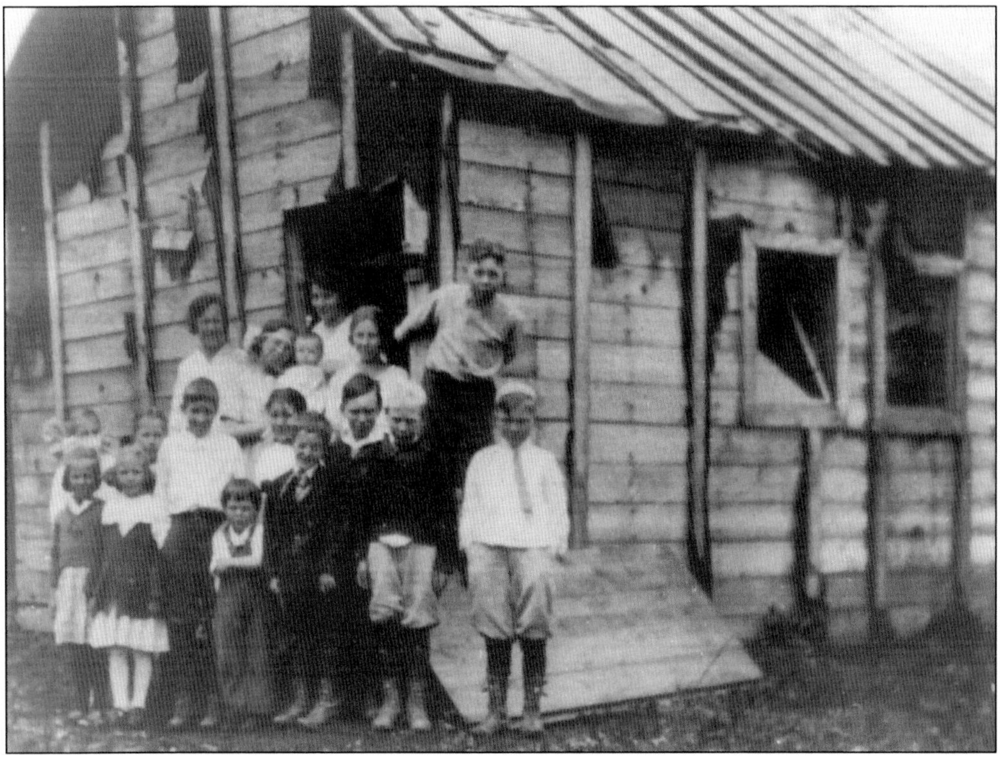

This tarpaper shack became the first school on Harrison Flats on land donated by Charles F. Custer. Built as a temporary logging bunkhouse, the building was skidded from a neighboring farm to the school site. The building was only used for about two years. It was used as a woodshed when a new school was built in 1920–1921.

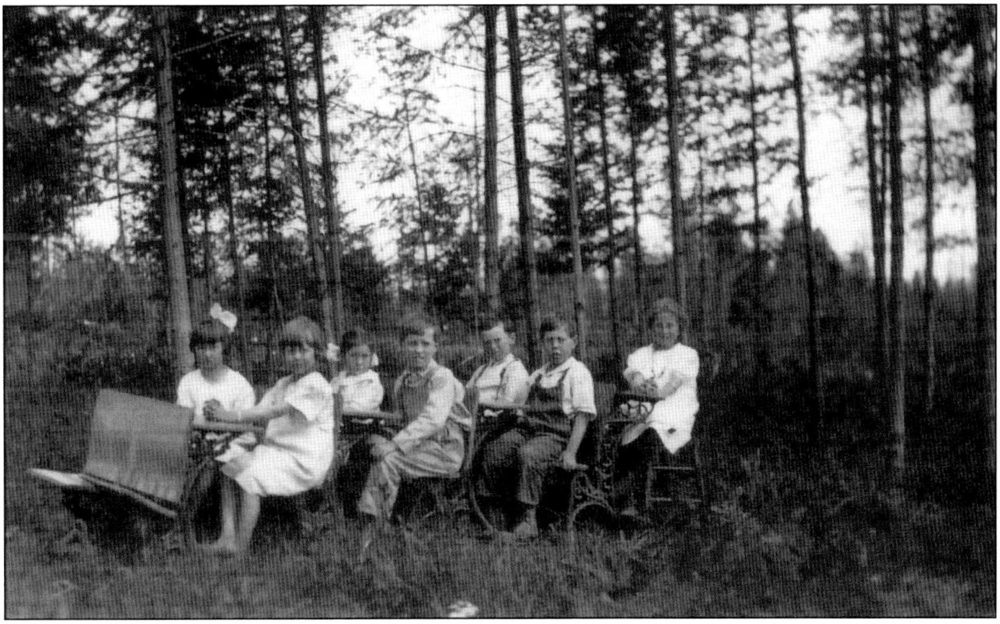

These happy Harrison Flats scholars in 1918 attended school *el fresco*, in the fresh air. It is possible that the outdoors was preferable to the gloomy tarpaper shack.

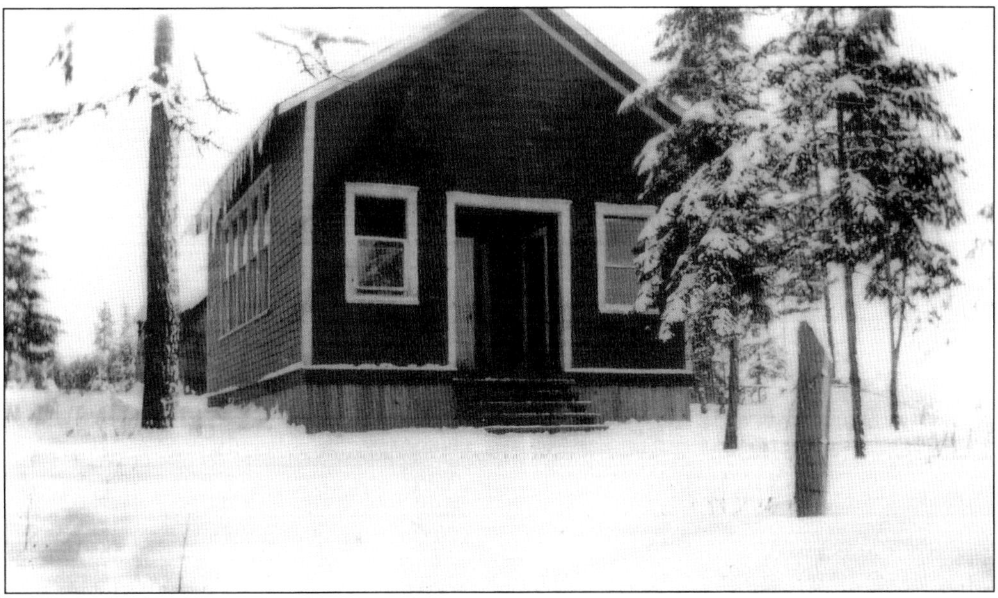

The new Harrison Flats School, later known as the Brown Jug School, replaced the tarpaper shack shown on the previous page. It boasted a closet for coats and boots, a shelf for lunches, a shelf for the water bucket, a wooden box to keep the firewood, a bookcase, and a shelf for the dictionary. In the winter, inkwells were stored at night in a box of sawdust to keep them from freezing and breaking. This picture was taken in 1926.

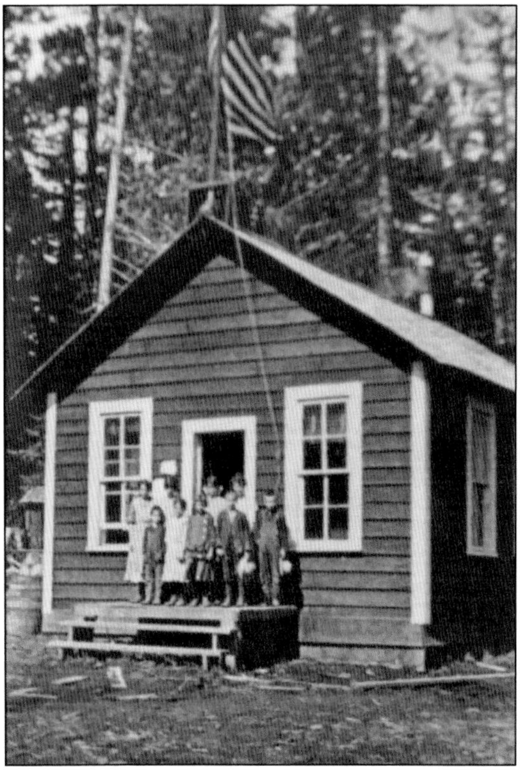

The Van Dusen School is shown here in 1915, a couple years after it was built. As with all one-room schools, the blackboard was the focal point; spelling words were posted, and arithmetic problems were solved. Playground equipment was unheard of. Children played games in good weather and went sledding in the winter. The school functioned until 1937.

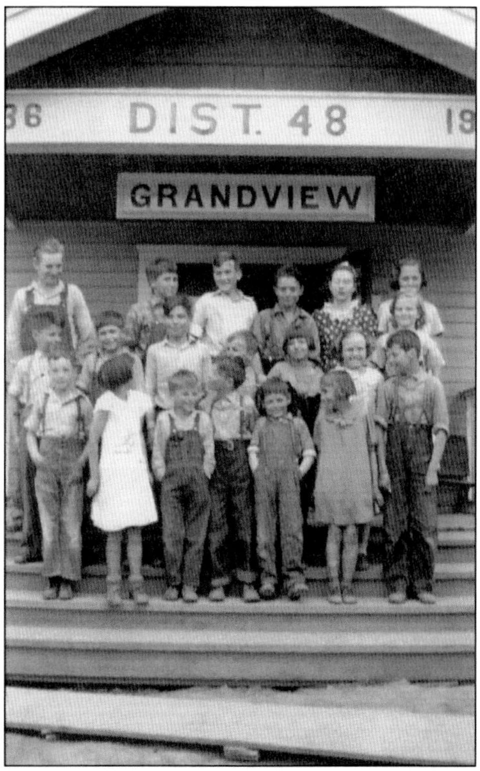

The *Harrison Searchlight* from Friday, June 5, 1908, ran the following notice: "District No. 61 [later District No. 48] calls for school bonds in the amount of $800. Said bonds to be sold for the purpose of building a schoolhouse in said district." Pictured here is the class of 1936 at Grandview School.

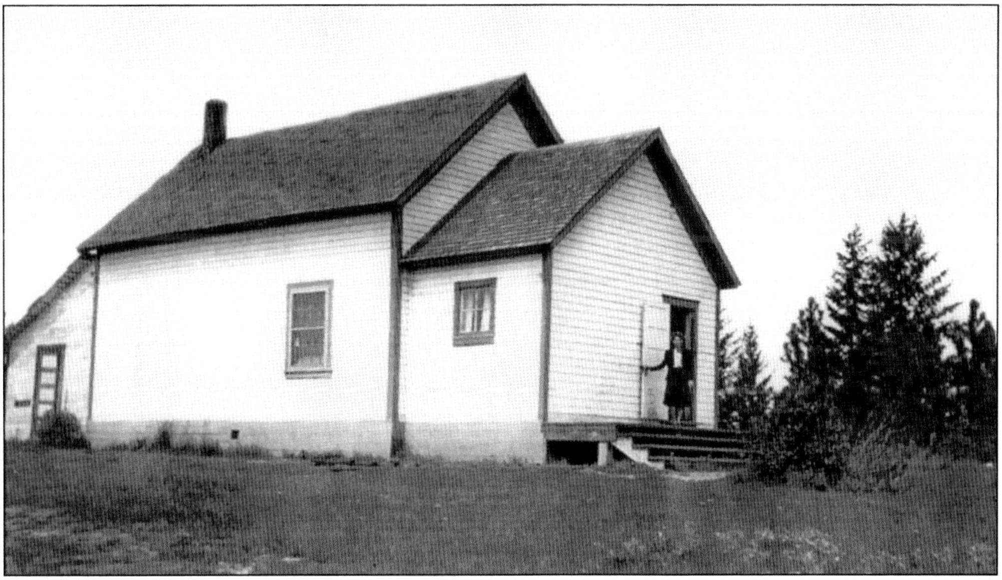

East Point School was built in 1900 on what is now called Bell Bay Road on the Powderhorn Peninsula, about five miles north of Harrison. Teacher Bonnie Sanders is shown during the last term in 1944–1945. The building later was used by local ranchers Arthur and Vernon Jensen to store hay.

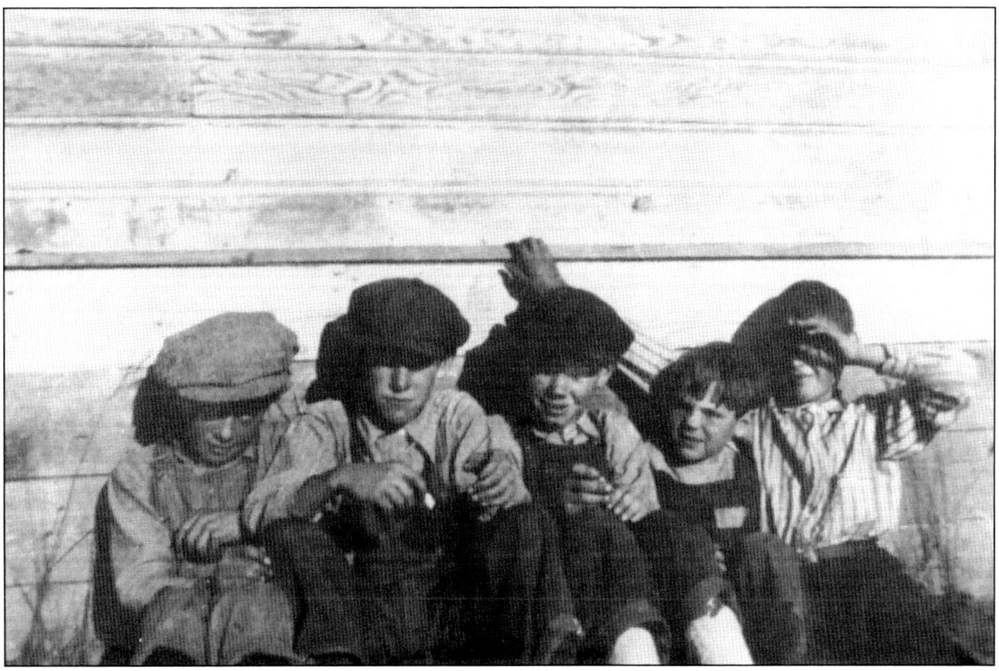

Teacher Esther Nelson taught these five students at East Point School: from left to right, Herb Wilson, Johnny Roberts, Al Lund, Jack Wilson Jr., and Vernon Jensen. As was the custom, the teacher boarded with a local family. Esther boarded at the home of John and Ida Fisher while she taught the school year 1925–1926.

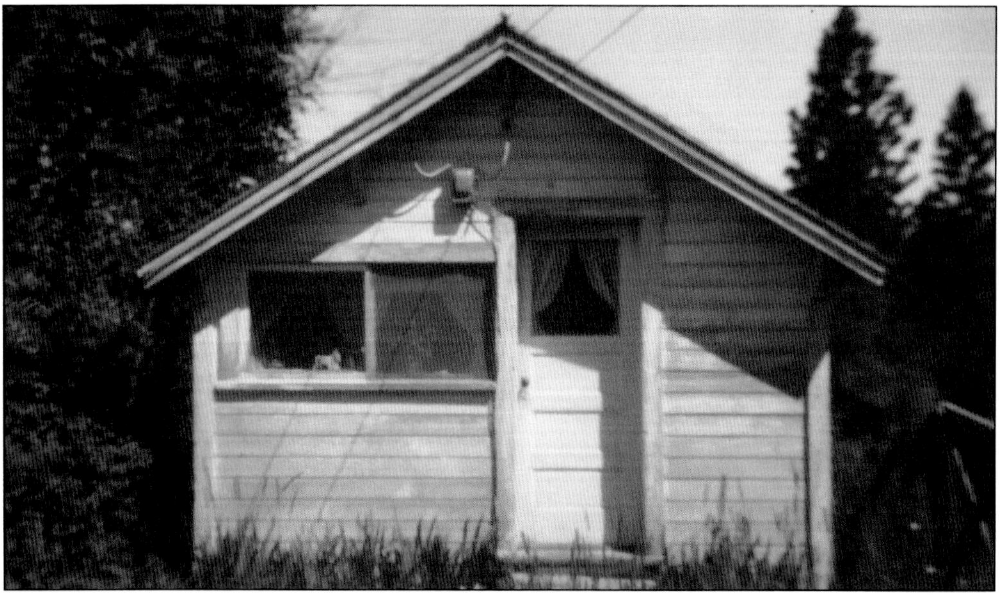

Carlin Bay's first school was built of logs. It was later replaced by Upper Carlin School and Lower Carlin School. This is the teacherage (teacher's residence) from the Upper Carlin School. Some of the teachers who taught at this school were Mrs. Hutchisson, Lorine Wilkinson, Estelle Salisbury, Margaret Oaks, and Alice Moore.

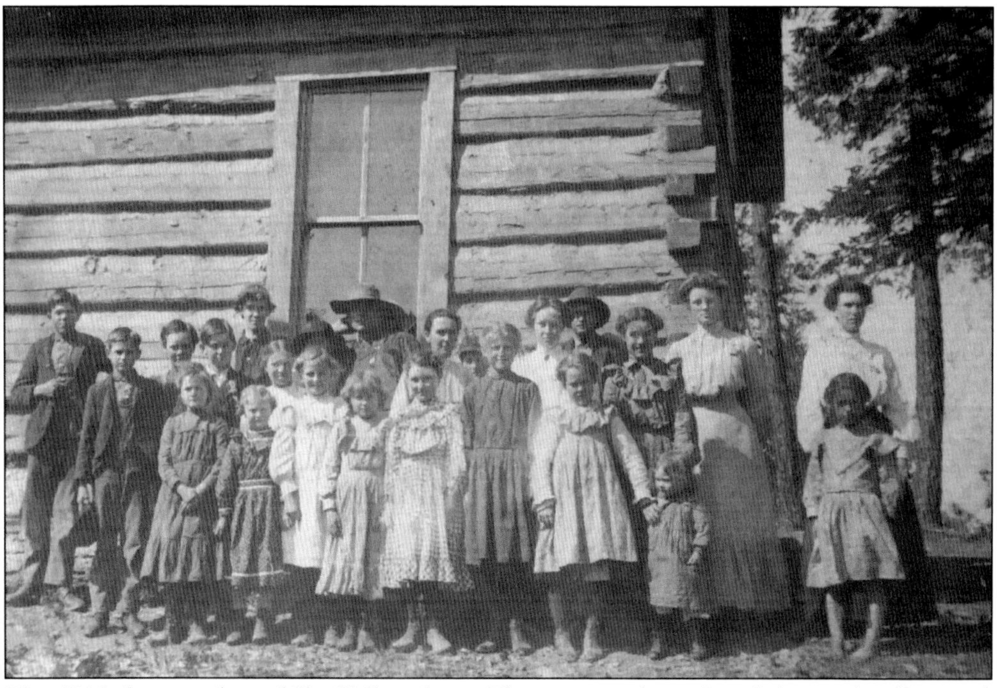

This 1905 photograph is of Sky Hill students. Those pictured are, from left to right, (first row) Cora Seat, Besie Cowan, unidentified girl, Lulu Seat, Rose Cowan, Mattie Hollingsworth, Amy Wells, Iva Hollingsworth, and Thelma Cardwell; (second row) George Cowan, Isaac Cowan, Peter Wells, Charley Seat, William Hollingsworth, Harry Wells, Cynthia Cowan, Mabel Waldo, Marvin Cowan, Elizabeth Hollingsworth, Miss Fennell (teacher), and Ora Hollingsworth.

Six

Businesses and Buildings

The new townsite saw a lot of activity in 1891—the first building, the first industry, and the first home. The first business was a general store in 1892, owned by Addison A. Crane. From that beginning, the town burgeoned. Soon other businesses followed: drugstores, hardware stores, grocery stores, general merchandise stores, restaurants, saloons, hotels, rooming houses, jewelry stores, furniture stores, photography studios, and barbershops. Undertakers, shoemakers, tailors, blacksmiths, doctors, dentists, attorneys, sundry other professional offices, small retail establishments, and construction businesses also came to town. Besides businesses, there were churches, a school, an opera house, fraternal orders, and private residences. According to the 1900 census, Harrison was credited with being the largest town in Kootenai County, with a population of 702 people. By 1903, there were 1,200 permanent residents. The town would mushroom to 2,000 when the mills were running at full capacity.

In 1892, a printing press was brought from Farmington, Washington, and Edwin W. Crane, the third son of Silas Crane, started a newspaper. The Cranes started the first newspaper called the *Fog Horn*. Another weekly, the *Mountain Messenger*, began publishing in 1897. In 1900, these two papers consolidated under name the *Harrison Searchlight*. The *Harrison Searchlight* was published weekly until 1925.

A Spokane company installed a water works system in 1901. In the same year, Kimmel Brothers built an electric light plant. A telephone line giving Harrison long distance service was installed in 1902.

As with all cities, buildings were built, demolished, and rebuilt. Businesses changed hands, moved, closed, or re-opened as a different type of business. The 1917 fire that destroyed businesses and homes changed the face of the city. In this book, no attempt has been made to trace the history of a particular parcel, because a lot of the details have been lost. However, as much as possible, a general location will be given. What is presented here is only a sampling of the many businesses and entrepreneurs who took part in Harrison's development.

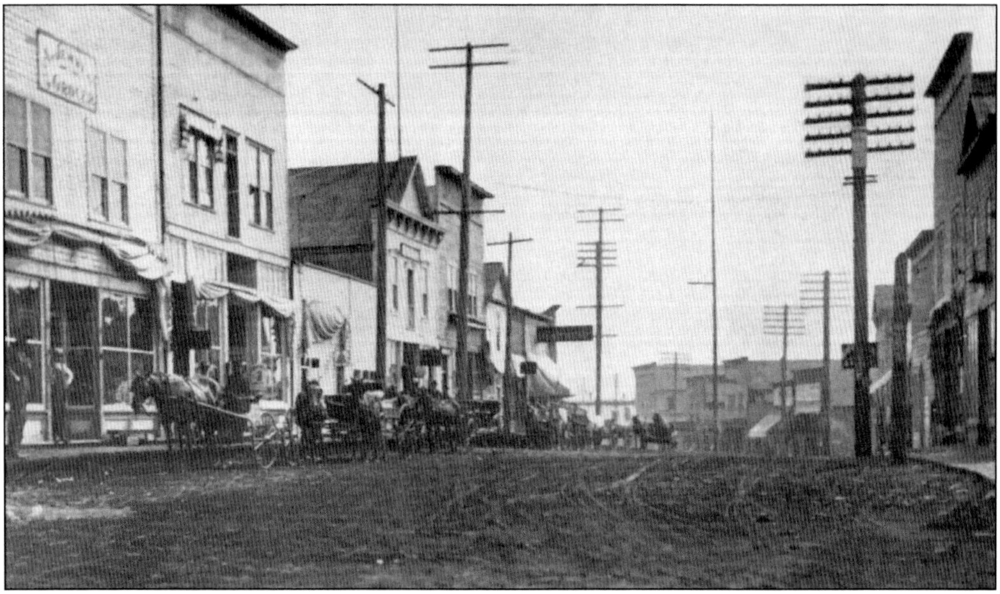

Taken from the north end of town looking southwest, this photograph is of the main street of Harrison in 1910. Those businesses on the left side are August & R.S. Jensen Bros., Corskie Drug, Ed Harris Barbershop, unidentified, Jimmie Jones's Café, the Telephone Office, and Ribstein Hardware. And those on the right side are Lamb's Blacksmith Shop, Lafferty Bakery (the tall building), the opera house, and Frank Smith's Pool Hall.

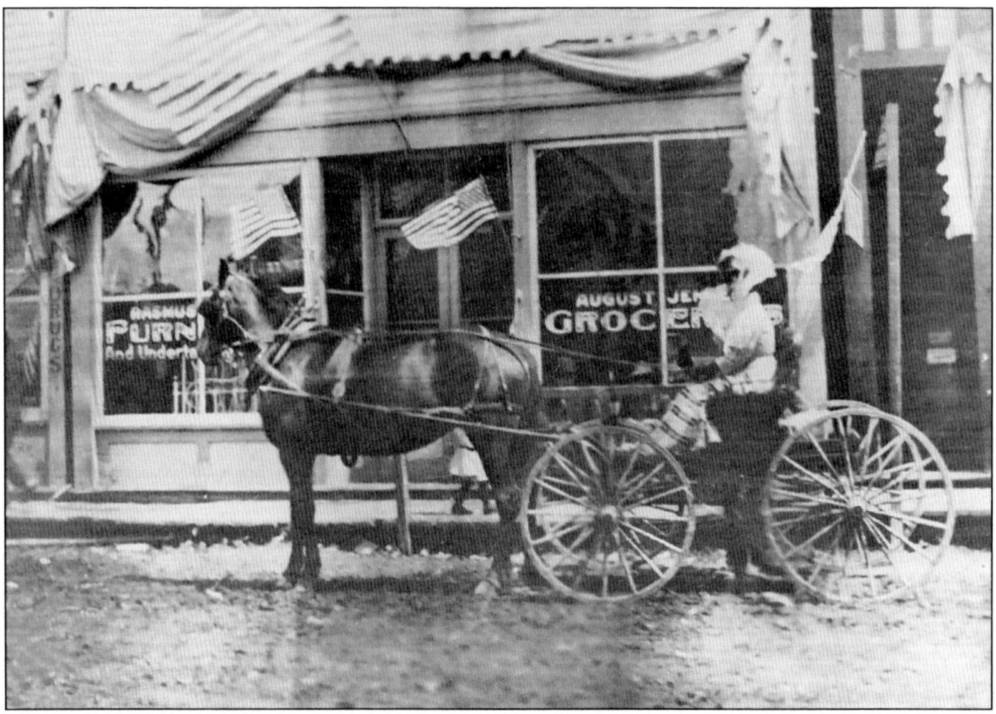

In this undated photograph, a carriage stands in front of the Jensen brothers' businesses. On the left is where Rasmus Jensen made furniture and was the undertaker. It was customary for a furniture maker to also make caskets. On the right is August Jensen's grocery.

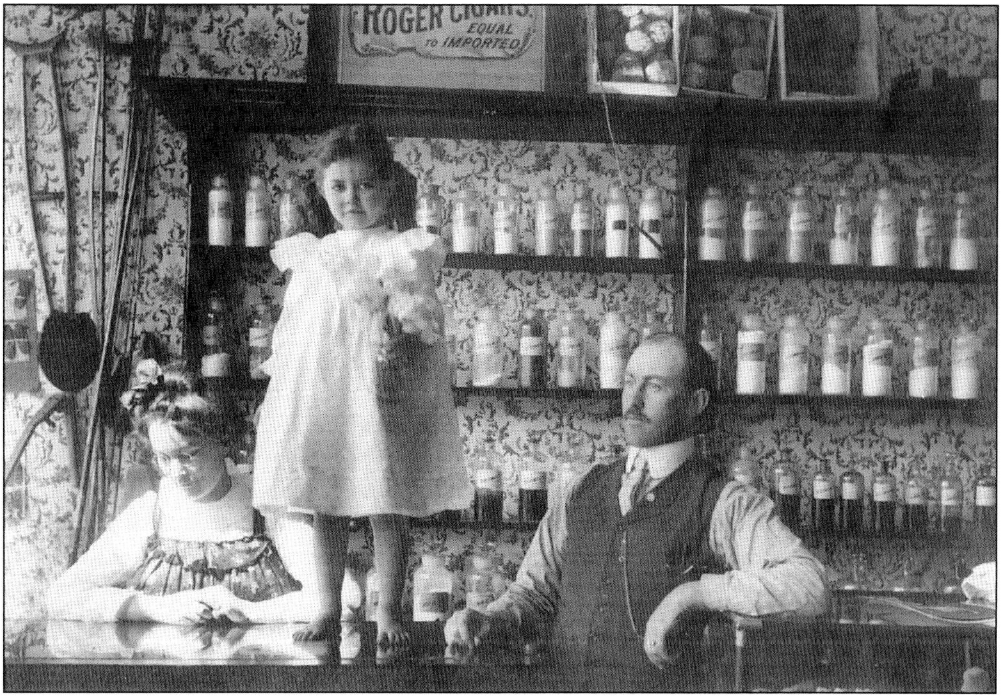

John A. Corskie, one of the first licensed druggists in Idaho, bought a store in Harrison with his brother James. John served as anesthetist for Dr. Finney and learned "doctoring" at the same time. In addition to operating the drugstore for more than 50 years, he was the bank president, a city treasurer, and a civic volunteer. Josephine, Dorothy, and John Corskie are in the store around 1901.

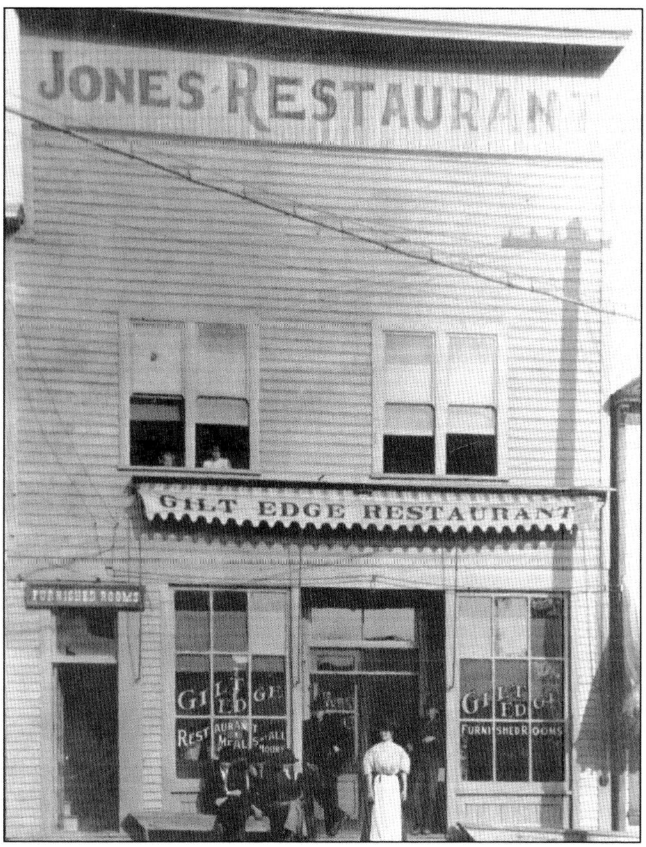

There are many tales about why Jimmy Jones's Gilt Edge Restaurant was called Greasy Jones's Café. However, it was claimed he had the cleanest kitchen in town, where meals were 25¢. They advertised as the best $1-per-day rooming house. It was located on the east side of the highway, located toward the north end of town and next to Lamb's Blacksmith shop. It operated from 1907 to 1917.

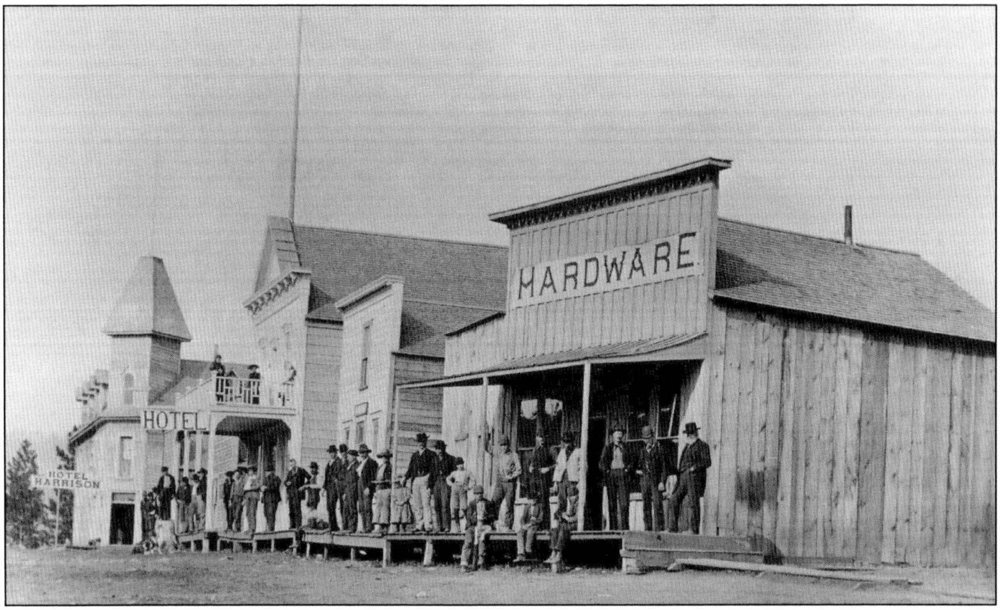

This part of the main street was the only block in 1911 without a saloon. The building on the far left is a church.

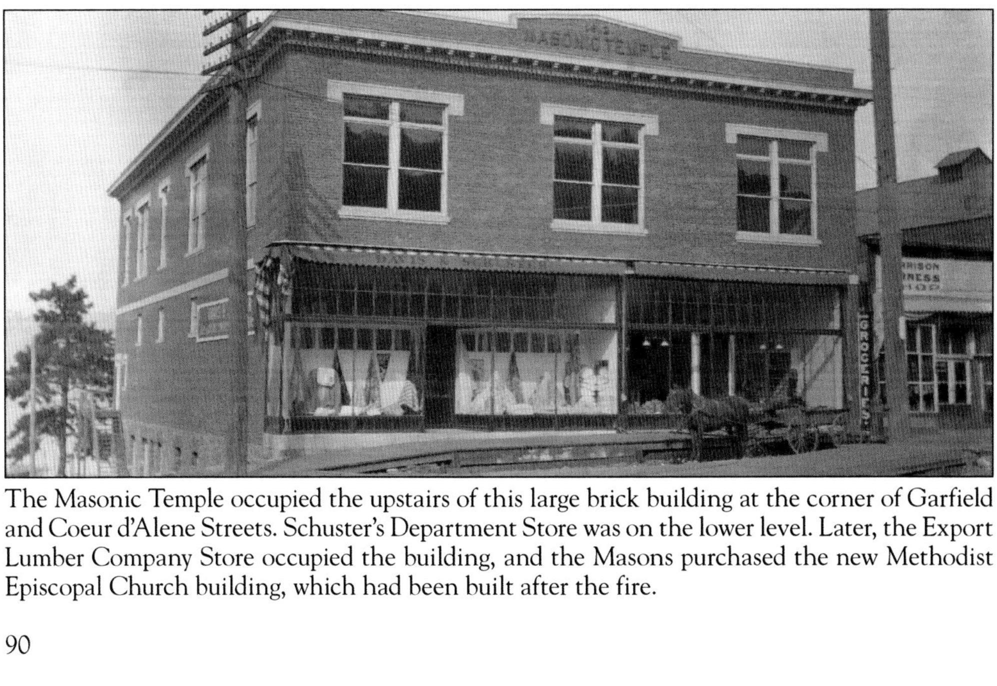

The Masonic Temple occupied the upstairs of this large brick building at the corner of Garfield and Coeur d'Alene Streets. Schuster's Department Store was on the lower level. Later, the Export Lumber Company Store occupied the building, and the Masons purchased the new Methodist Episcopal Church building, which had been built after the fire.

Silas W. Crane (1833–1908) was a native of Ohio who came west with his parents by overland train in 1852. Records show that in 1891 he and his three sons, William E., Addison A., and Edwin W., settled on land that would become Harrison. He owned a photography studio.

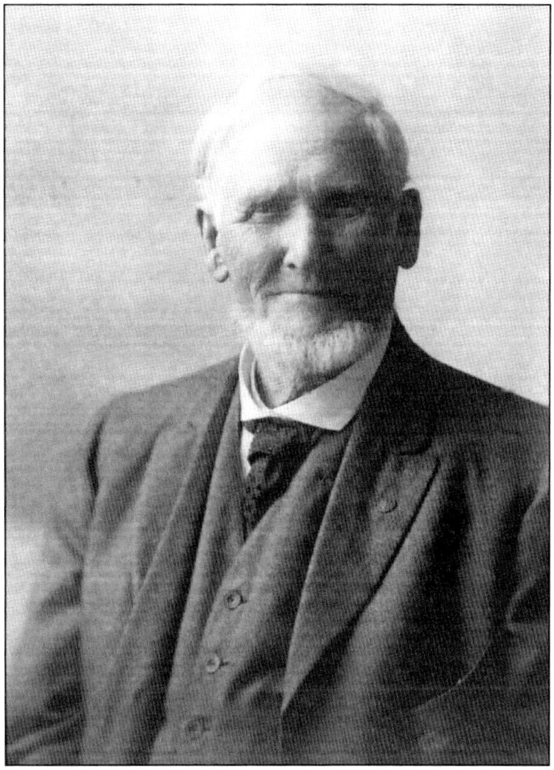

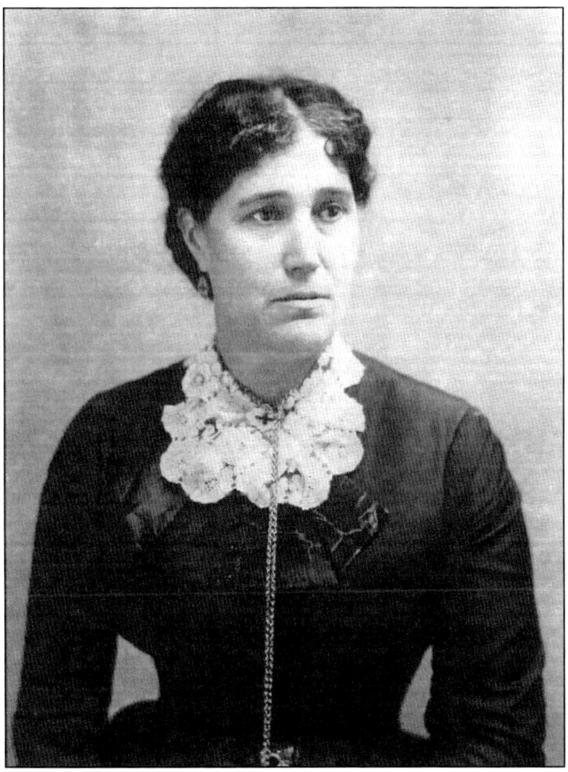

Elizabeth Crane (1838–1911) was the wife of Silas W. Crane. She had also traveled west with her parents by overland train. Her father George Jones was with the Cranes when they selected the Harrison townsite. She had three sons who owned businesses in Harrison, a daughter Helen, and a niece Mary, who was raised as a daughter.

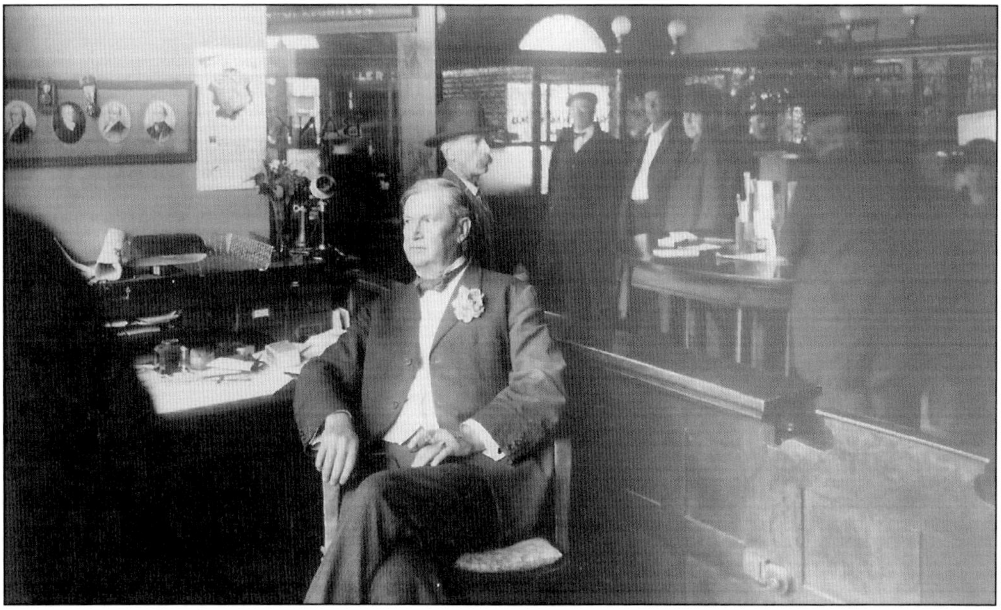

The First Bank of Harrison began in 1902 with O.B. Steward as president. In 1905, it was incorporated with Barney O'Neil as president. Addison A. Crane, an original shareholder, was president from 1912 until he moved to Coeur d'Alene in 1915 to become the president of a bank there. This photograph is of Addison A. Crane around 1912.

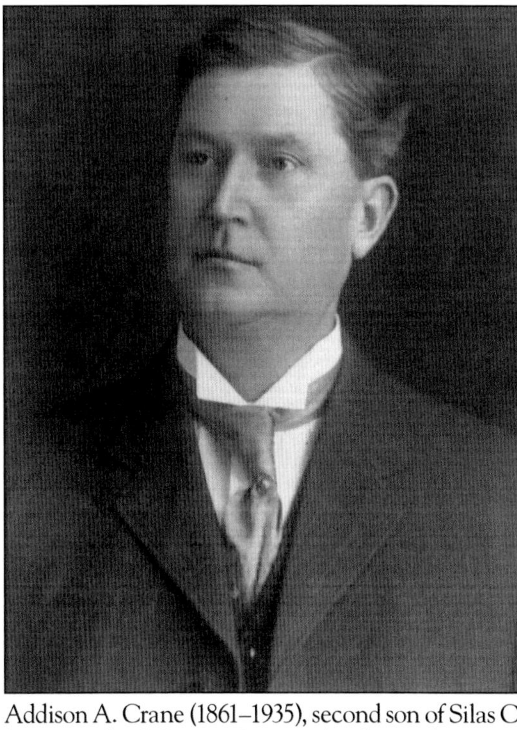

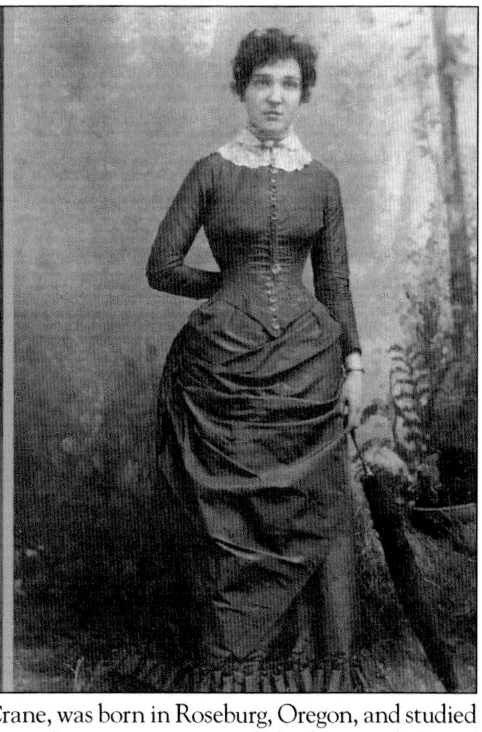

Addison A. Crane (1861–1935), second son of Silas Crane, was born in Roseburg, Oregon, and studied law in Portland, Oregon. He was a bank president, attorney, business entrepreneur, the first city clerk, and served as a state legislator. Helen (Crane) Wark (1868–1904) was Silas Crane's daughter. Her son Earl, the first child born in Harrison after it became a city, was born in the first home built in Harrison.

Edwin W. Crane, third son of Silas Crane, was publisher of the newspaper. He owned property at the mouth of the Coeur d'Alene River, where he installed a sorting works to sort logs that were being driven down the river. In 1907, he sold the property where his home stood to the school district to build a new brick schoolhouse. He is shown here with his wife, Clara.

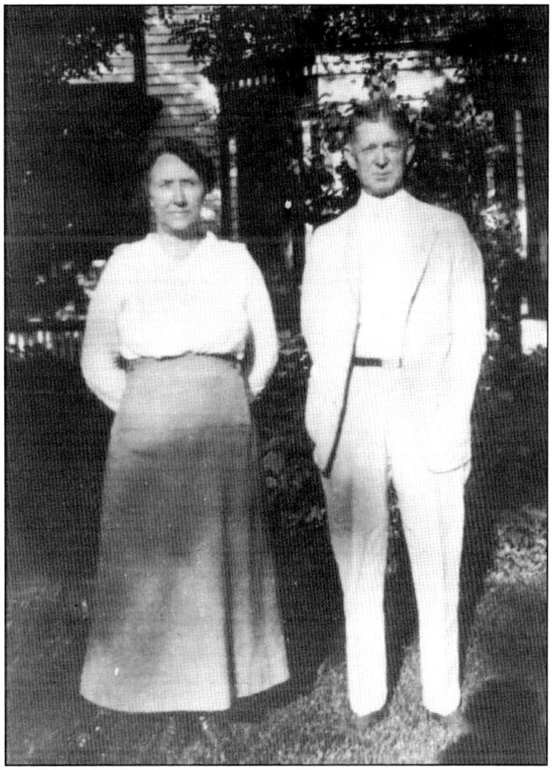

In 1891, a post office was established with William E. Crane, Silas Crane's oldest son, as postmaster. Early post offices usually did not have their own quarters but occupied a corner of a store. The boy on the left is unidentified. William is in the center. The boy on the right is Earl Wark, the son of William's sister Helen.

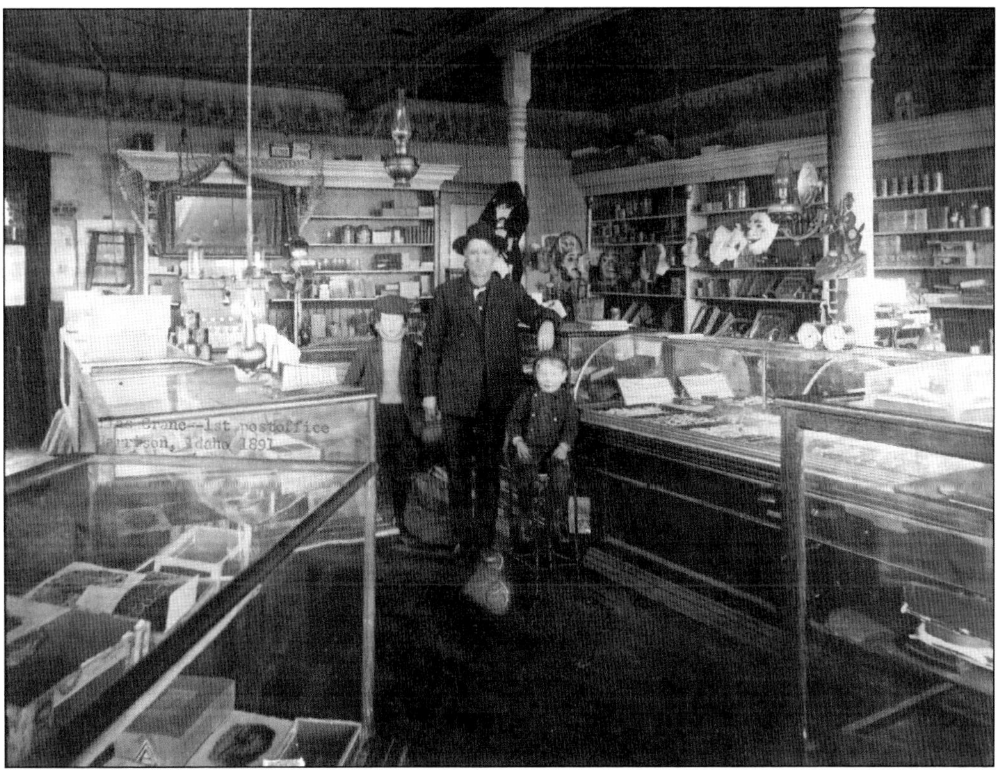

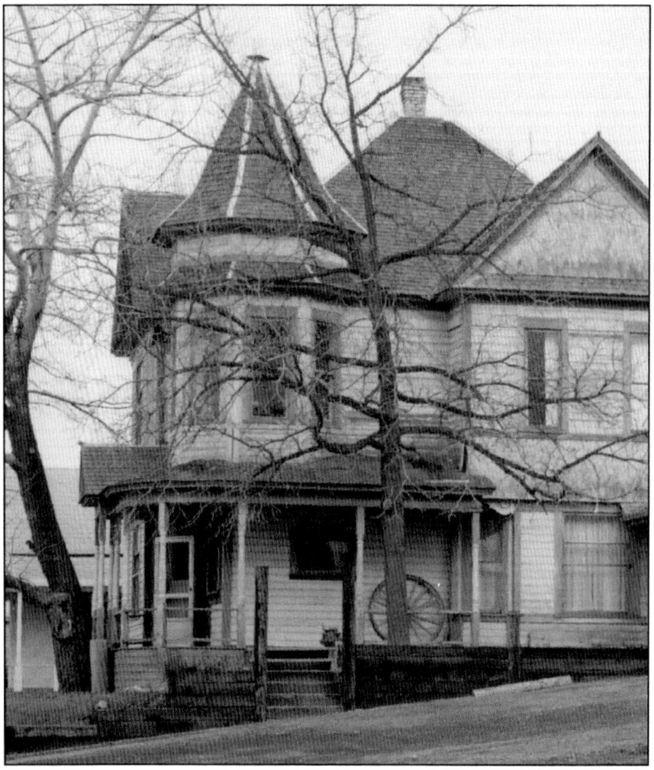

Dr. John Busby built this grand Victorian home in 1904. A small cottage next door was his office. He sold his home three years later, presumably to raise funds to build the floating hospital at St. Joe City, open a hospital in Harrison, and hire an assistant physician. His home later became the Baptist parsonage.

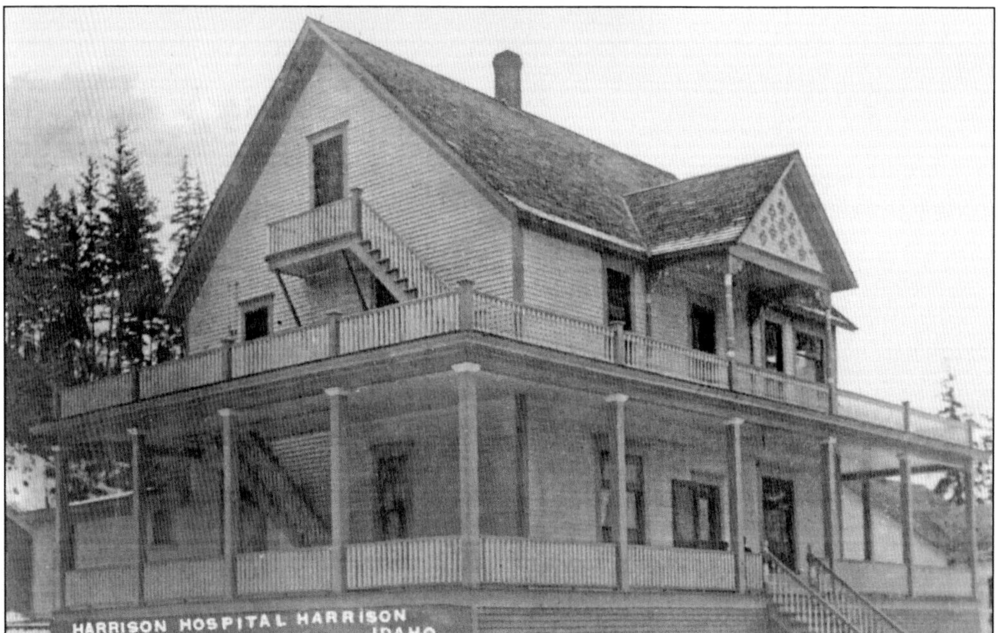

The Harrison Hospital, located on Garfield Street at the top of the hill, was operated by Dr. Busby along with the St. Joe Hospital. The latter was a raft that followed the railroad construction crews by water from St. Joe City to Chatcolet Lake, a distance of 30 miles. Eventually, both hospitals were abandoned, and this building was the family's home until it was destroyed by a kitchen fire in 1909.

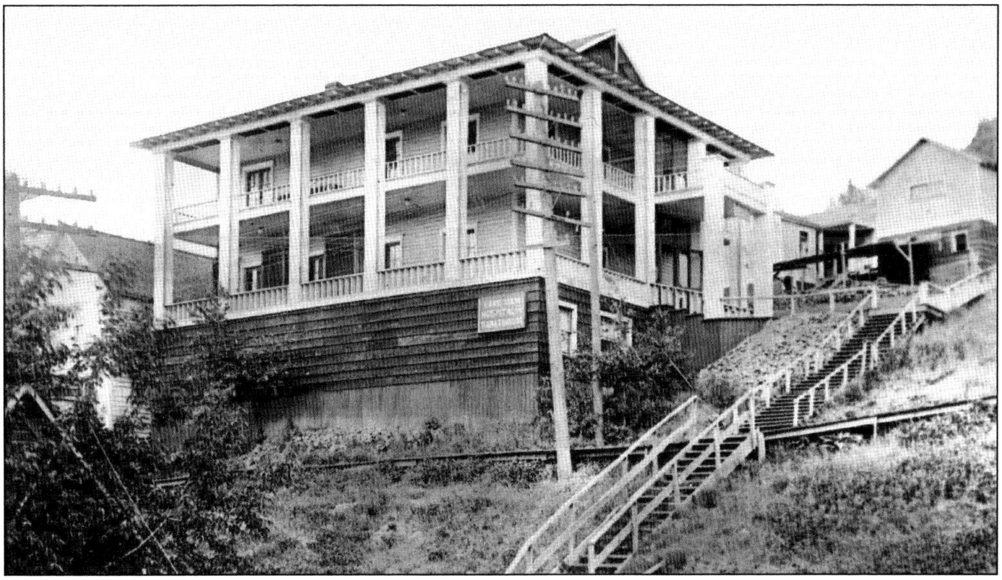

Dr. John M. Finney arrived in Harrison in 1910. The Ohio native was a young man of 29 and a recent medical school graduate. He built this Lakeview Hospital and Sanitarium. The stairs led from the street below (now Highway 97). Dr. Finney was active in politics, serving as city health officer and county coroner, and is credited with solving the local typhoid epidemic of 1918.

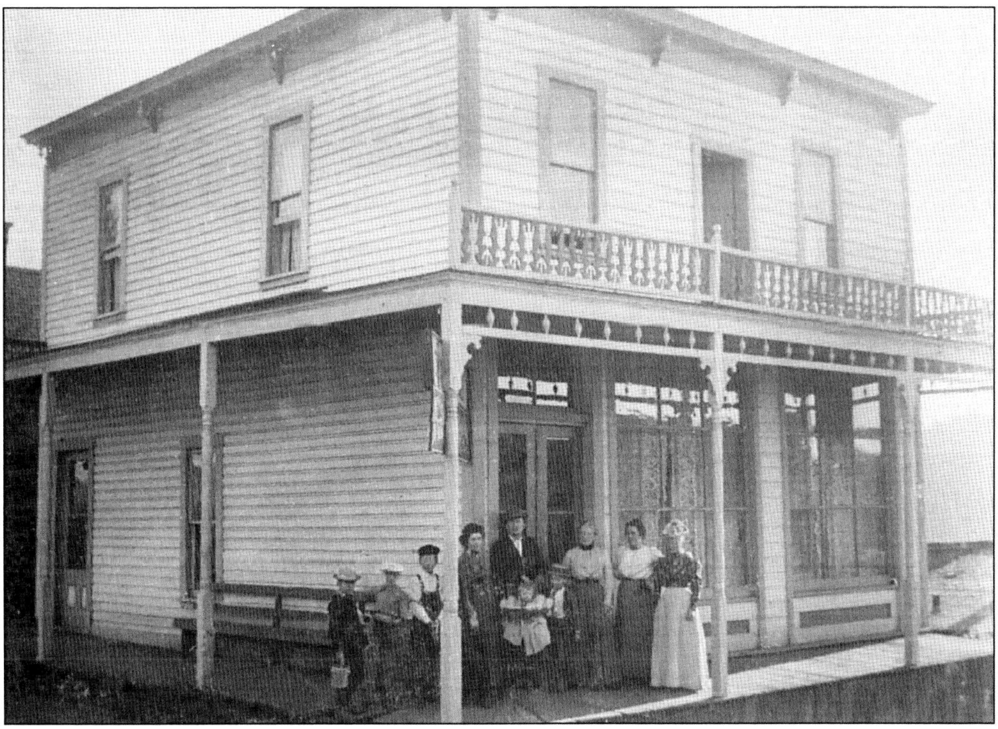

This 1898 photograph is of the Harrison Hotel. On November 25, 1892, Harrison's newspaper reported, "Mr. Cash Cole will open the new hotel next Tuesday. Everything will be first class and satisfaction guaranteed. Mr. Cole will give a dance here next week to celebrate the event. At Christmas, Mr. Cole intends to entertain us with a grand ball at the Harrison Hotel."

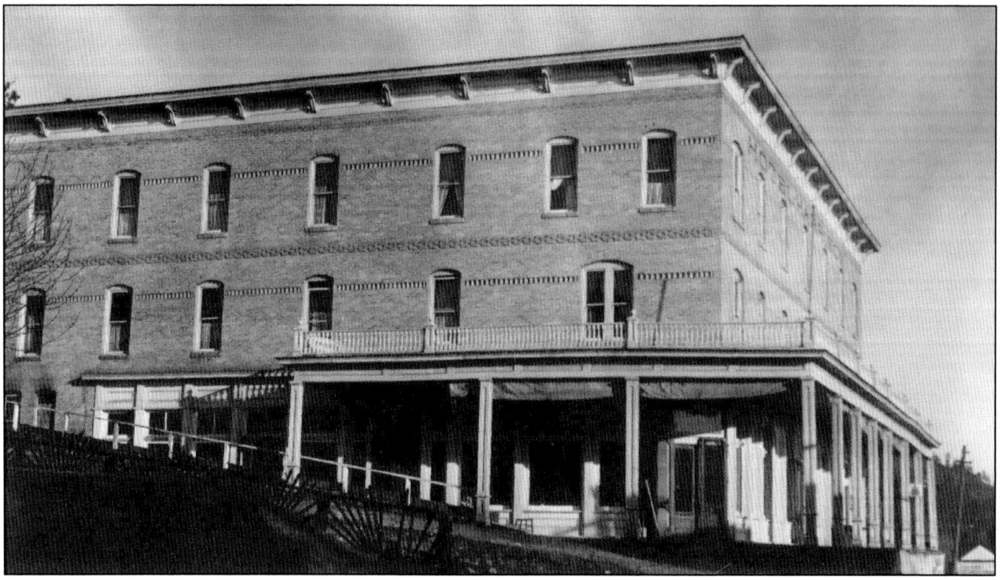

In April 1905, a new hotel, the Hotel Harrison, was built south of the main business district on the site of the former Harrison Hotel. Built by J.W. Jamison for a cost of $25,000, the frame building with a brick veneer covered 10,000 square feet. The hotel was razed in the 1930s, and the material was used by Jessie B. Manifold to build homes on Harrison Flats.

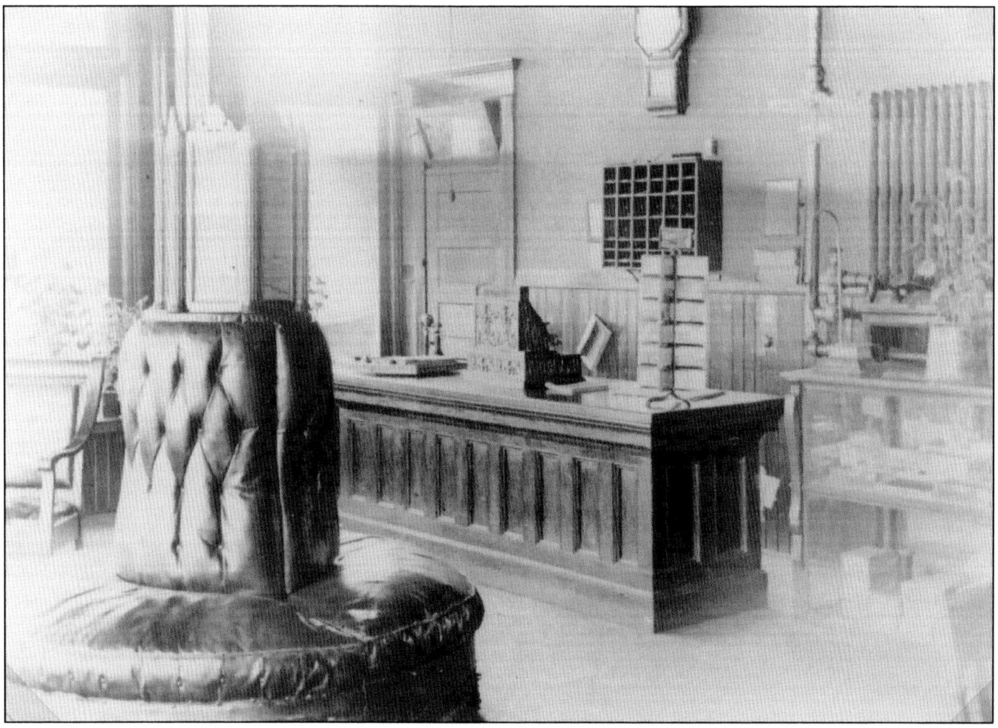

This is the lobby of the Hotel Harrison. The hotel's registers for the year from September 1914 to September 1915 shows guests were from all over the United States (New York City, Chicago, New Orleans, and Kansas City), as well as Canada and Mexico. Guests also came from as far away as Cairo, Egypt; Calcutta, India; Manila, Philippines; England; and Hong Kong.

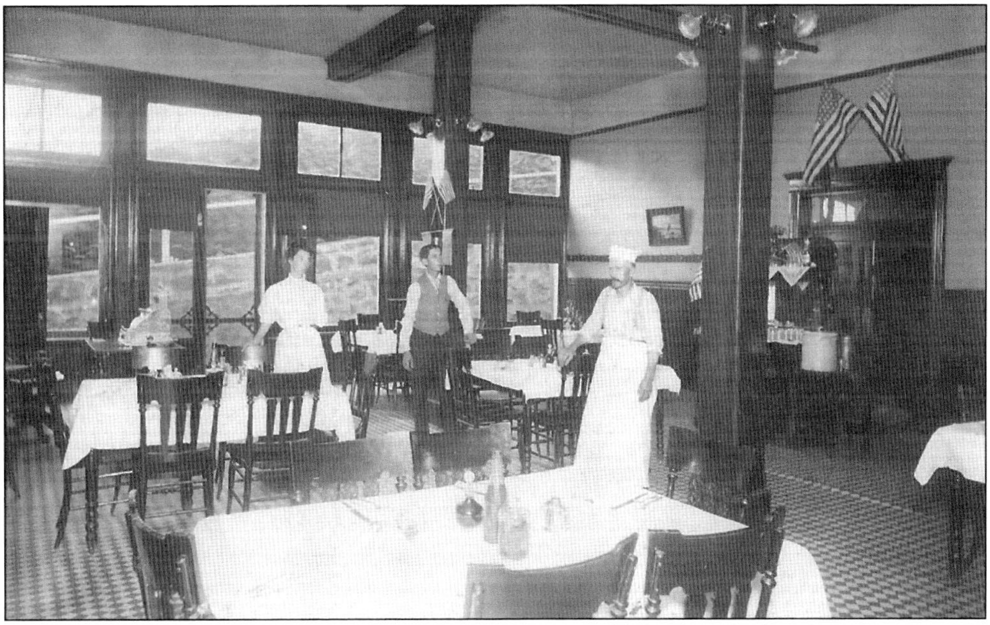

On January 19, 1906, it was reported in the *Harrison Searchlight* that the hotel's proprietor sent out 300 invitations announcing a grand ball. This dining room was for travelers and better-dressed clientele. A separate dining room was for anyone wearing work clothes. The hotel also contained two offices, a kitchen, sample room, parlor, barbershop, 80 sleeping rooms, a number of baths, and a barroom.

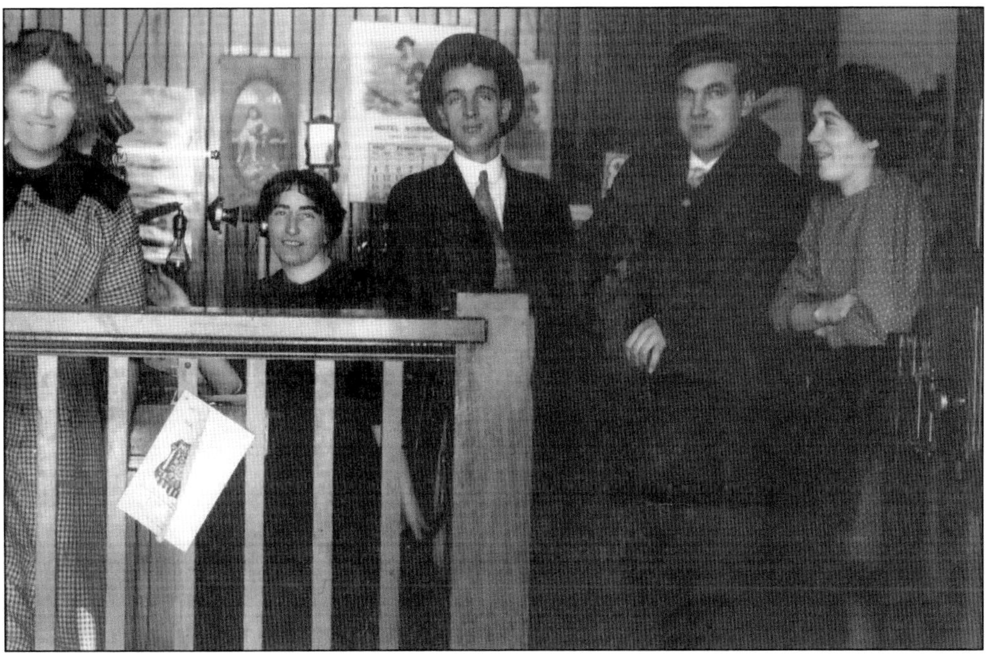

The Telephone Office was located in the Hotel Harrison. This photograph, taken about 1912, shows, from left to right, Hazel Ashton, Ines Redfield, Paul Morin, Art McCain, and Nellie Doyle. The Telephone Office occupied various locations throughout the years. Unusual for the time was a telephone in every room of the hotel.

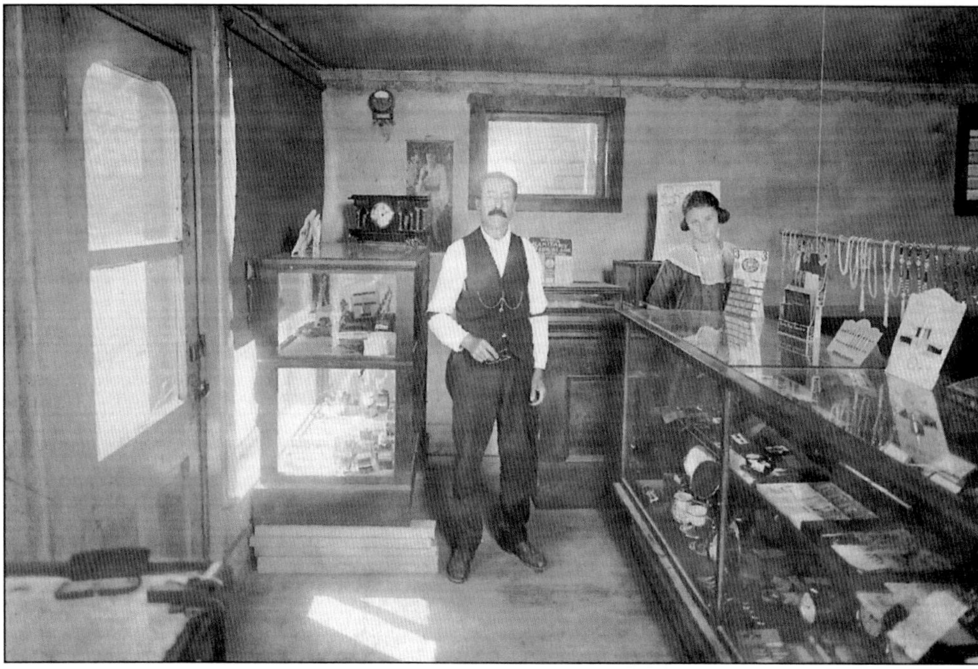

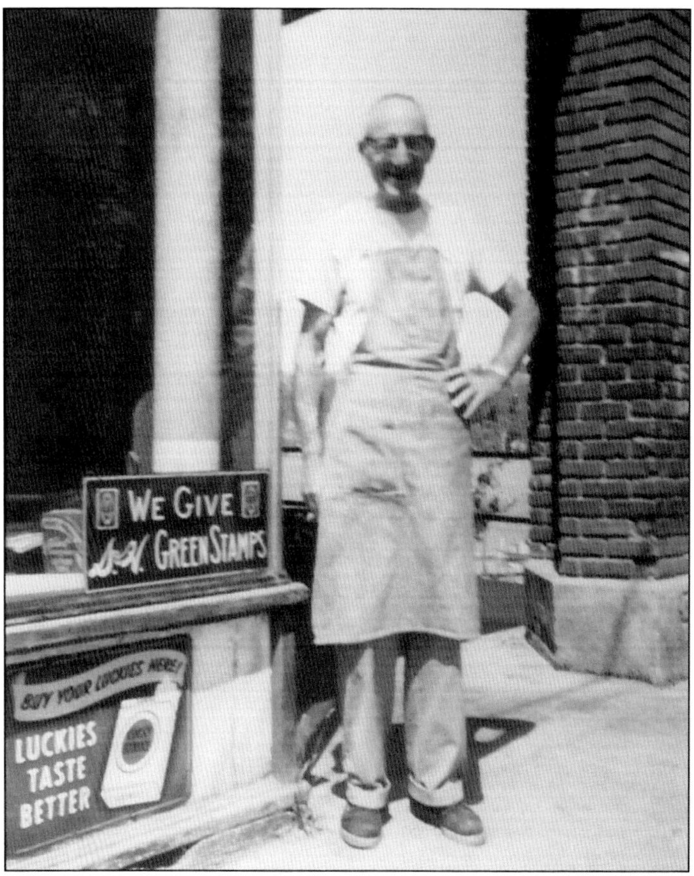

John E. Fisher and his teenage daughter Effie Fisher, the ninth of 11 children, are pictured around 1922 in the Fisher Jewelry Store on the main street in Harrison. Fisher was a self-taught watch repairman, having learned the business from a book. The Fishers also had a farm on East Point.

Silas William "Bill" Cope and his wife, Alice, arrived in Harrison in 1901. They owned the Cope Confectionery and Drugstore. Their son Ralph W. "Curley" and his wife, Luella (Wygant), owned and operated Cope's Mercantile until they retired in 1972. Ralph is in front of their store, located in the International Order of Oddfellows (IOOF) Building.

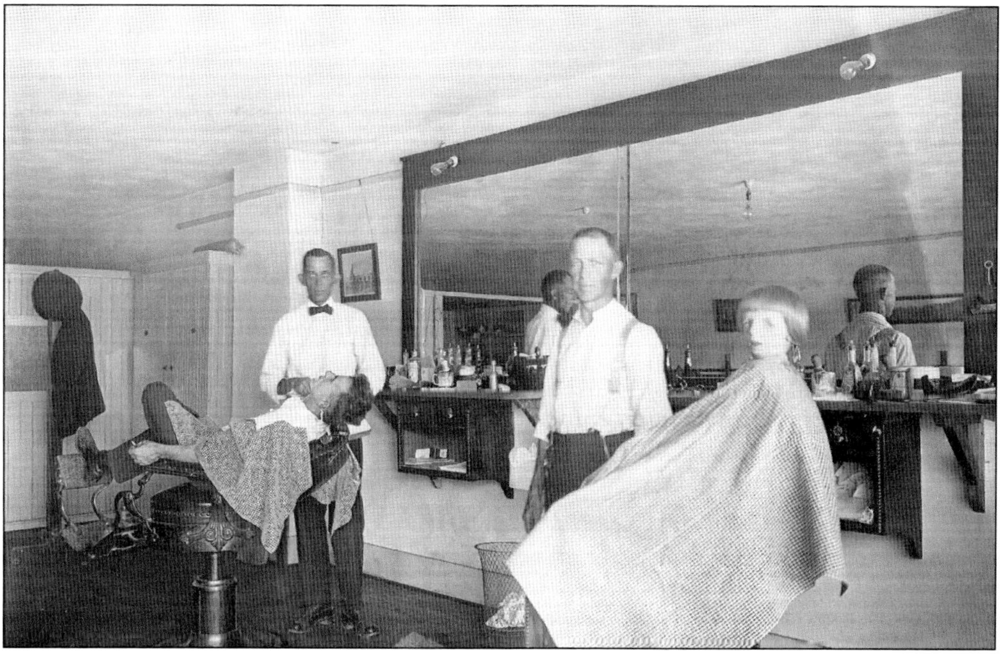

Milton Flatt's Barbershop was next to the old post office site in the IOOF Building. In this 1929 photograph, Charles Cleveland is standing at the left, with Milton Flatt at right. Barbershops included tubs for bathing, as bathtubs in homes were rare. A wood stove heated the water.

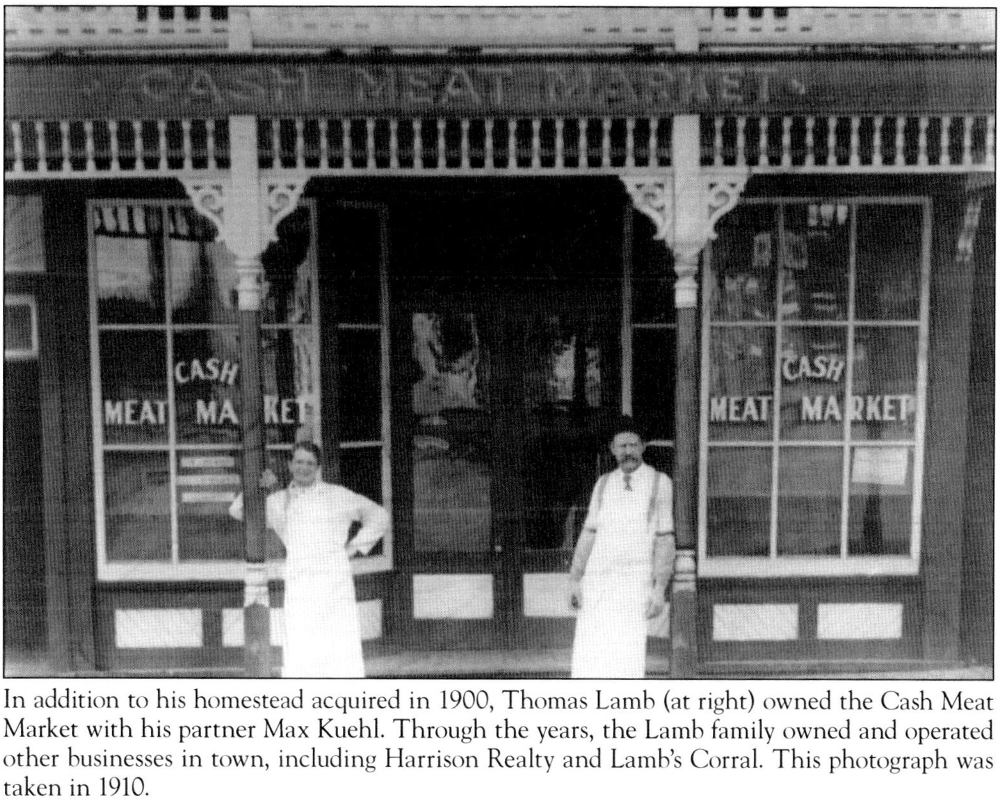

In addition to his homestead acquired in 1900, Thomas Lamb (at right) owned the Cash Meat Market with his partner Max Kuehl. Through the years, the Lamb family owned and operated other businesses in town, including Harrison Realty and Lamb's Corral. This photograph was taken in 1910.

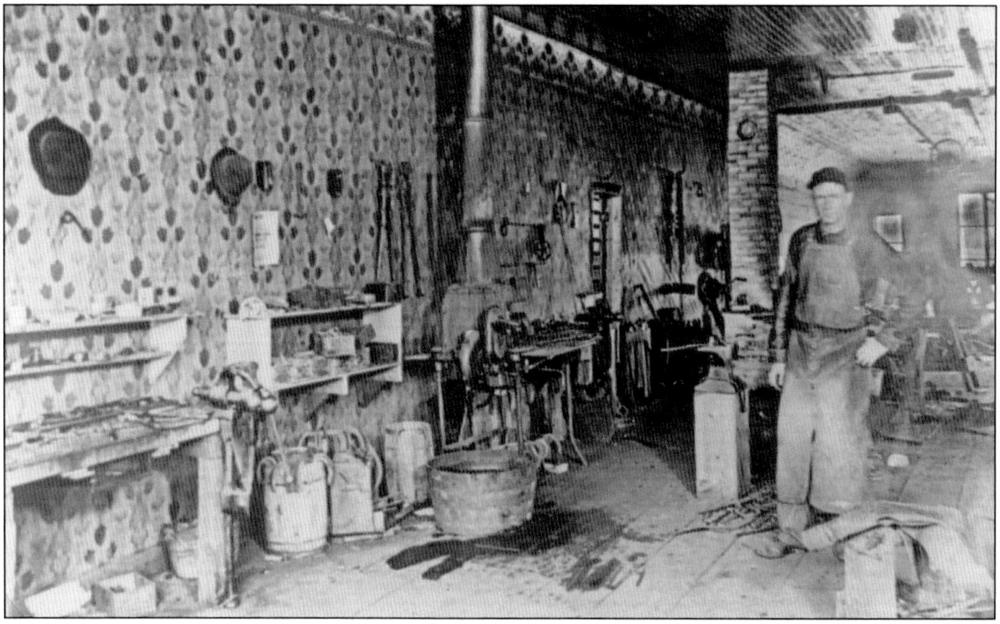

Thomas Lamb and his brother Joseph opened a business in the former Wygant Blacksmith Shop. Thomas operated a machine shop in the rear, and Joseph a blacksmith shop in the front. This photograph, taken about 1914, is of Joseph Lamb in the machine shop. Note the lovely wallpaper.

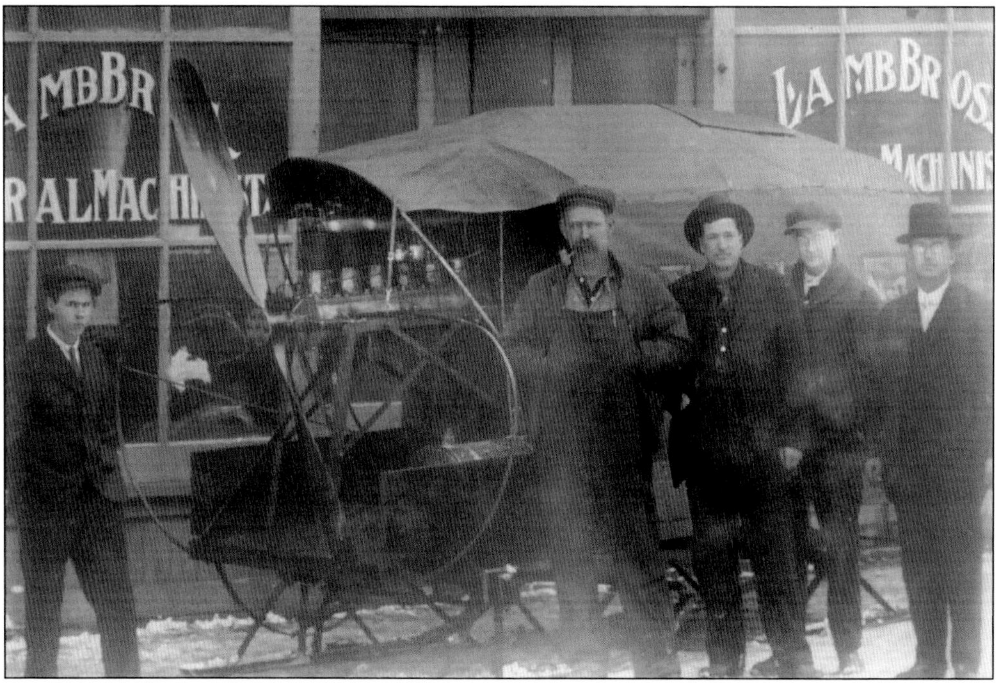

Thomas Lamb built this "aero-sleigh" parked in front of Lamb's machine shop in 1913. Those pictured are, from left to right, Hallis Beasley, Thomas Lamb, Mr. Reader, Phillip Drissen, and Mr. Riley, the designer of the sleigh. The motorized sleigh was built with the idea of running mail in Alaska. Stock was used to pay for materials and labor. One day, reportedly, Mr. Riley and his machine left town, never to be seen again.

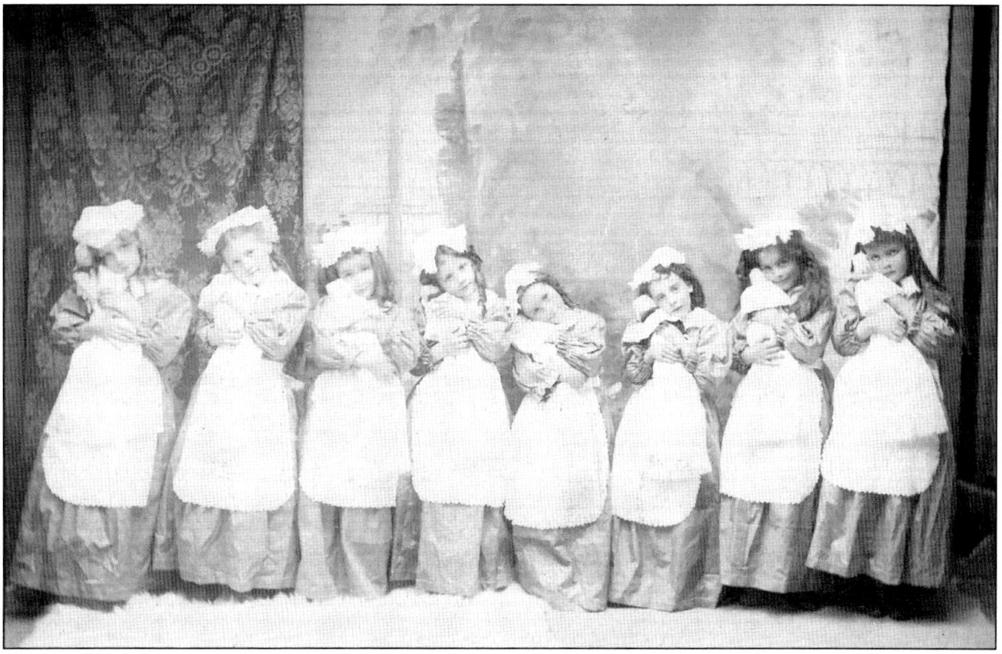

These local actresses played in the opera house in 1898. From left to right are Edna Stuve, Mamie Russell, Florence Mason, Gertrude Bridgeman, Byrl Frownfelter, Bertha McFadden, Goldie Lockwood, and Violet Packer. The opera house, which seated 400 people, was owned and operated by Benjamin S. Lafferty, who also ran the Harrison Bakery.

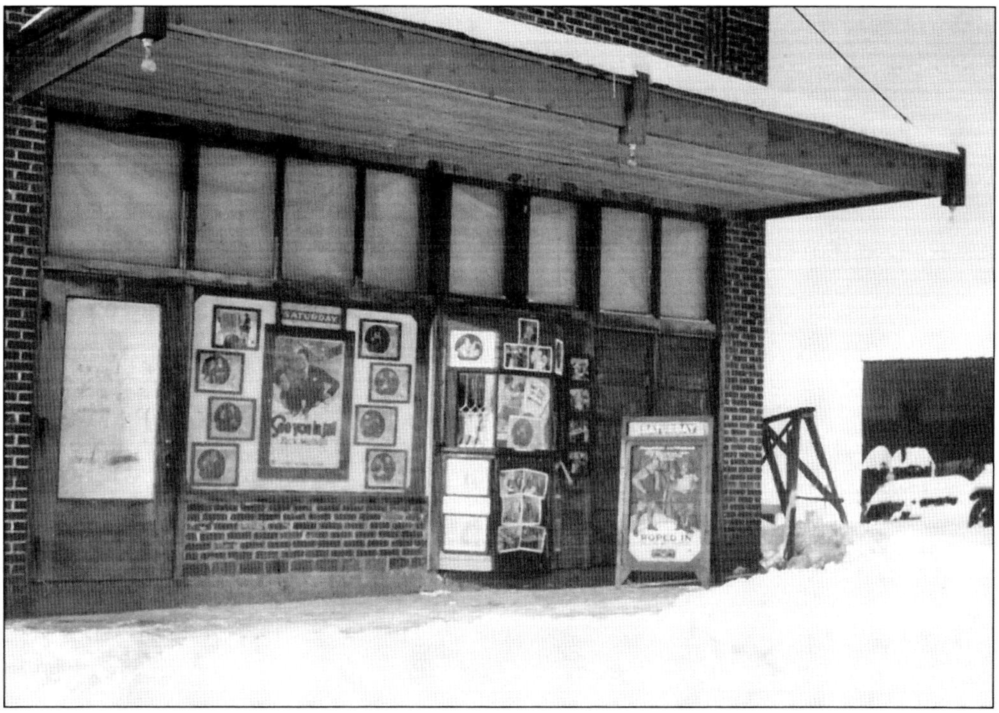

In the 1920s, the opera house was converted to a theater. The building, located on the highway on the north edge of the business district, later became Duke Patterson's garage.

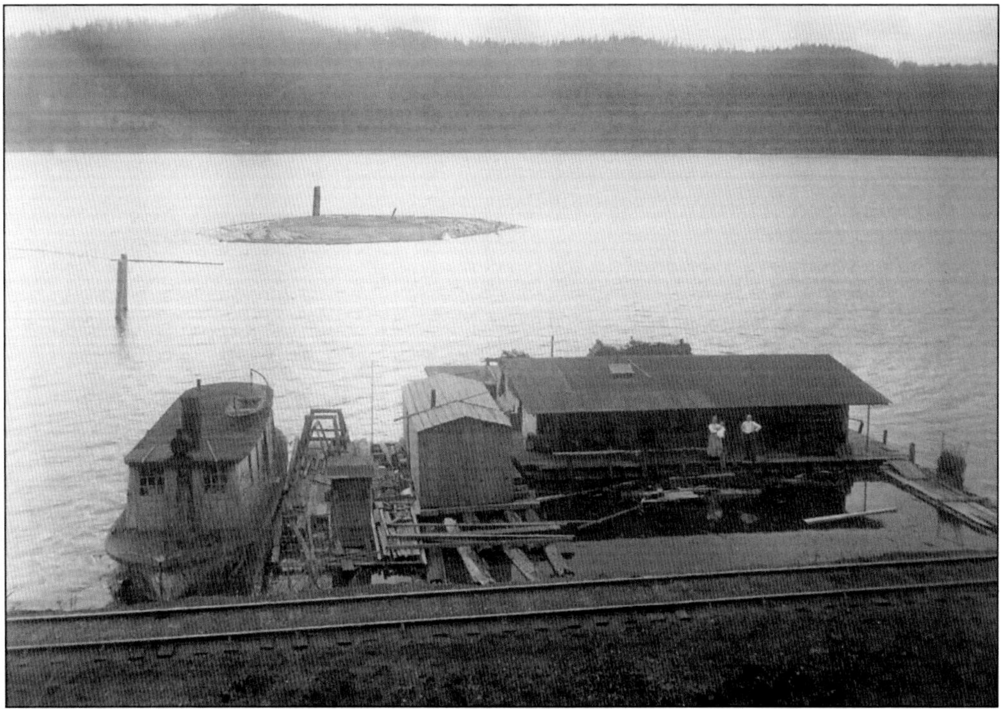

Homes, as well as mills and businesses, were located along the waterfront. This is the Anderson's float home in the early 1900s. William Knaggs cut and delivered cordwood for the steamers at the going rate of $4 per cord. His boat is moored at the dock.

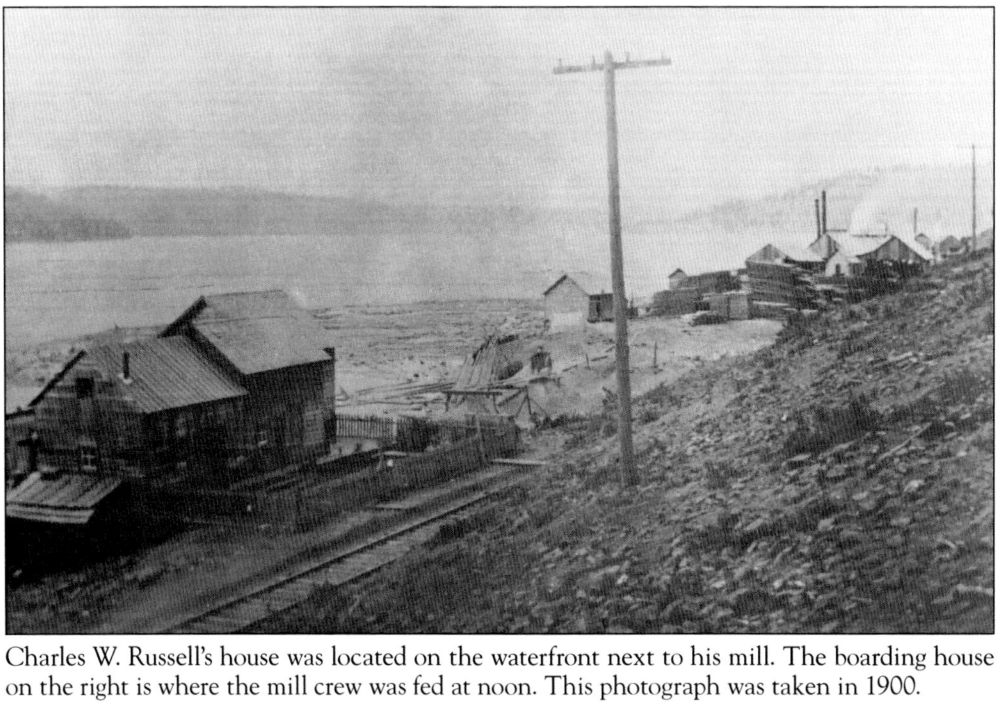

Charles W. Russell's house was located on the waterfront next to his mill. The boarding house on the right is where the mill crew was fed at noon. This photograph was taken in 1900.

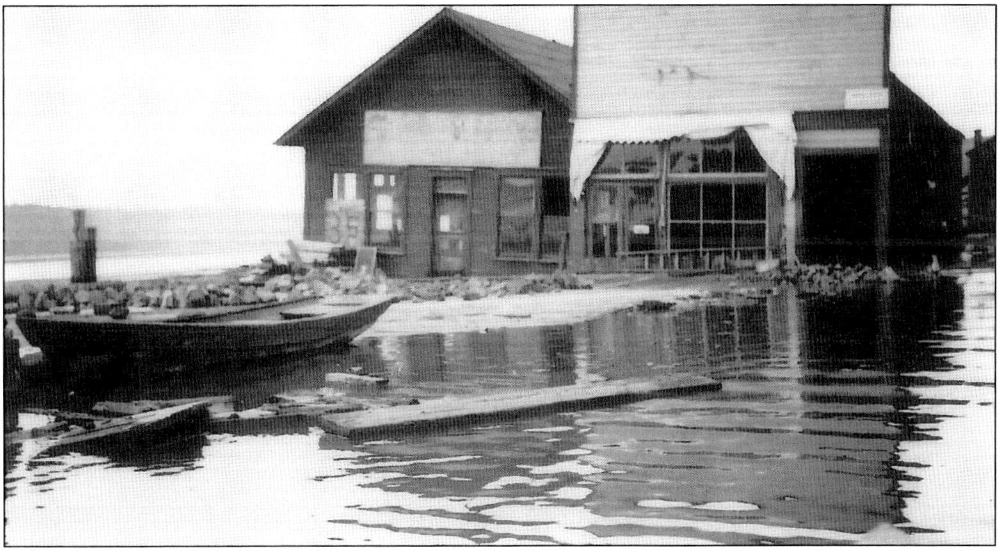

Mr. Apostolou arrived in 1908 and bought Burley's Dock Café and Bar. It was the custom to give newly arrived foreigners more Americanized names. Thus, Pamjiotis Apostolou became well known locally as "Pete the Greek." His brother-in-law Dimitri Petrou, "Jim the Greek," arrived in 1909 and opened the Dock Confectionery. Jim had a wheel cart and would meet the trains and sell fruit to the passengers. In 1921, Pete's sister Diamondo "Mandea" was able to join her husband. These photographs, taken about 1920, show Pete's Dock Café and Bar on the dock. In the lower photograph, the steamer *Harrison* is docked at the waterfront with Pete's building on the right. Bill Sutton's Steam Laundry is on the left.

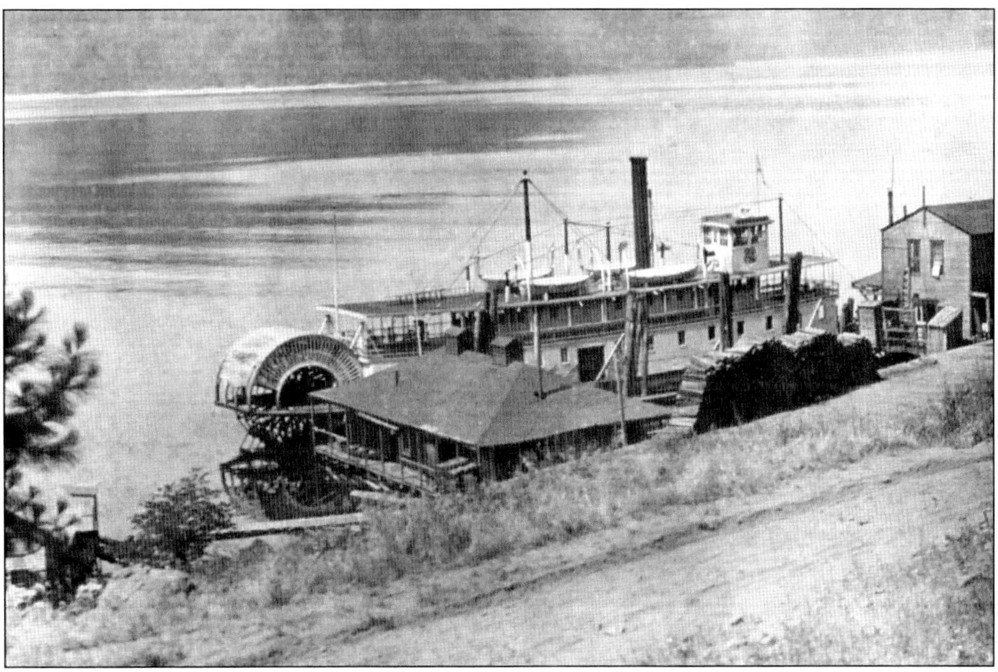

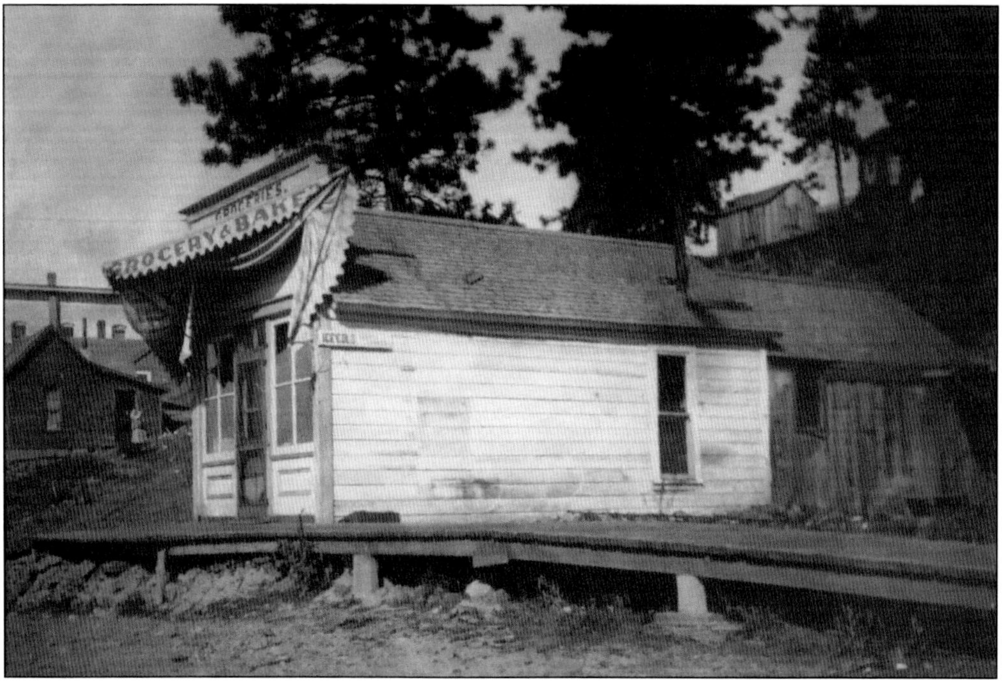

Benjamin Lafferty, who also owned the opera house, owned this bakery and grocery. This picture was taken about 1905, which was after the Harrison Hotel (the large building at the left) was built. Later, in 1910, it is noted that Lafferty owned a bakery on the main street.

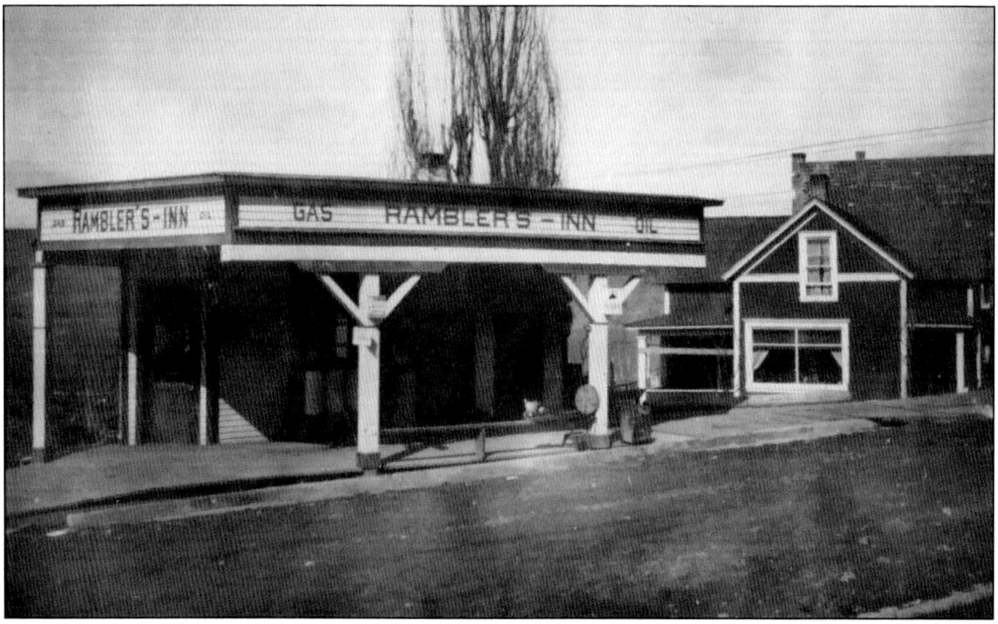

The Rambler's Inn, pictured here around 1930, was located on the main highway at the south end of the business district. William Knaggs built it in the early 1920s. In addition to being an auto repair and gas station, the building was equipped with counters, two tables, and a kitchen for serving hamburgers. The inn changed hands throughout the years, and in the early 1960s, the building was razed.

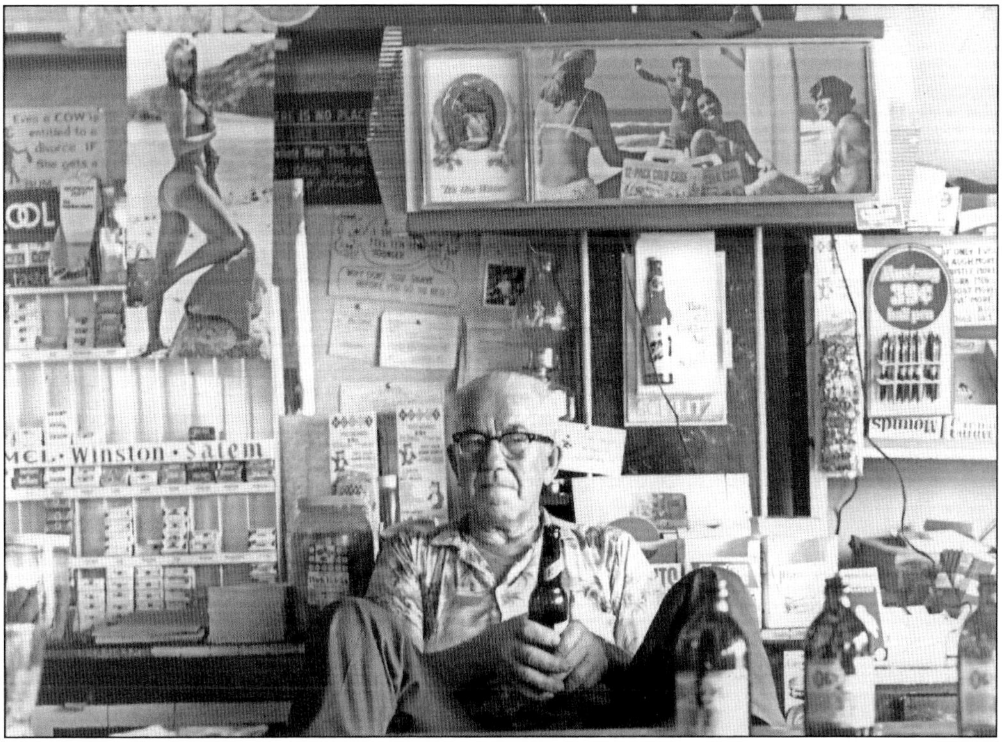

Through the years, the IOOF Building, located on the main street, has held many businesses, including groceries, mercantile stores, barbershops, a dentist office, and the post office. In 1949, Charles Jenecik, a Czechoslovakian immigrant, purchased this building and for 25 years operated a bar/restaurant there, which became well known as "One Shot Charlie's." The business has changed owners, but the name remains legendary.

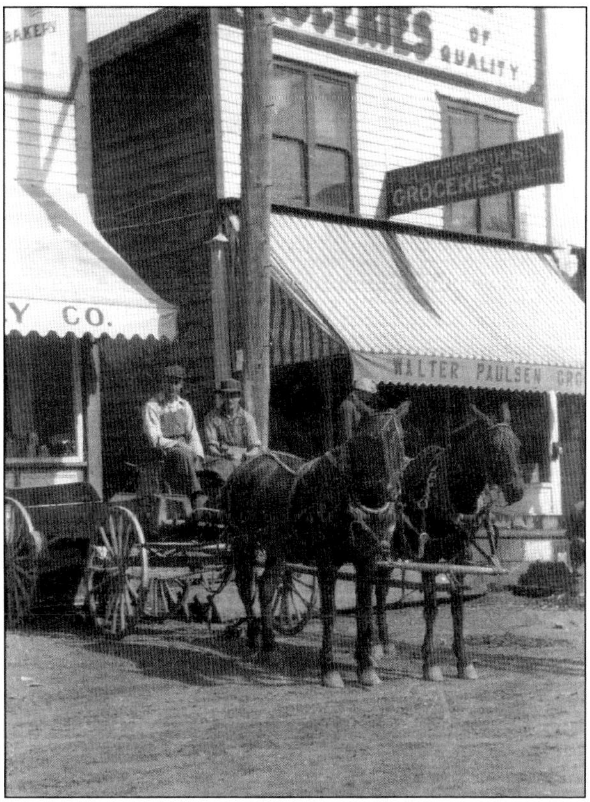

Not all businesses were located in the main business district or the waterfront. Clifford Lavigne, seated on the left in this photograph taken about 1920, operated a dray service. He met boats and trains at the dock and delivered supplies to businesses uptown. Clifford was one of nine children of Joseph and Anna Lavigne, who came to Harrison about 1911.

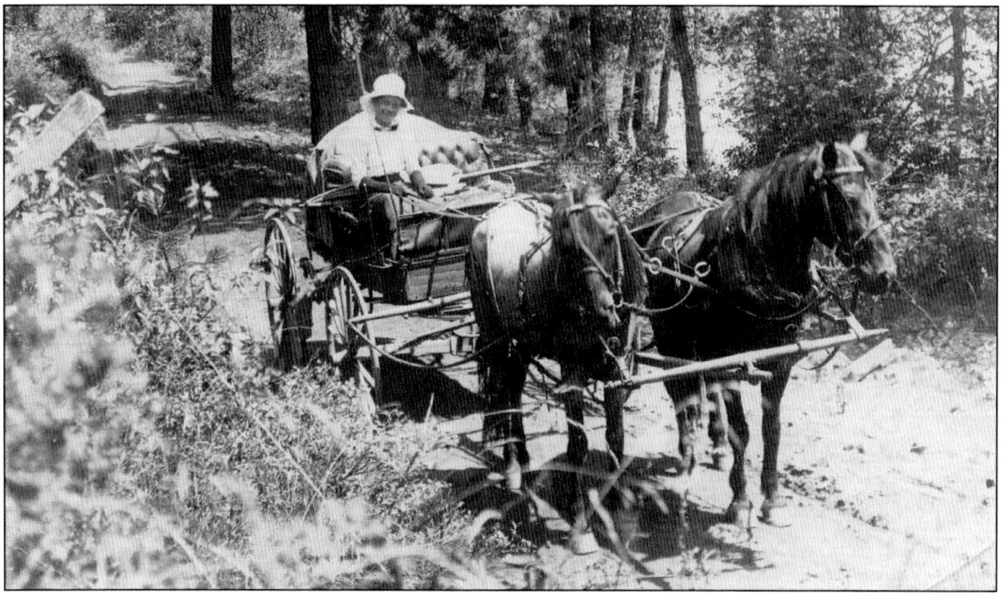

Anna Fabricius, shown here about 1918, delivered milk from East Point to Harrison. In the beginning, her father rowed across the lake, then carried two three-gallon cans by a yoke on his back. After the trestle bridge was built, 14-year-old Anna took the daily 45 minute drive to Harrison to deliver 25 to 30 gallons of milk to 75 customers, including the hotel and restaurants, before going to school.

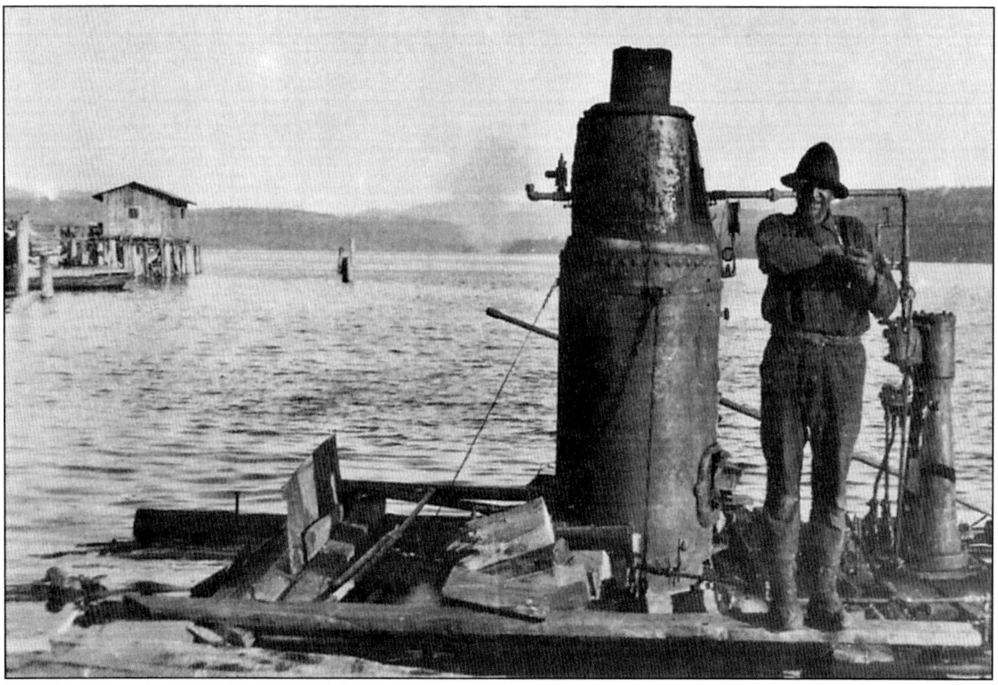

Russian Joe is pictured here in 1921. No one knew his last name, where he came from, or where he went. For about 13 years, he moved from bay to bay building and repairing engines. He lived and worked on his log raft propelled by three old gas motors. His knowledge of gas engines, unusual for the time, led some to suspect he had a technical education in Russia. Russian Joe was featured in the book *Calked Boots and other Northwest Writings* by Bert Russell.

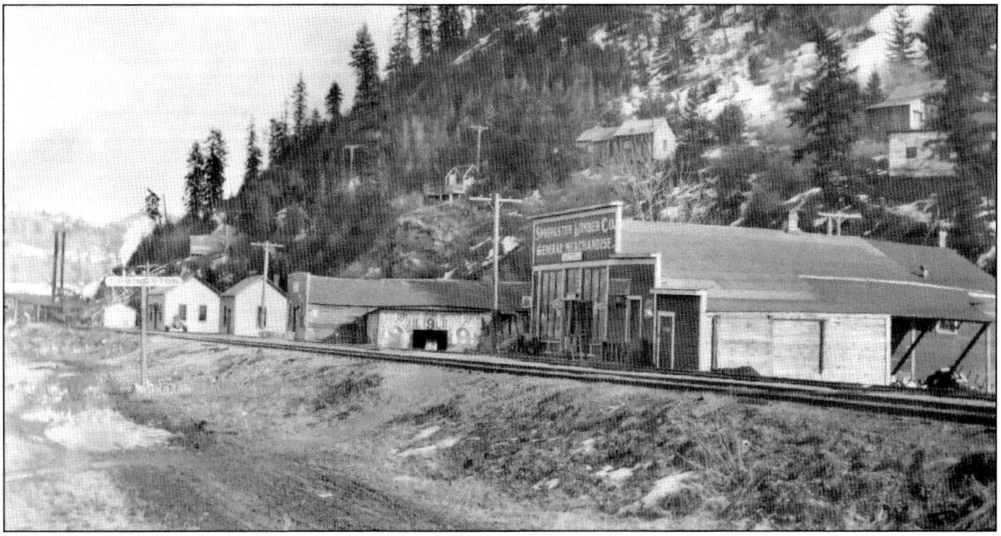

Springston, located three miles up the Coeur d'Alene River from Harrison, consisted of worker housing, a school, the post office, a company store, company offices, and warehouses. The photograph above was taken in the 1920s. The mill is in the background to the left, the home and office of the Union Pacific agent are in the center, and the company store is on the right. None of the houses at that time had running water or electricity. Water for drinking and cooking was carried from a spring. Water for laundry and bathing was taken from the river. The photograph below, taken in 1944, shows that little had changed in 20 years. However, when the Russell and Pugh mill closed in 1962, the town disappeared along with it.

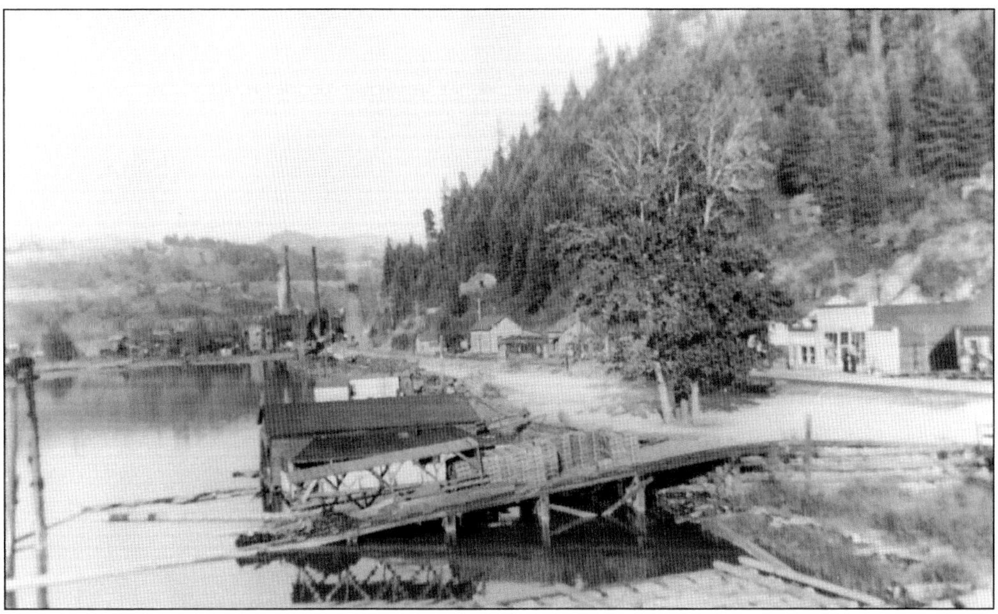

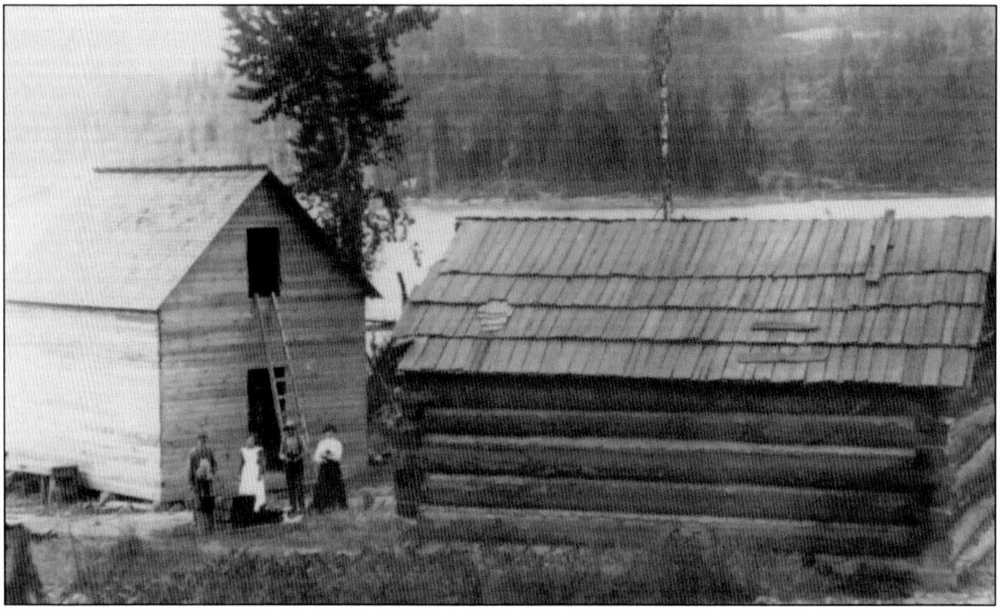

The Waldo family arrived in Harrison around 1901. They soon moved to Carlin Bay, clearing land up the hill from the lake. Roland Woodhall Waldo built a store on the lakeshore supplying his customers with what he thought they needed, not necessarily what they wanted. He became Carlin Bay's third postmaster, a position he held from 1928 to 1936. The photograph above is the Carlin Bay Store and Post Office in 1918. About 1935, a new store with gas pumps and the big house were built slightly west and further from the lake. Roland's sons Henry and Herman were the last of the Waldos to operate the store and gas station. Carlin Bay was the last post office along the marine route. The post office closed in 1965.

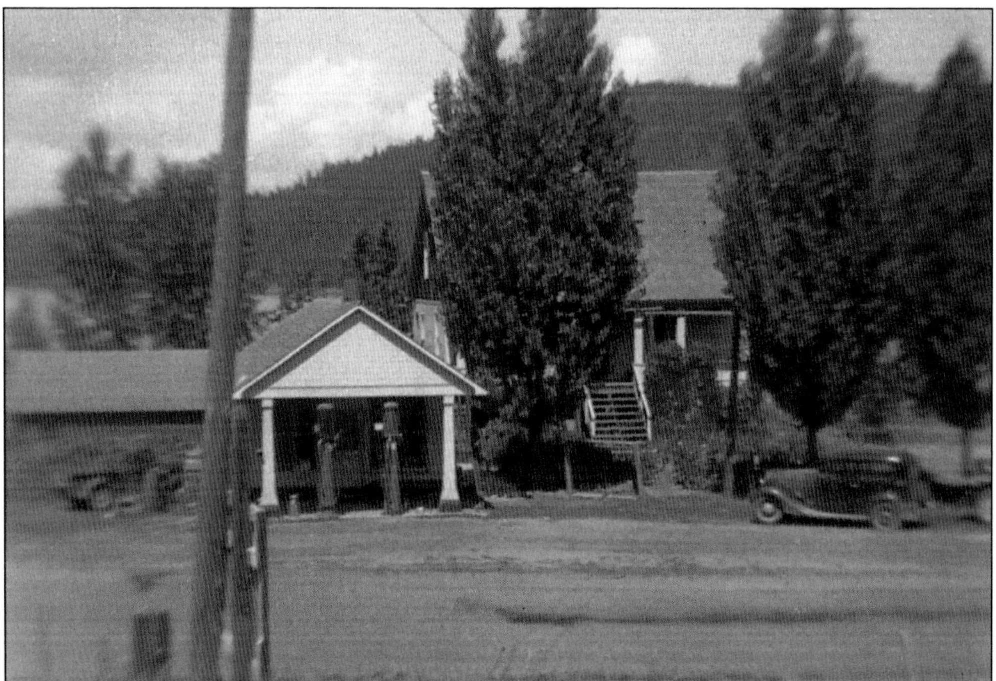

Seven

FIRES

Fires were all too common in early 20th-century towns. Large fires that destroyed mills in Harrison occurred in 1900, 1902, 1913, 1915, 1916, 1917, 1919, and 1920.

The most destructive fire, of course, started at 8:00 a.m. on July 21, 1917, in the drying kilns of the Grant Lumber Company. A strong southwesterly wind carried sparks to awnings on the fronts of the businesses on the main street and spread to the north side of town from there. By nightfall, the business district and a good portion of the town were gone.

Harrison did have water hydrants and volunteer firefighters, but their efforts were hampered by low water pressure and the fact that the fire was so hot it dryed out the canvas hoses, some of which burned. One of the volunteer firemen reported later that the fire moved too fast to control.

The Grant Lumber Company was destroyed, along with part of the Harrison Shingle Company, 25 dwellings, 30 businesses, 4 churches, 2 meeting halls, the water works, the utility company, the city clerk's office, and a boarding house. These buildings were all wood frame construction and burned rapidly. Several citizens were injured; fortunately, no one was killed. The loss was equal to about $500,000 in 1917 dollars with about half of the losses covered by insurance.

Harrison never fully recovered from the 1917 fire. Some businesses did rebuild, and in 1918, six new buildings constructed of fire-resistant bricks were completed. These still stand today.

Fires impacted the city in other ways, too. After a fire in 1919, one of the largest mills relocated to the small town of Springston, about three miles east of Harrison.

The city park now covers the site where the Grant Lumber Company Office and 10 businesses were razed. Included were saloons, restaurants, a meat market, a confectionery, a barber, a cobbler, and a newsstand—all destroyed in the great fire of 1917 and never rebuilt.

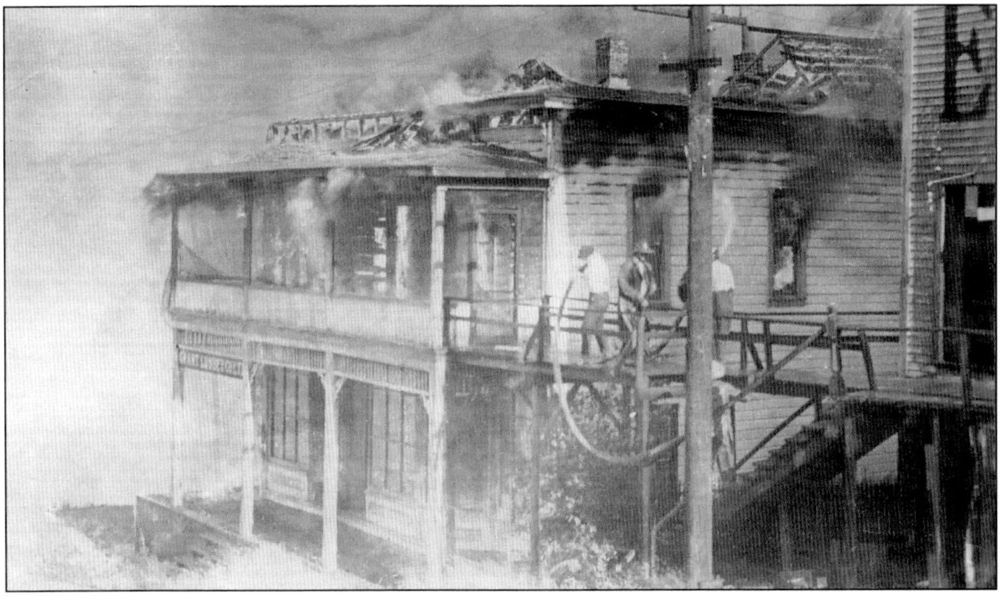

The 1917 fire started at the Grant Lumber Company Mill. All mills had some sort of plan for fighting fires. Barrels of water and buckets of sand were placed in strategic locations throughout the mills. Workers were trained in firefighting techniques using hose carts with steam-driven pumps. Help was usually available with workers from other mills coming to assist whenever the fire whistle blew. These pictures are of the Grant Lumber Company Office. In the second picture, one can see how the fire had progressed.

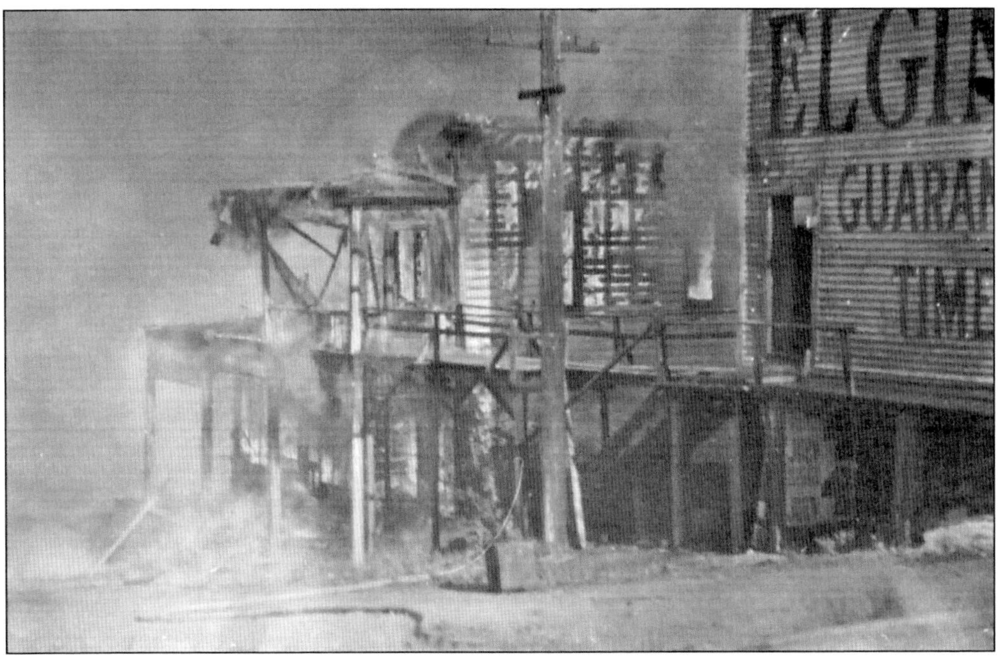

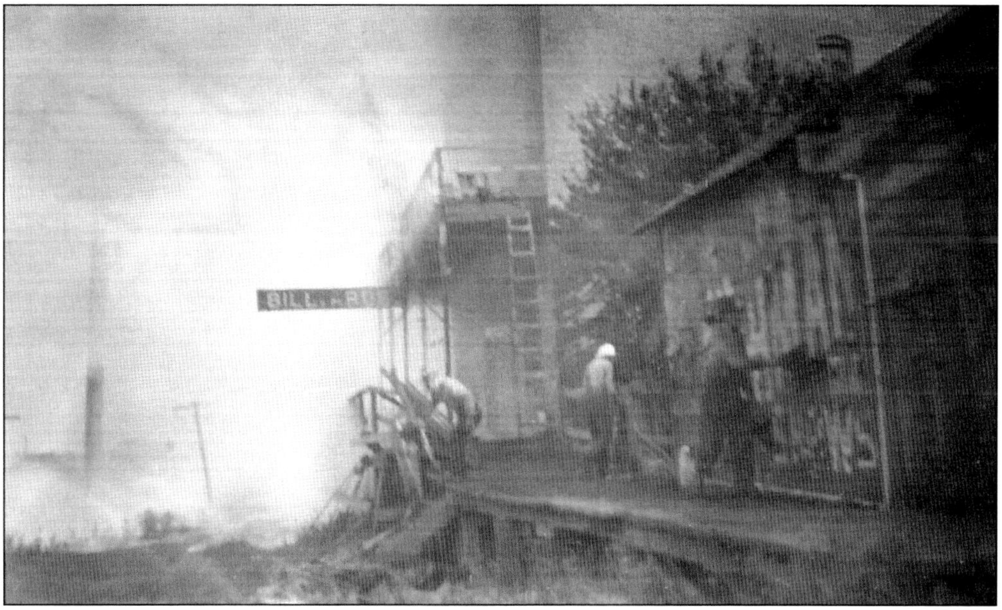

The mills frequently had fires, but they remained contained at the waterfront. When it became evident this fire was moving toward the city, volunteer firemen responded immediately. The city had a municipal water system. Water from both a spring and the lake was pumped to two 52,000-gallon tanks located on a hill above the city. Pipes from the tanks ran to mains in the business district. Hydrant pressure was usually good and deemed sufficient to handle most fires. The fire company, hose carts, and fire hoses were always in readiness. All these preparations, however, failed. This fire quickly got out of control, the site was abandoned, and the firefighters pulled back to try to save adjoining properties.

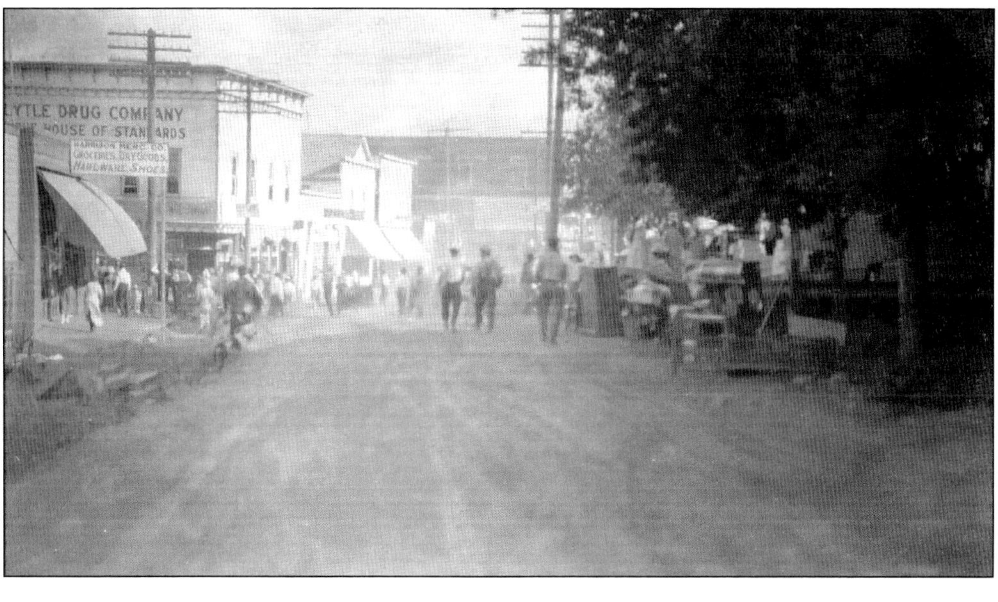

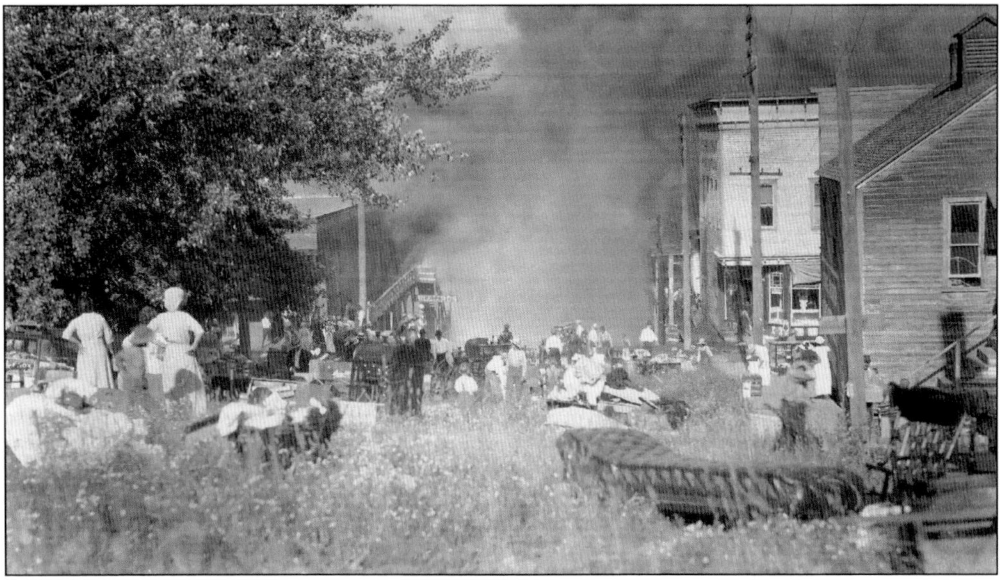

People in the city, fearing their homes might catch fire, moved their valuables out to the street and as far away from wooden structures as possible. Since looters were nonexistent in those days, their personal goods were safe.

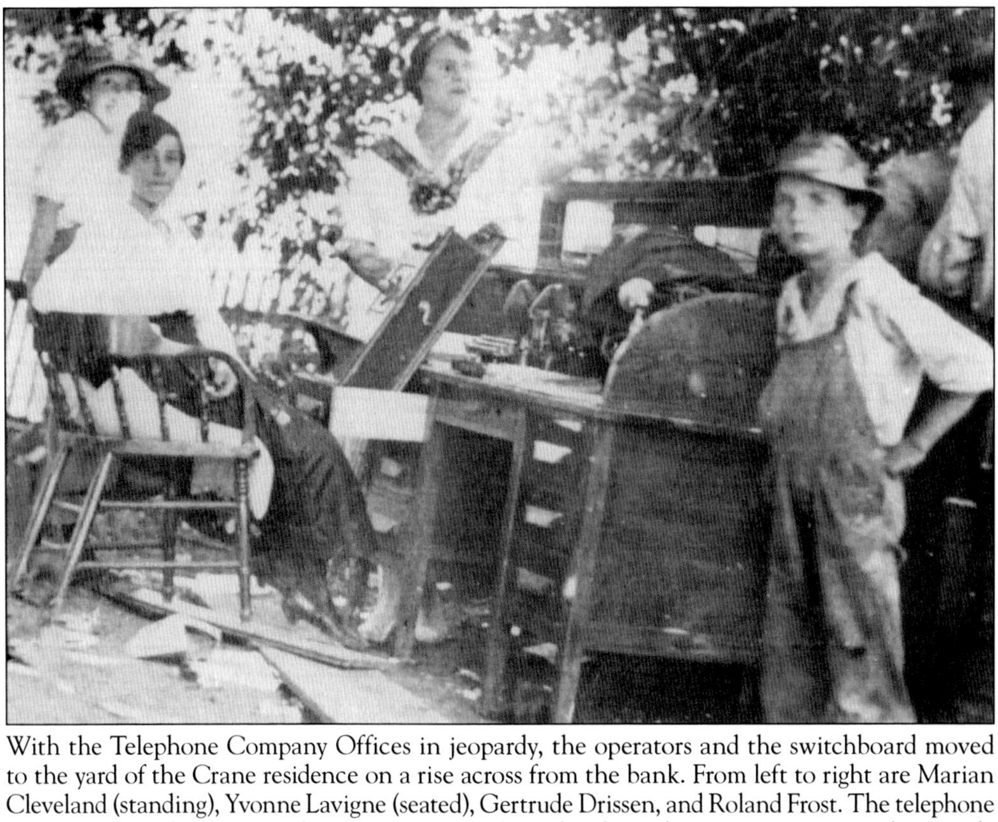

With the Telephone Company Offices in jeopardy, the operators and the switchboard moved to the yard of the Crane residence on a rise across from the bank. From left to right are Marian Cleveland (standing), Yvonne Lavigne (seated), Gertrude Drissen, and Roland Frost. The telephone company immediately started stringing wire, and in a few days, phone connections to the outside word were re-established.

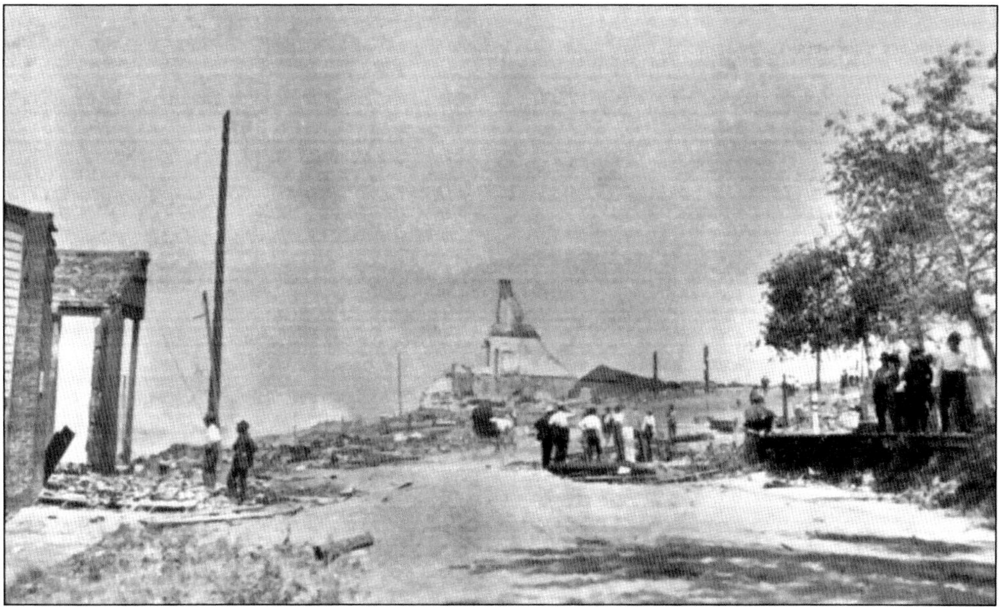

Much of the timber in the Coeur d'Alenes was resinous. Sawdust shavings and other waste products were highly flammable. This material, wooden structures, and a great amount of lumber in sheds and yards represented a real fire hazard. Fast moving machinery heats up quickly when oil or grease runs dry, and an overheated bearing can cause a fire, and often did. Open-sided waste burners, inadequate spark arrestors, exploding boilers, and faulty fireboxes were responsible for starting more than one fire. These pictures of the fire's aftermath reflect the results.

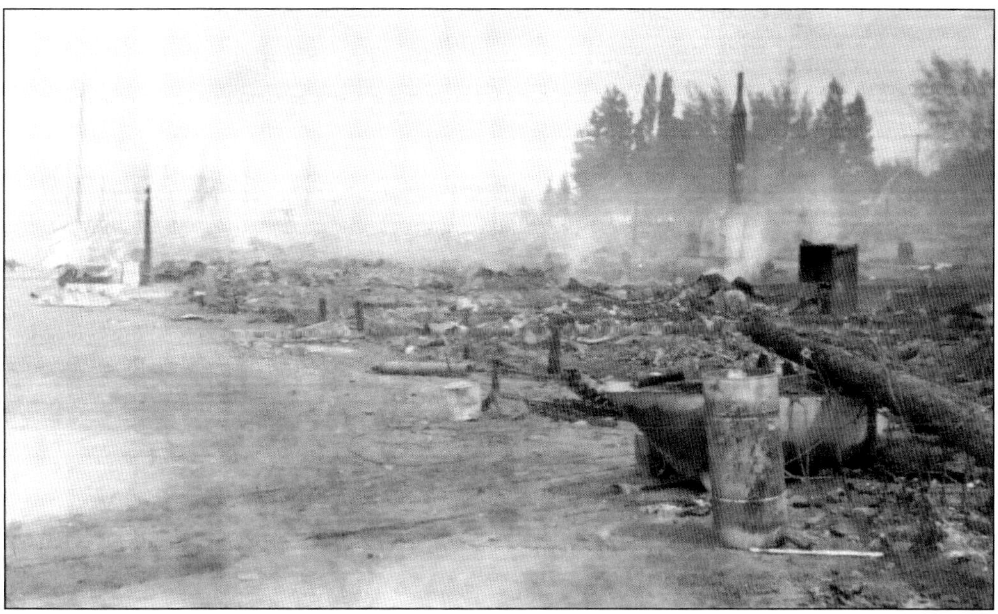

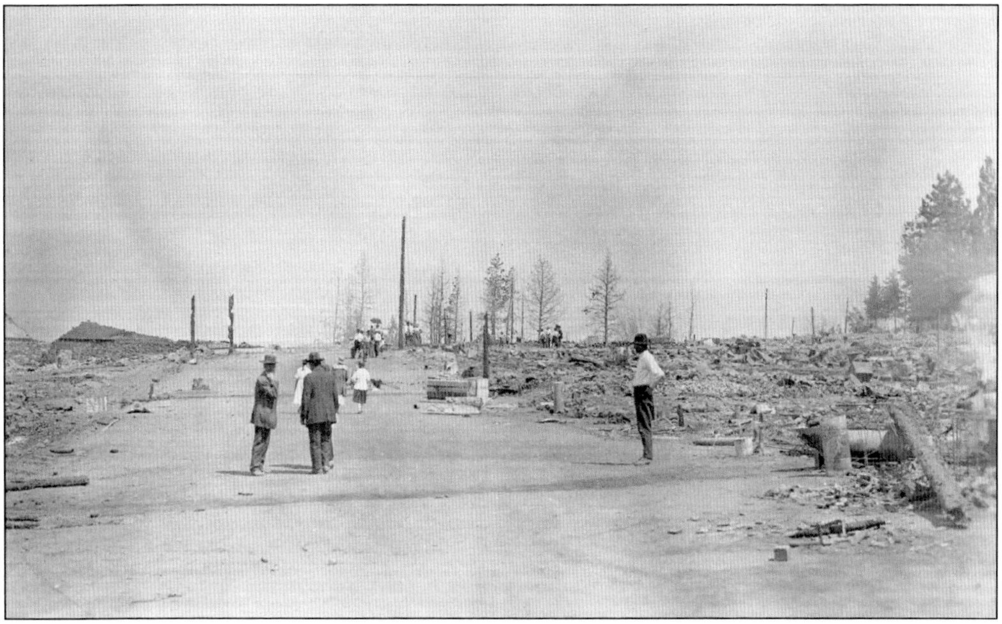

In 1917, there was unrest in the mines and mills of North Idaho. William Dudley "Big Bill" Heywood, a chief organizer of the Industrial Workers of the World (IWW), a Socialist labor union, incited his followers, known as Wobblies, to acts of violence and sabotage. The fire was firmly believed, at the time, to be a work of arson on the part of the Wobblies or a disgruntled employee.

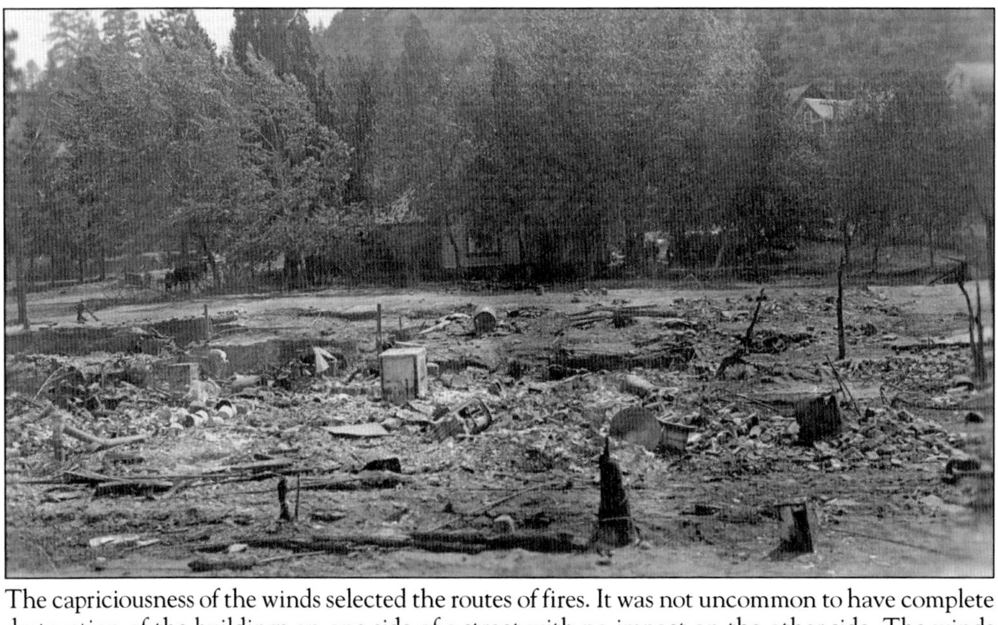

The capriciousness of the winds selected the routes of fires. It was not uncommon to have complete destruction of the buildings on one side of a street with no impact on the other side. The winds blew north and east, passing the homes and businesses on the southern end of town. In this picture, one can see debris with spared homes in the background among the trees.

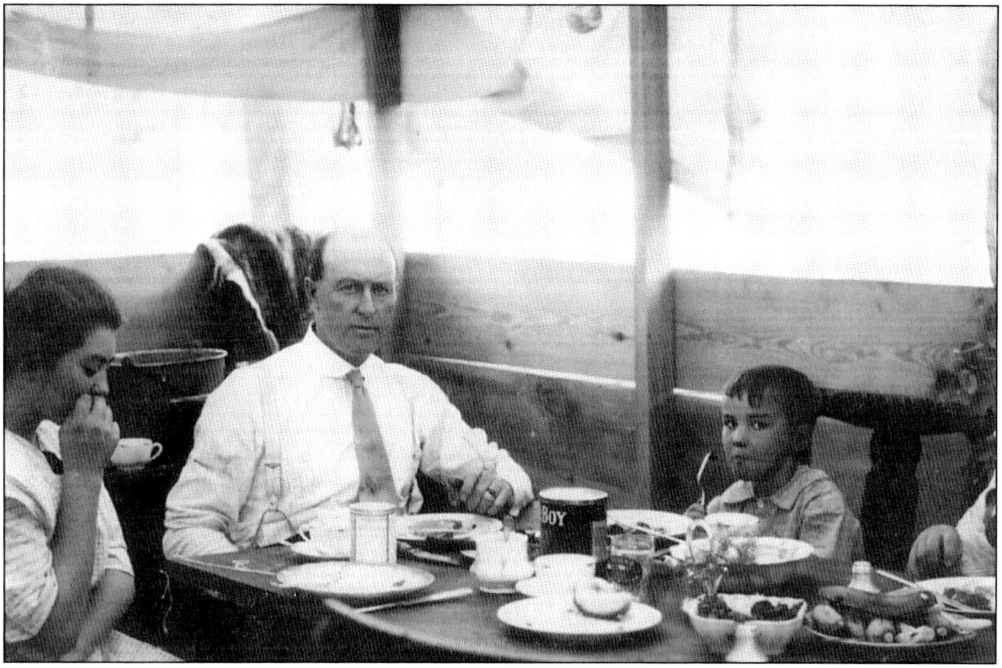

The home and drugstore of John and Josephine Corskie were destroyed. They decided to remain in Harrison and rebuild. During construction, they lived in tents supplied by surrounding cities. One tent was used for sleeping and the other for general living quarters. Corskie family members are seated inside a tent. From left to right are Dorothy, John, and Don. Josephine, Jeanne, and Betty are not shown.

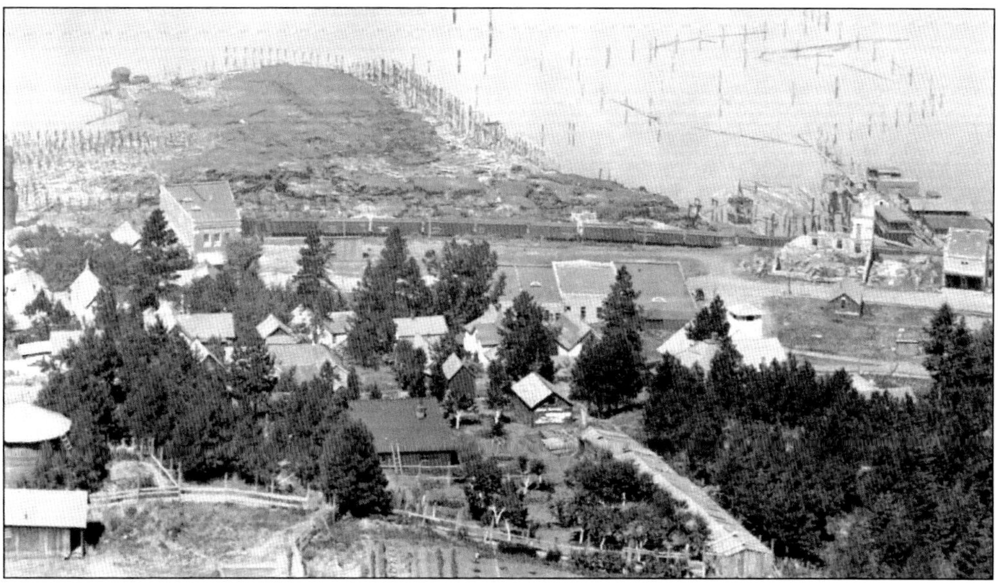

Looking down on Harrison one can see the destruction and the beginnings of rebuilding. At the left is the burner, which is all that remained of the Harrison Shingle Mill. The trapezoidal shaped IOOF Building has been rebuilt. Some businesses and the Methodist church are new. The general store on the corner is still rubble. The Baptist church has not yet been rebuilt. The opera house, at far right, remains standing.

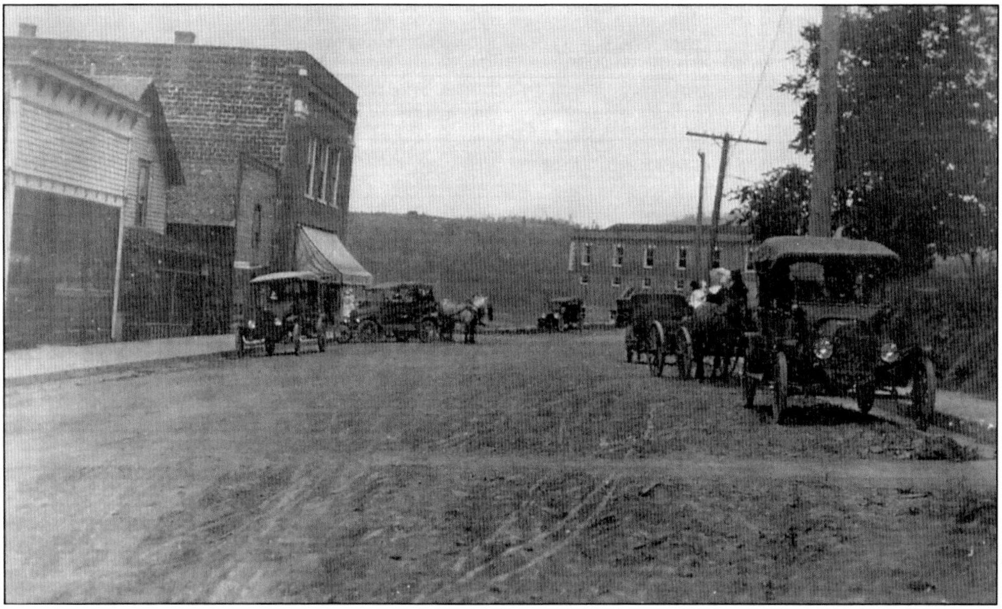

This is the main street (Highway 97) in 1921. The brick building on the corner of Harrison Street belonged to the International Order of Odd Fellows. The brick building at the right is the General Store on the corner of Garfield Street. They were rebuilt. The businesses in between, all made of wood, were not. This space between the buildings later became the city park

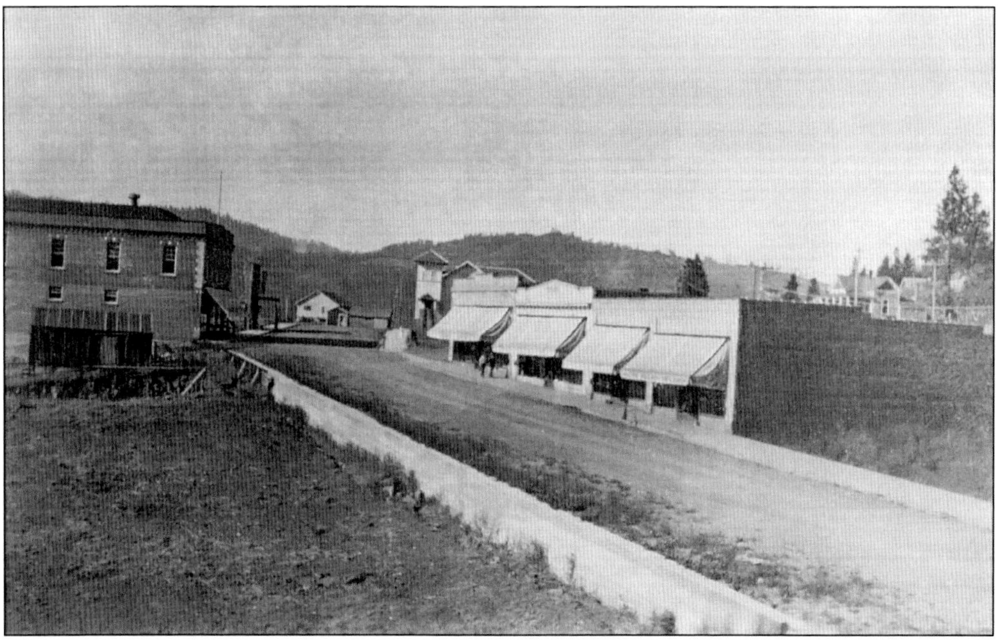

After the 1917 fire, some businesses rebuilt under more stringent fire codes, and brick was the primary material used. This photograph shows part of the business district in 1922 or 1923. From left to right are Bridgeman Hardware, Corskie Drug, Fick and Sala Meat Market and Grocery, and the pool hall (later the feed store). At the far end of the street are the rebuilt Corskie home and the bell tower of the Baptist Church. These buildings stand today and are all in use by local businesses.

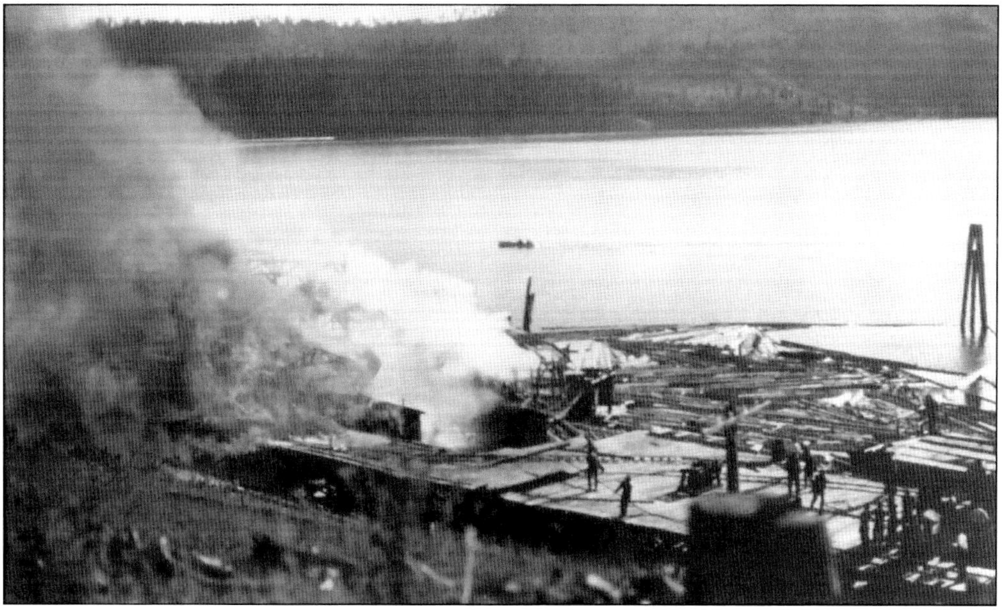

Mill fires such as these were common. In 1919, the Russell and Pugh mill at the south end of town caught fire, leaving the destruction pictured at right. Owners then purchased the Springston Lumber Company and moved their operations to Springston, which is along the Coeur d'Alene River three miles from Harrison. Note that the John Pugh home, which was on the hill above the mill, was spared.

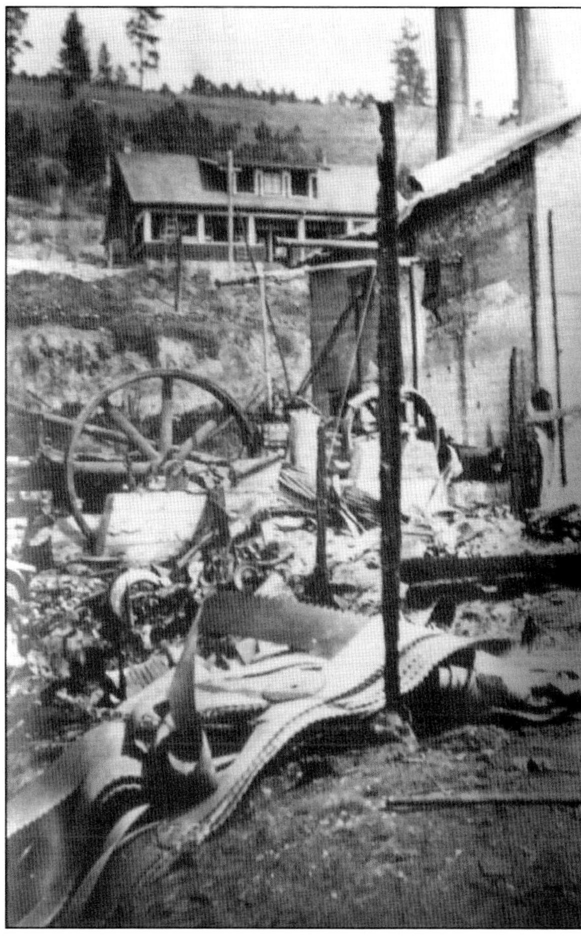

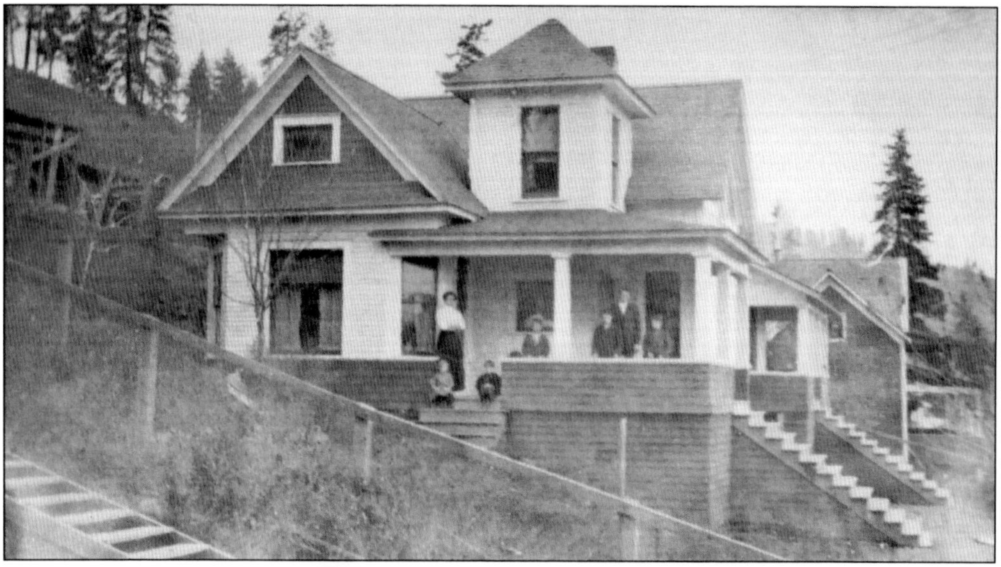

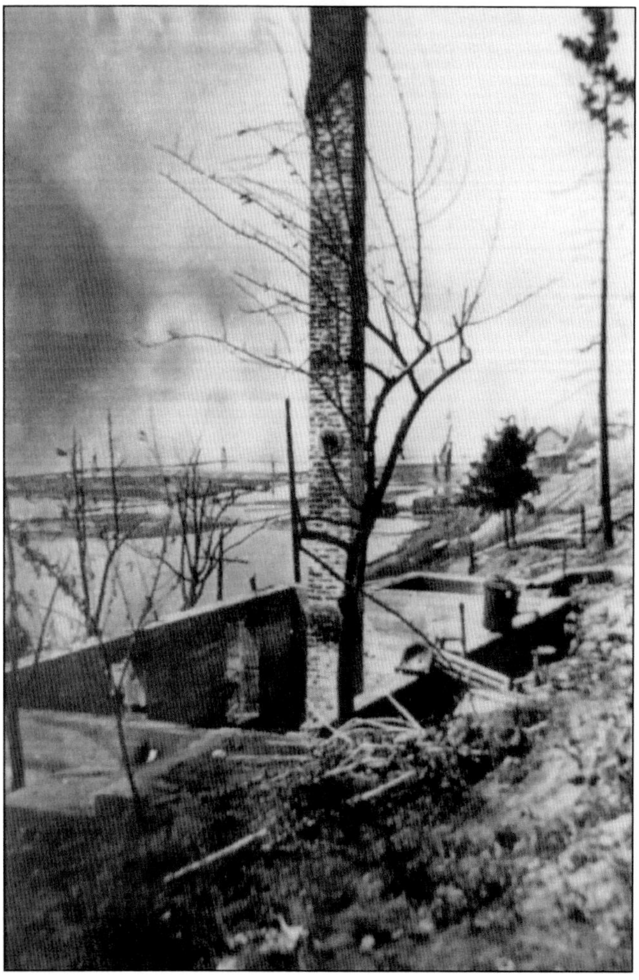

This photograph is of the Guy Russell home, which stood next door to the Pugh home. The Russell home was newly finished and furnished just before the fire started.

These are the remains of the Guy Russell home after the mill fire burned it. The capriciousness of the winds was selective, again. The Pugh home was spared; the Russell home was not.

Eight

COMMUNITY

Throughout this book, the working side of early Harrison, logging, sawmills, farming, transportation, and commercial businesses, is portrayed. But a community is more than brick and mortar or industry. A community is made up of people. Harrison is a true melting pot. The 1910 census shows that people came from no fewer than 15 countries. They cooperated on community projects, which were paid for by fundraisers and donations. They built churches and schools and joined together in fraternal organizations. The *Illustrated History of North Idaho*, dated 1903, lists 11 national societies as having a chapter in Harrison. Groups gathered together in clubs to pursue common interests.

The community held together through floods, fires, deaths, and world wars. But Harrisonites have also had their share of disagreements. Some are amusing today, such as this report in the June 8, 1893, copy of the *Harrison Fog Horn*: "A petition was circulated Wednesday afternoon among the men of leisure, namely mill hands out of employment, on account of high water, protesting against the blowing of the Bacon-Herron whistle so early in the morning, 6:30 o'clock, setting forth that it disturbed their peaceful slumbers, making it a public nuisance and hence should not be tolerated."

Of course, there were the unsavory events such as a shooting or two, which have been told and retold into legends. Many citizens deplored the darker side of early Harrison, which included saloons, brothels, and rowdiness that discouraged ladies from venturing out at night. When Prohibition was introduced, the countryside boasted its share of moonshine stills.

The community also had fun—an opera house that seated 400, a theater, community bands, picnics in the park, parades featuring prize winning floats, sports teams, and a local theater troop. From the beginning Harrison loved the lake for its boating, lake cruises, and Fourth of July celebrations on the waterfront.

This is just a small cross-section of the people of Harrison.

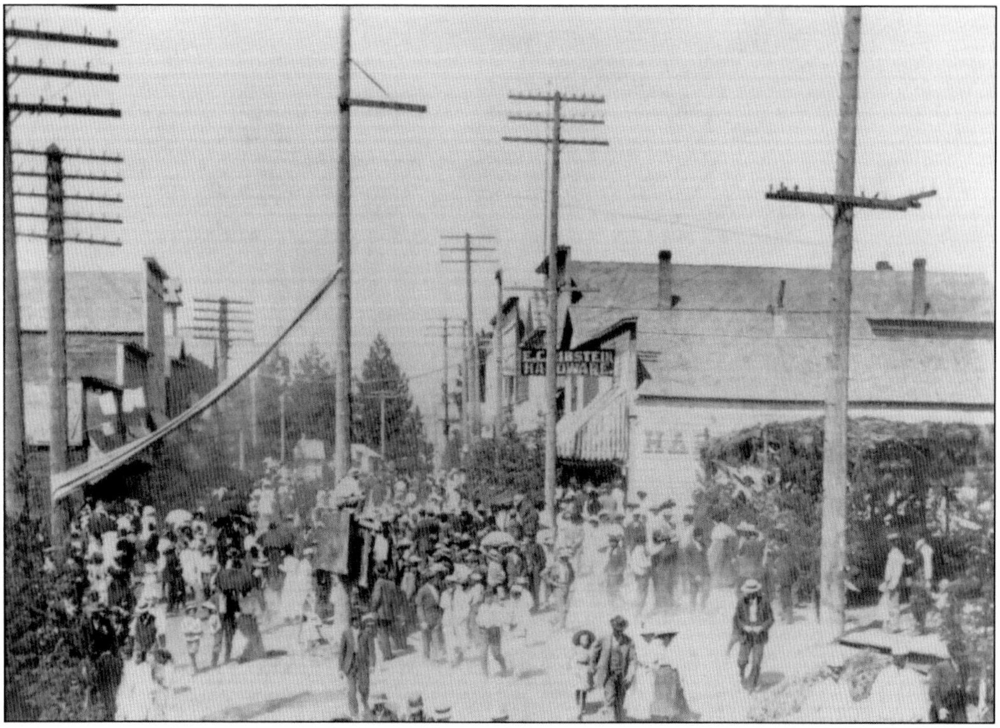

This is a busy street scene in Harrison around 1903. The people of the Harrison Area worked hard, so when there was a scheduled celebration, everyone came to enjoy the day.

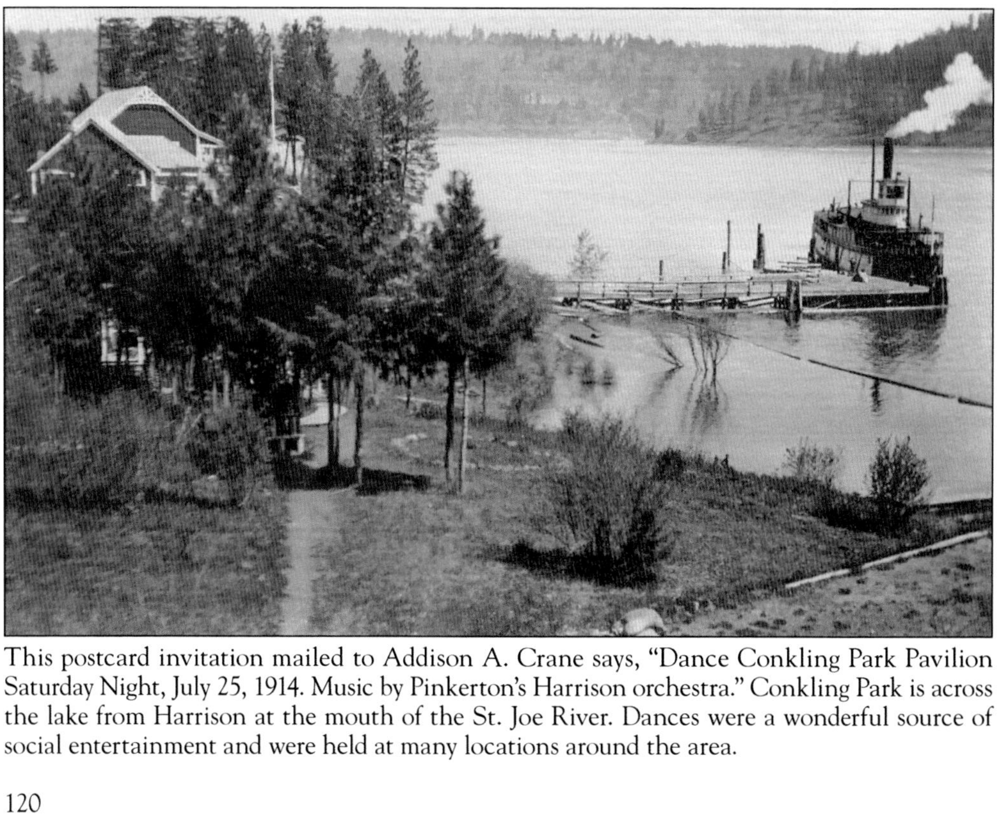

This postcard invitation mailed to Addison A. Crane says, "Dance Conkling Park Pavilion Saturday Night, July 25, 1914. Music by Pinkerton's Harrison orchestra." Conkling Park is across the lake from Harrison at the mouth of the St. Joe River. Dances were a wonderful source of social entertainment and were held at many locations around the area.

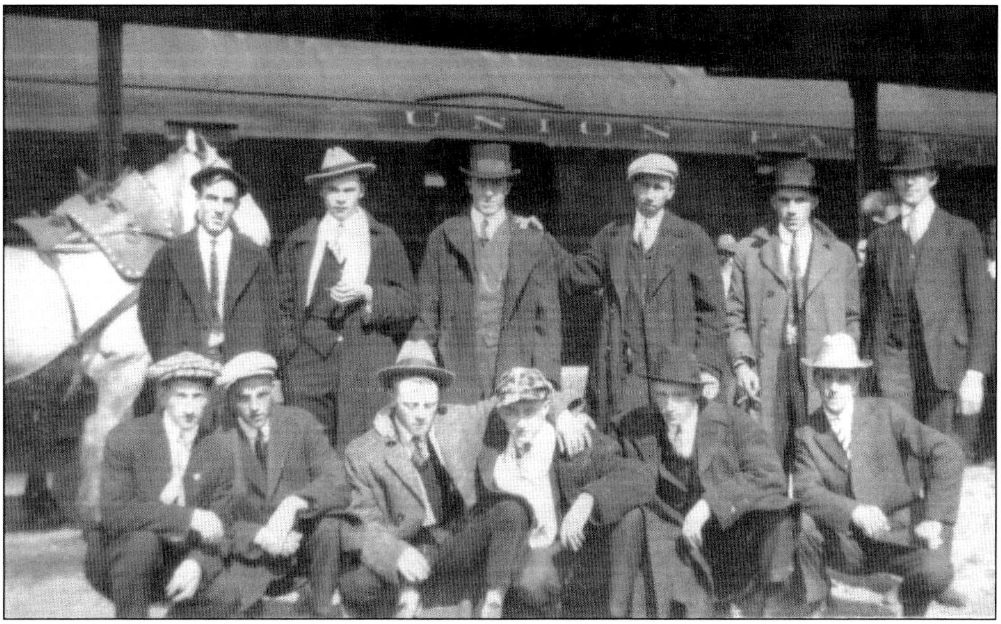

Volunteers leaving for World War I are, from left to right, (kneeling) John Pedro, Martin Peterson, Harry Rice, Doug Doty, Alvin Doty, and Bill Haner; (standing) Vic Lavigne, Guy Stuart, Leslie McCarthy, Mike Naglin, Bill Lavigne, and Harry Hamm. According to an article in the *Harrison Searchlight*, a national magazine (*Colliers* or *Post*) stated that it is possible Harrison produced more volunteer soldiers per capita than any other city in the United States.

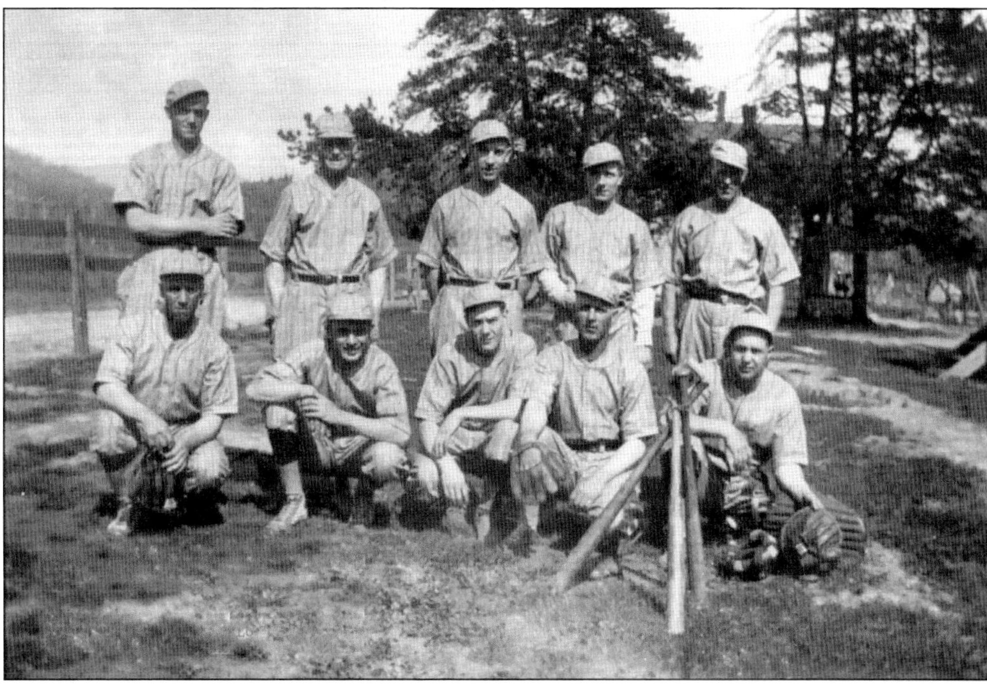

Springston baseball team members in 1925 are, from left to right, (first row) William Reynolds, Jack Turner, Joe Wark, Claude Newton, and Claude Knaggs; (second row) Larry Hansen, Charlie Downey, Gene Lowe, Irwin Lapore, and Oran Wilson.

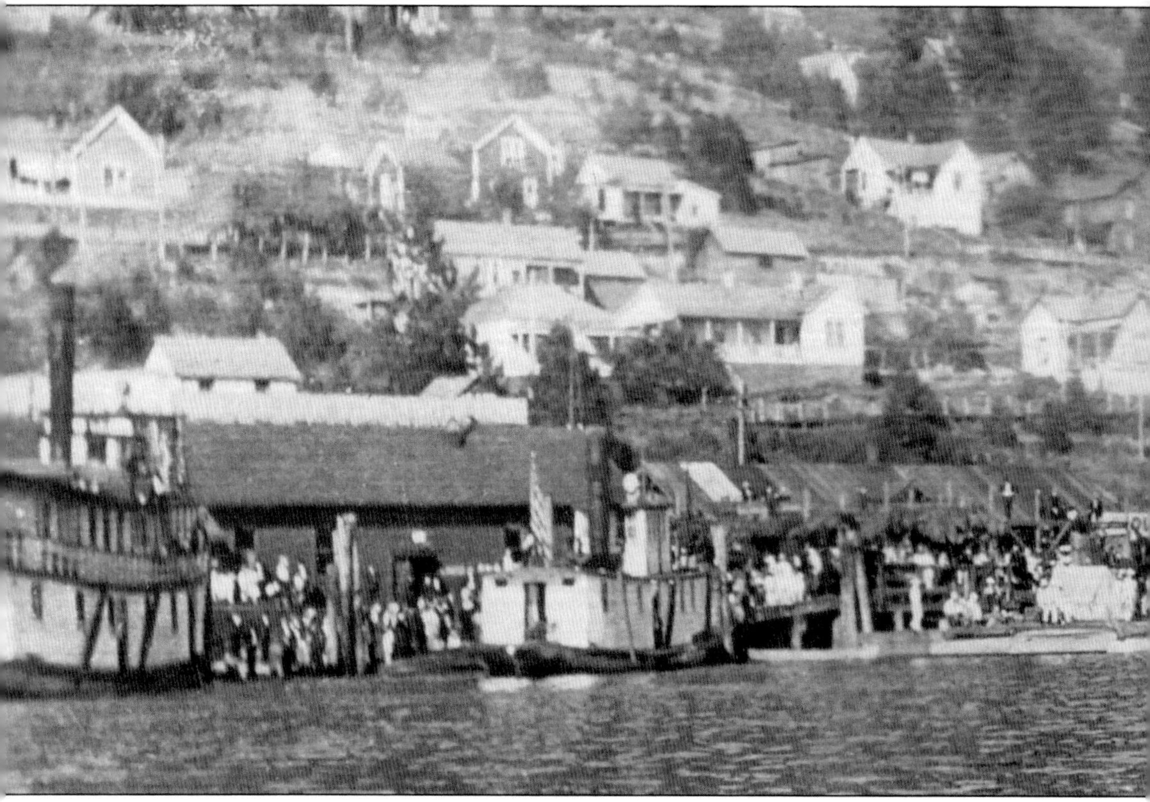

This is a panoramic view of a pre-1917 Fourth of July celebration on Harrison's waterfront. The

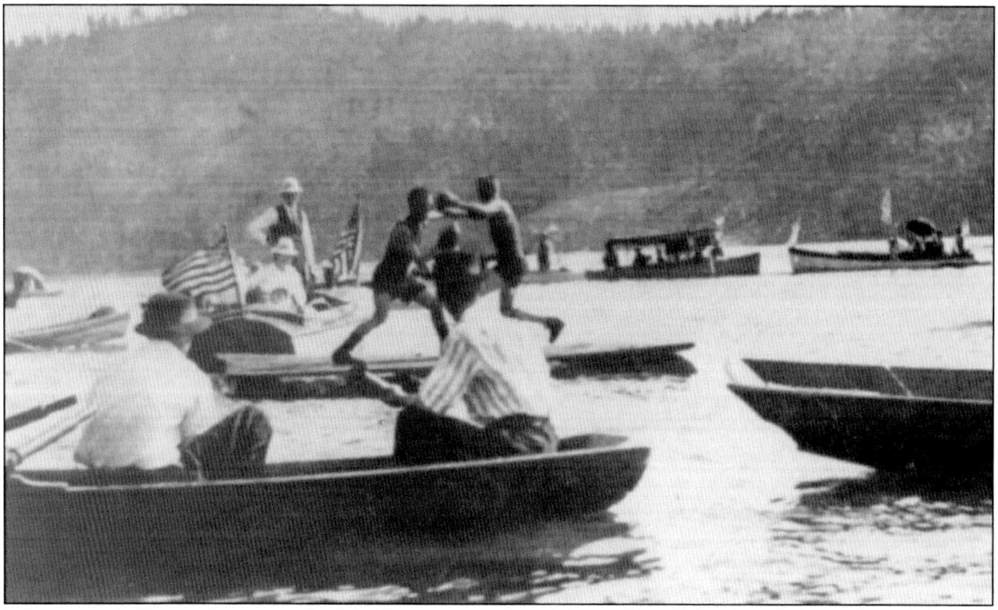

Boxing was a favorite sport. When Jack Dempsey was on tour in the 1920s, William "Bill" Nearing sparred with him. These boxers took the sport one step further by moving the ring to a floating dock on the lakefront at Harrison.

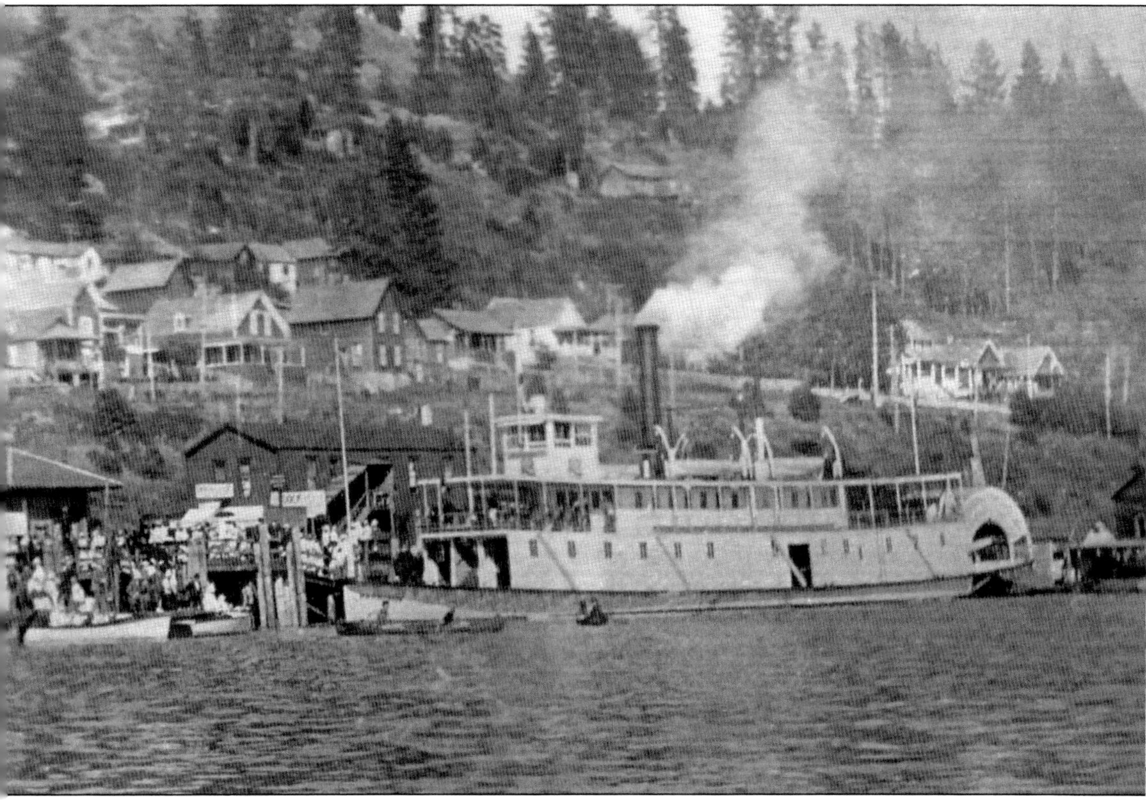

passenger boats *Flyer*, *Wallace*, and *Harrison* brought people to share in the festivities.

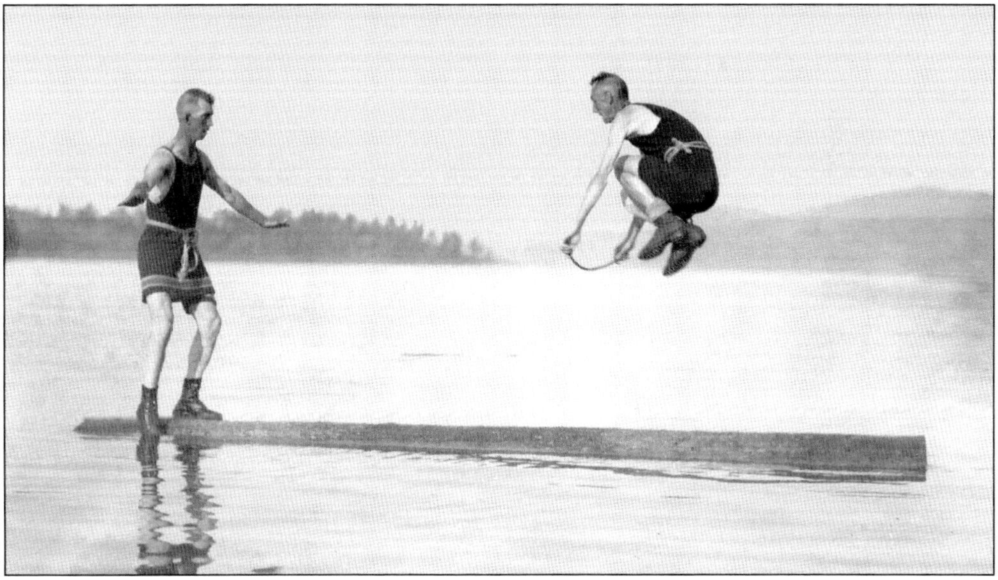

Henry Morin is jumping rope in 1912, while his brother William holds the log steady. These antics, along with log rolling (the art of staying on top of a floating log while "rolling" the log by walking), were loved by "river rats" who enjoyed the competition to see who was the best. The Morin brothers were champion log rollers.

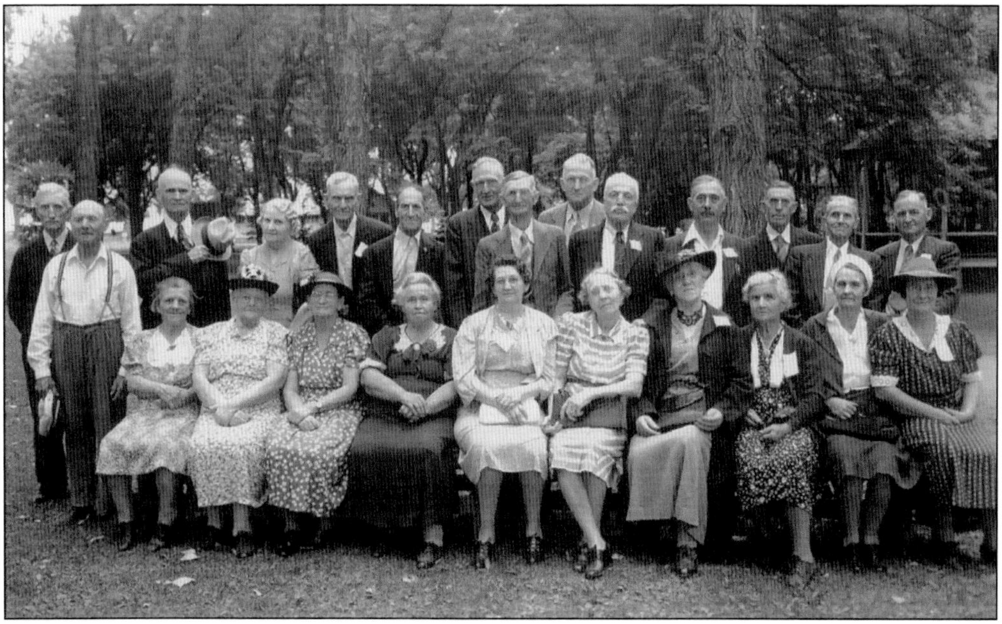

Here is a 1938 Harrison picnic on Coeur d'Alene. Those pictured are, from left to right, (first row) Mrs. Harp, Mrs. Copsy, Ida Fisher, Kirstine Jensen, Grace Walton, Mrs. Crane, Olivia Sala, Mattie Murray, Dolly (Slayton) Newman, and Stella (Fisher) Knudson; (second row) Jay Doty, Hans Jorgenson, Ike Thompson, Cora Lee, Ben Thompson, Tony Tonti, Joseph Lamb, Chris Arnold, George Lamb, Matt Sala, Tony Dire, Rasmus Jensen, August Jensen, and Col. Will Edelblute.

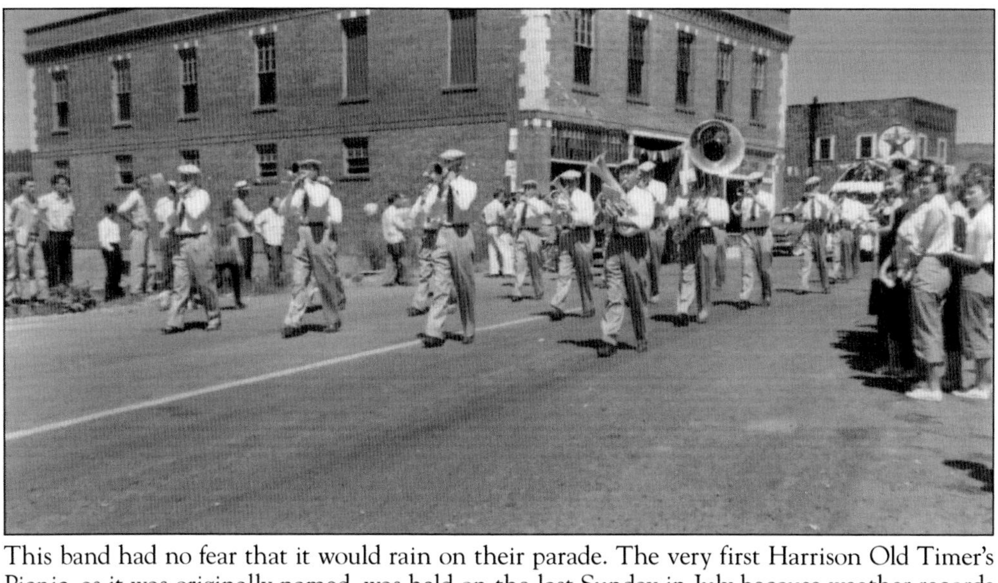

This band had no fear that it would rain on their parade. The very first Harrison Old Timer's Picnic, as it was originally named, was held on the last Sunday in July because weather records showed that it had not rained on that date for 50 years. That record still holds, except for two light sprinkles in later years. This Harrison tradition continues today.

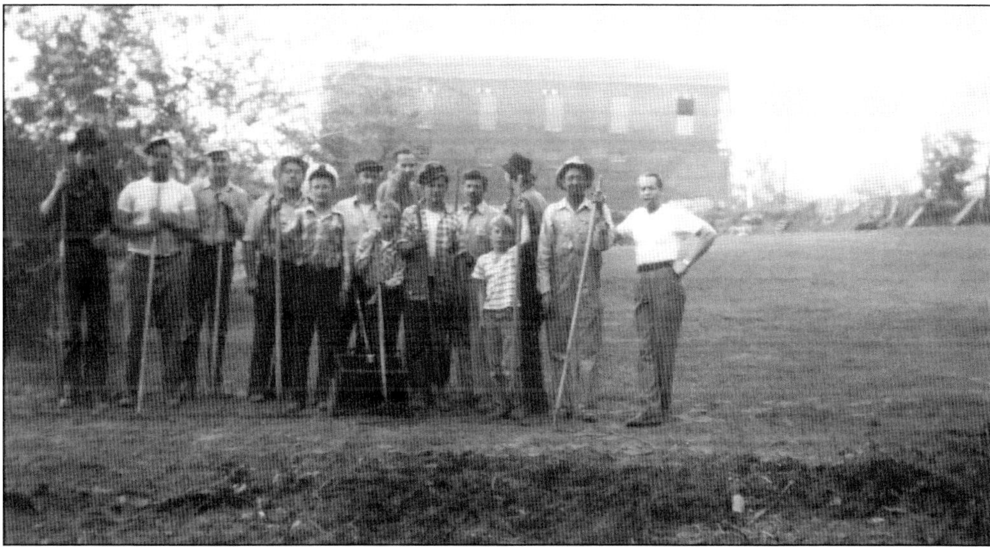

This area had been a hazard since the 1917 fire left it in rubble. Inspired by Tom Collier, the Old Timer's Picnic Committee spearheaded building a city park so the annual picnic could be moved from Coeur d'Alene to Harrison. Also, with the mills replaced by a boat launch and marina bringing in visitors, a general sprucing up was warranted. In 1953, volunteers began renovations from rubble to park, and the picnic was held there that year.

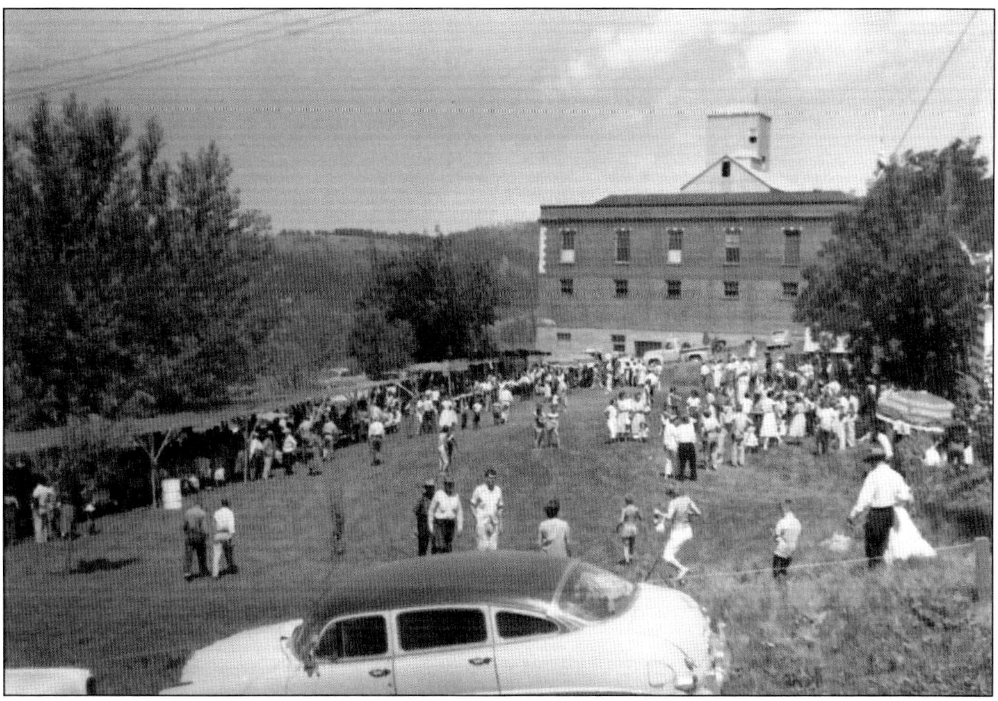

In 1956, the city park hosted the annual Old Timer's Picnic, later renamed the Old Time Picnic, an event still held each summer. People come from all over the world to spend the weekend with old friends and neighbors. Today, the park has mature trees for shade, picnic tables, benches, restrooms, an outdoor kitchen, and a large gazebo.

About the Organization and Authors

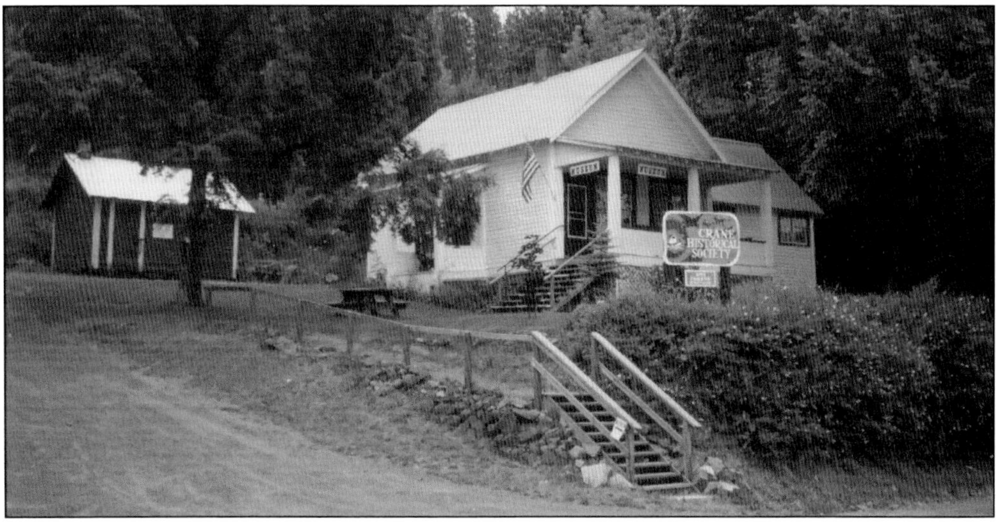

On May 5, 1984, a group of 12 met to form a historical society. Incorporation and election of officers and trustees followed. Its mission was to preserve the history of the Harrison area and to make it available to the public.

Howard and Geraldine Russell donated a building for a museum. This building was the first home in Harrison, built in 1891 by the city's founders. It had remained in the Crane family until 1936.

A Russian elm in the front yard was planted in 1891 by N. B. Willey, the second governor of Idaho, a testimony to the prominence of Harrison.

The small 12-by-16-foot building on the left is the Harrison jail. Constable Claude Knaggs built it in 1925 by laminating two-by-fours together. Seeing little usage—everyone in Harrison was apparently law-abiding—the building was sold. John Procopio used it as a storage shed on his ranch. When William and Shirley Bunton became owners, they donated the building, and it was moved back into town.

The museum contains artifacts and memorabilia from Harrison's early settlers. Local families have donated displays. The museum store carries books by several authors and oral histories preserved on CDs. The society also publishes calendars, booklets, and pamphlets on various subjects relating to Harrison's history.

Through the years, dedicated members have given their time and energy on museum projects to further its goals. In 2010, the museum joined with Arcadia Publishing to produce this book. Mary Mills collected and cataloged the photographs. Josephine Prophet was the author, in collaboration with Roberta Arnzen, Eileen DuHamel, Florence Farber, Marian Jones, Mary Mills, Jerry Prophet, and Marie Russell. Husbands critiqued and supported.

BIBLIOGRAPHY

Carns, Iva Hollingsworth. *Steamboats and Memories.* Coeur d'Alene, ID: Century Publishing Company, 1990.

Custer, Charles Joseph. *I Did My Damnest.* Coeur d'Alene, ID: Estate of C.J. Custer, 2007.

Hult, Ruby El. *Steamboats in the Timber.* Portland, OR: Binfords & Morts, Publishers, 1952.

Museum of North Idaho. *In All the West No Place Like This.* Coeur d'Alene, ID: PageWorks Publication Services, 1996.

Pugh, John D. *Springston Idaho 1900–2003.* Corvallis, OR: self-published, 2003.

Russell, Bert. *Calked Boots and other Northwest Writings.* Harrison, ID: Lacon Publishers, 1967.

Russell, Bert. *Hardship and Happy Times.* Harrison, ID: Lacon Publishers, 1978.

Russell, Bert. *The Sawdust Dreams.* Harrison, ID: Lacon Publishers, 1990.

Russell, Bert and Marie Bert. *Rock Burst.* Moscow, ID: University of Idaho Press, 1998.

Scott, Orland A. *Pioneer Days on the Shadowy St. Joe.* Caldwell, ID: Caxton Printers, Ltd., 1967.

Shadduck, Louise. *At the Edge of the Ice; Where Lake Coeur d'Alene and its People Meet.* Boise, ID: Tamarack Books, Inc., 1996.

Strong, Clarence S. and Clyde S. Webb. *White Pine; King of Many Waters.* Missoula, MT: Mountain Press Publishing Co., 1970.